THE SIXTH GUN

BOOK 5: WINTER WOLVES

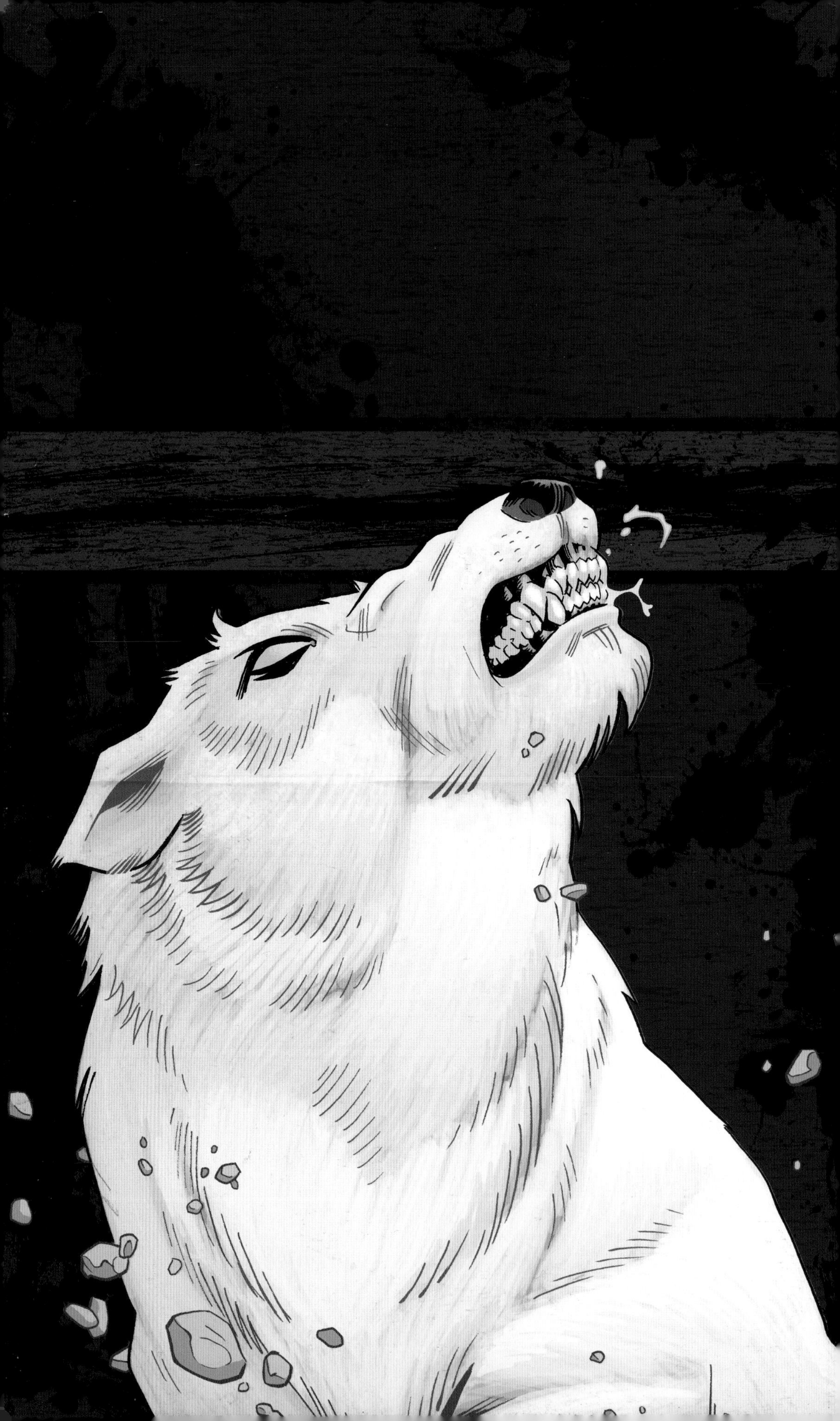

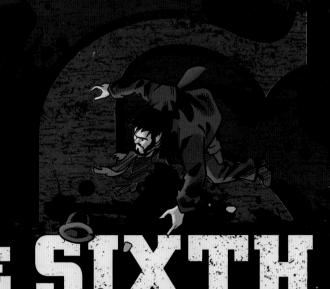

THE SIXTH GUN™

BOOK 5: WINTER WOLVES

WRITTEN BY

CULLEN BUNN

ILLUSTRATED BY

BRIAN HURTT

COLORED BY

BILL CRABTREE

LETTERED BY

DOUGLAS E. SHERWOOD

EDITED BY

CHARLIE CHU

DESIGNED BY

KEITH WOOD

The Sixth Gun™
By Cullen Bunn & Brian Hurtt

Published by Oni Press, Inc.

Joe Nozemack *publisher*

James Lucas Jones *editor in chief*

Keith Wood *art director*

Tom Shimmin *director of sales & marketing*

Jill Beaton *editor*

Charlie Chu *editor*

Troy Look *digital prepress lead*

Jason Storey *graphic designer*

Robin Herrera *administrative assistant*

THE SIXTH GUN: WINTER WOLVES, September 2013. Published by Oni Press, Inc. 1305 SE Martin Luther King Jr. Blvd., Suite A, Portland, OR 97214.

This volume collects issues #24-29 of the Oni Press series *The Sixth Gun*.

Oni Press, Inc.
1305 SE Martin Luther King Jr. Blvd.
Suite A
Portland, OR 97214
USA

onipress.com
facebook.com/onipress
twitter.com/onipress
onipress.tumblr.com

cullenbunn.com • @cullenbunn
briburtt.com • @briburtt
@crabtree_bill

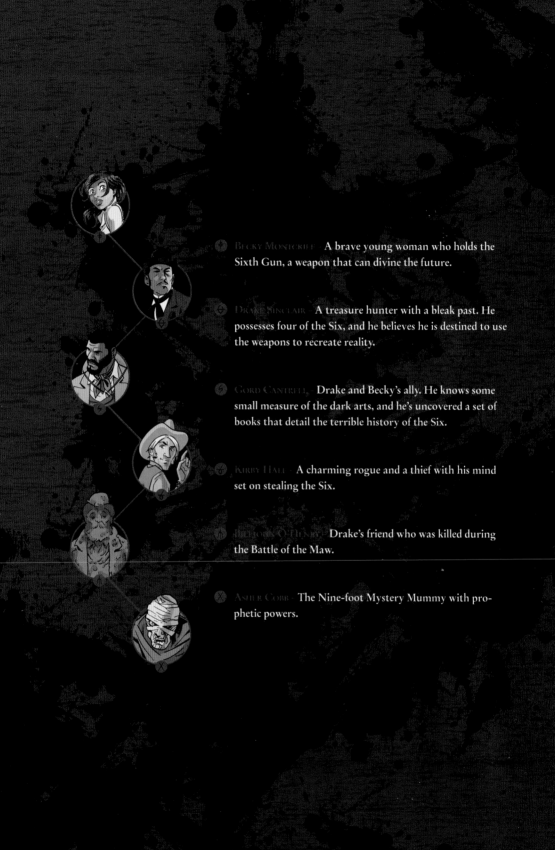

Becky Montcrief – A brave young woman who holds the Sixth Gun, a weapon that can divine the future.

Drake Sinclair – A treasure hunter with a bleak past. He possesses four of the Six, and he believes he is destined to use the weapons to recreate reality.

Gord Cantrell – Drake and Becky's ally. He knows some small measure of the dark arts, and he's uncovered a set of books that detail the terrible history of the Six.

Kirby Hale – A charming rogue and a thief with his mind set on stealing the Six.

Jeremiah O'Henry – Drake's friend who was killed during the Battle of the Maw.

Asher Cobb – The Nine-foot Mystery Mummy with prophetic powers.

CHAPTER ONE

For centuries, the Sword of Abraham has stood ready to turn back the tide of the apocalypse.

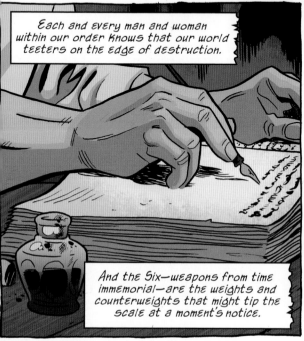

Each and every man and woman within our order knows that our world teeters on the edge of destruction.

And the Six—weapons from time immemorial—are the weights and counterweights that might tip the scale at a moment's notice.

We make ready for the time when we must take up arms and wage war. Not for our sake, not for the sake of the world...

...but for the fate of all creation.

The world is not as it once was.

It has been worn down and rebuilt time and again.

And with every re-creation it becomes less and less what God intended.

With each recreation it becomes more like Hell.

My grandfather served the cause, and he was ripped to shreds by gargoyles in France.

My father, even with his waning faith, followed the edicts of the Sword. It was edicts of a different nature—the laws of the ghouls—that cost him his life.

I came into this world as a member of the order, and I do not yet know how I will shed my mortal coil.

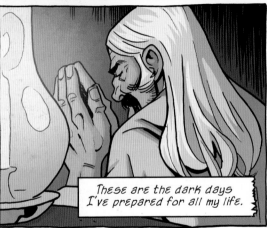

These are the dark days I've prepared for all my life.

And, Lord help me, I'm not ready.

Brother Roberto! Brother Roberto!

What is it?

Th-the *dreams*, brother! The dreams!

Did you not see *him* in your dreams?

I... I haven't slept.

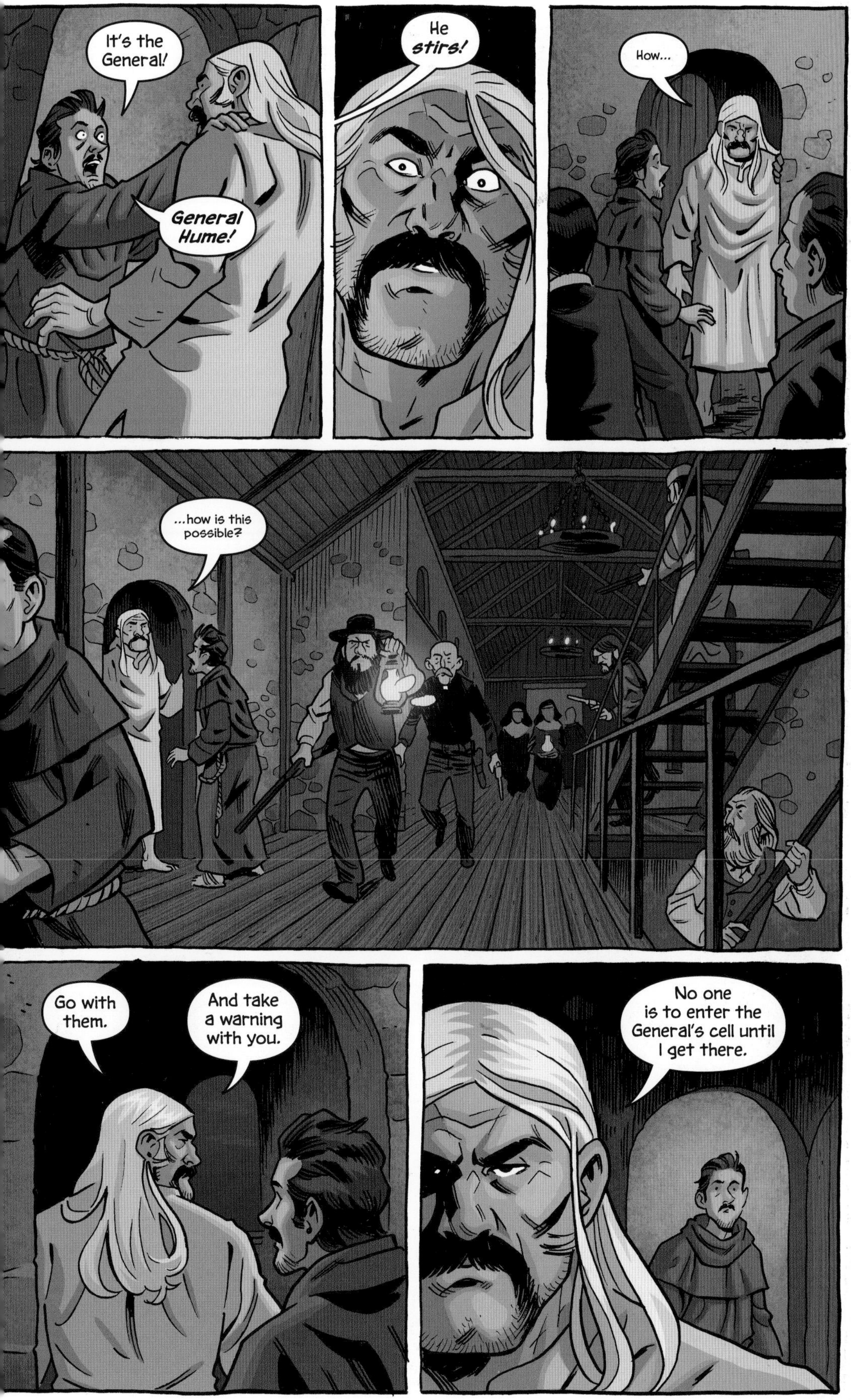
It's the General!
General Hume!
He stirs!
How...
...how is this possible?
Go with them.
And take a warning with you.
No one is to enter the General's cell until I get there.

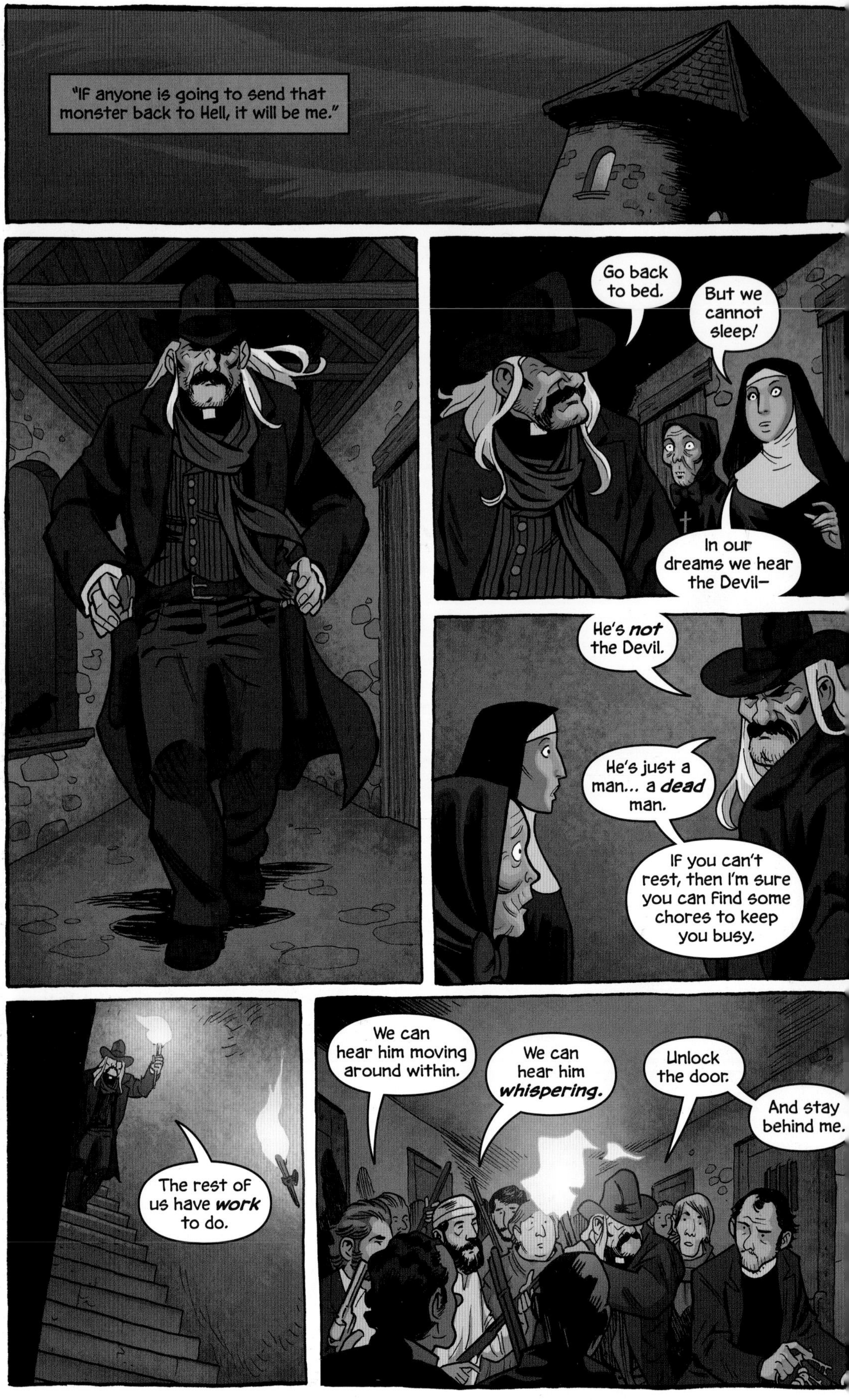
"If anyone is going to send that monster back to Hell, it will be me."
Go back to bed.
But we cannot sleep!
In our dreams we hear the Devil—
He's *not* the Devil.
He's just a man... a *dead* man.
If you can't rest, then I'm sure you can find some chores to keep you busy.
The rest of us have *work* to do.
We can hear him moving around within.
We can hear him *whispering.*
Unlock the door.
And stay behind me.

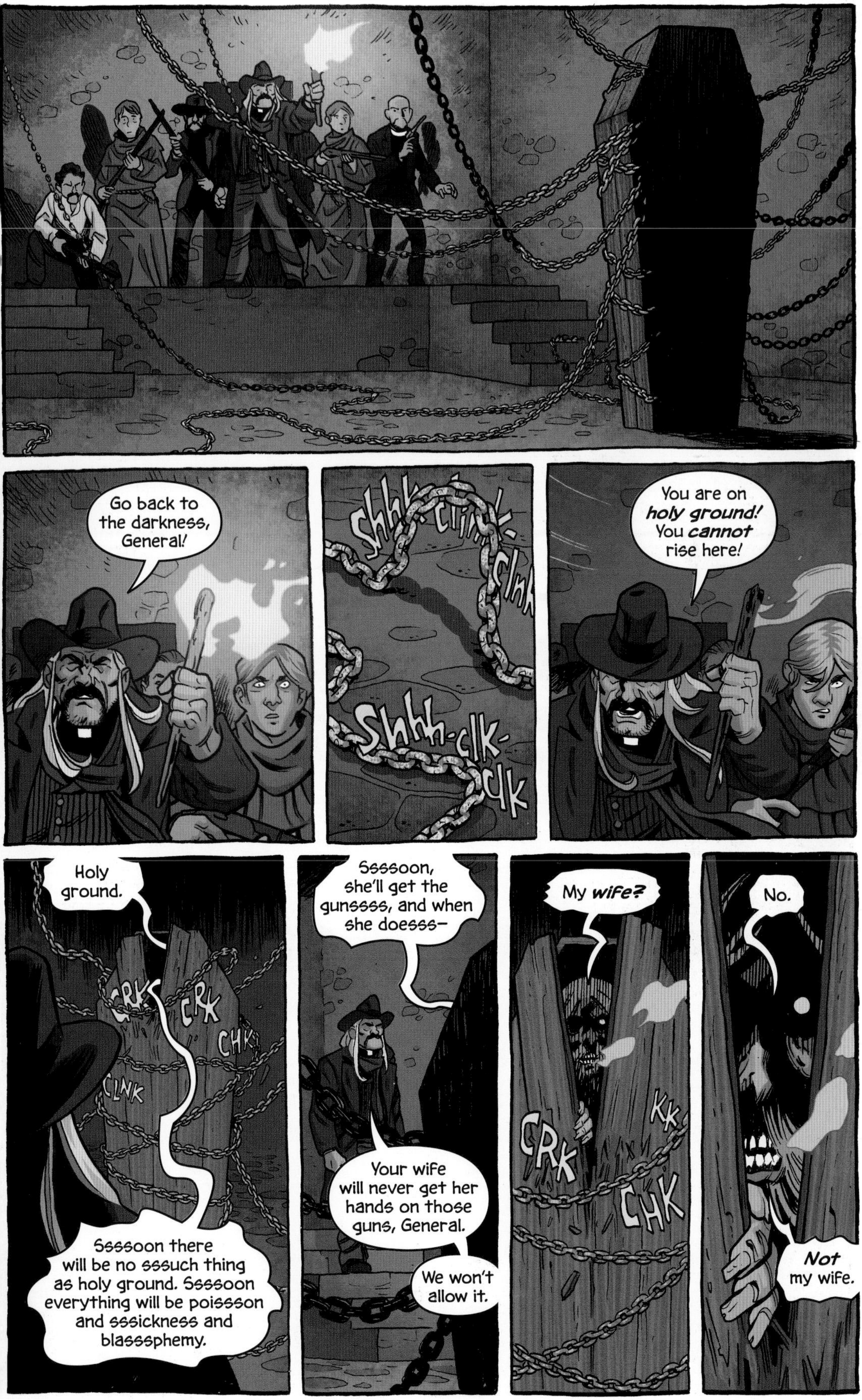
Go back to the darkness, General!
Shhk-clink-clnk
Shhh-clk-ck
You are on *holy ground!* You *cannot* rise here!
Holy ground.
CRK
CRK
CHK
CLNK
Sssssoon there will be no sssuch thing as holy ground. Sssssoon everything will be poissson and sssickness and blassssphemy.
Sssssoon, she'll get the gunssss, and when she doesss—
Your wife will never get her hands on those guns, General.
We won't allow it.
My *wife?*
CRK
KK
CHK
No.
Not my wife.

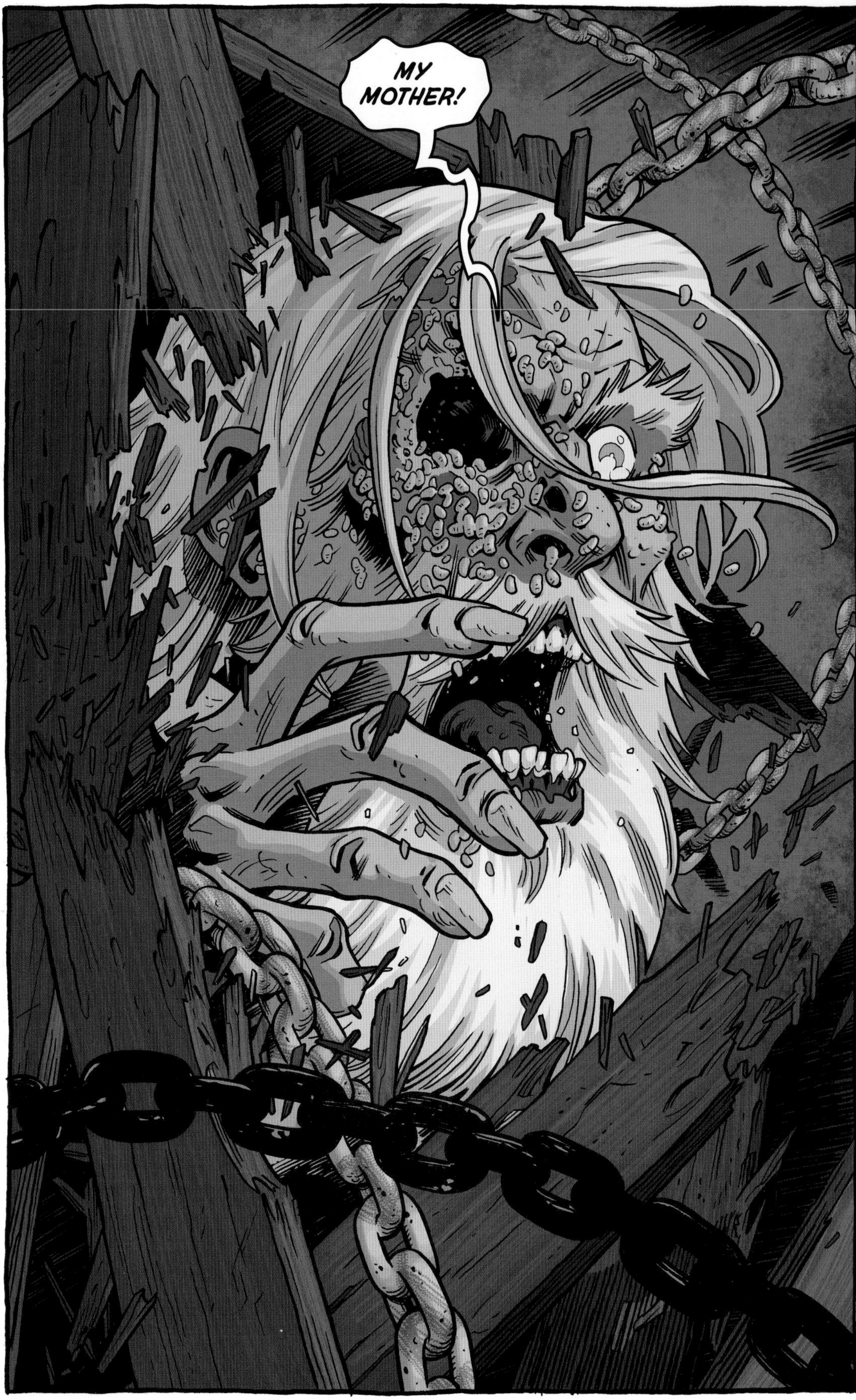
MY MOTHER!

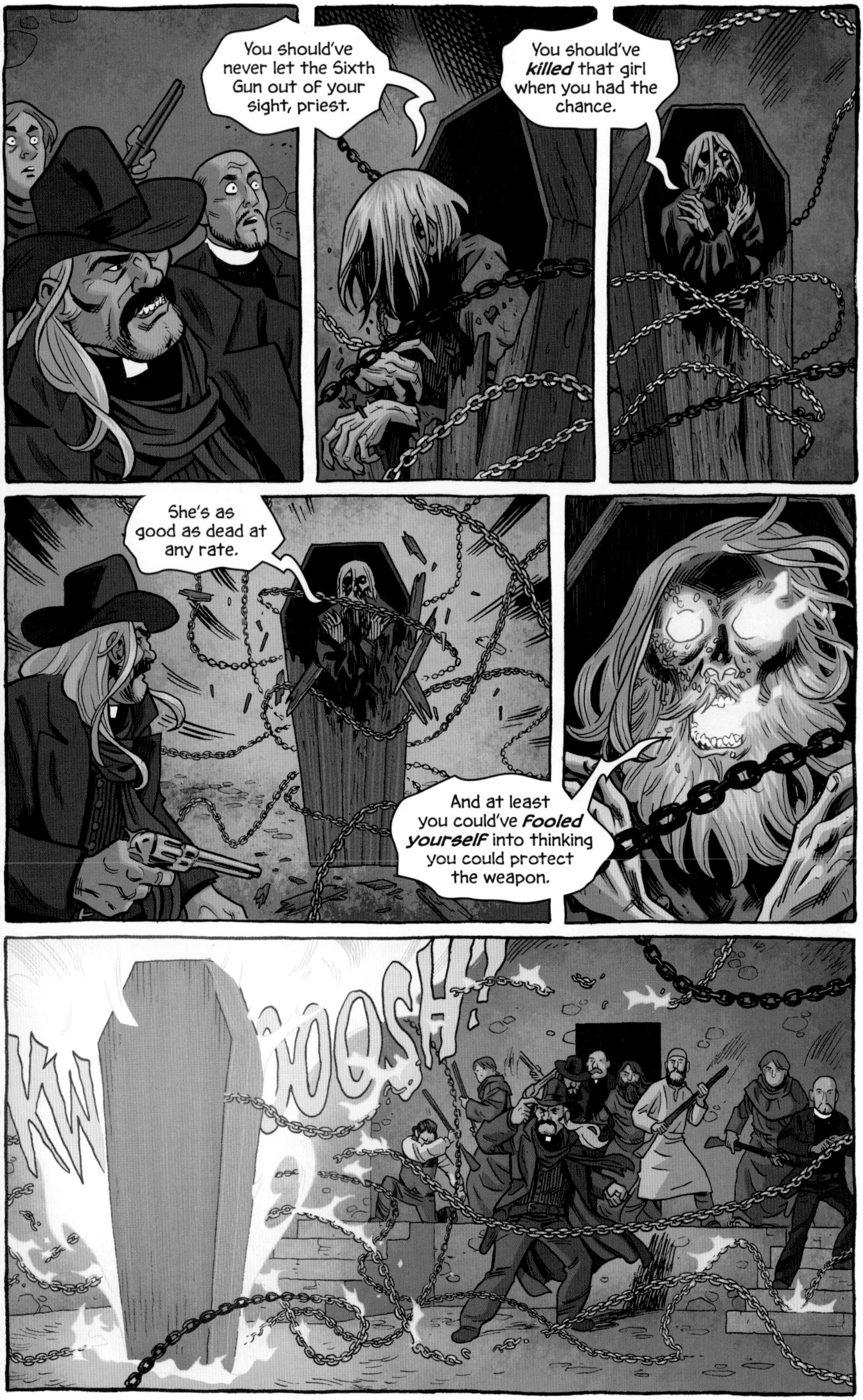
You should've never let the Sixth Gun out of your sight, priest.
You should've *killed* that girl when you had the chance.
She's as good as dead at any rate.
And at least you could've *Fooled yourself* into thinking you could protect the weapon.
KW
OOSH!!

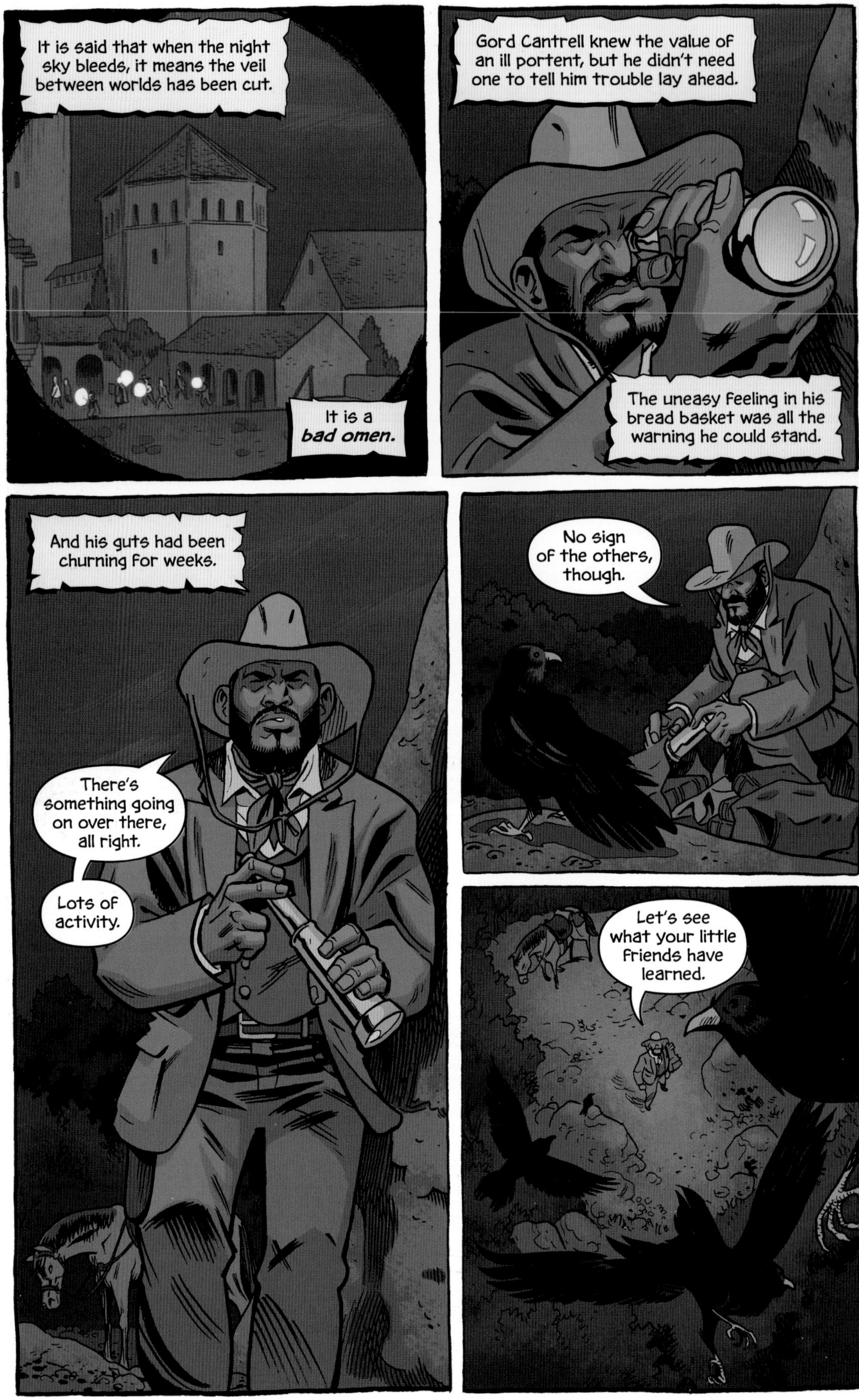
It is said that when the night sky bleeds, it means the veil between worlds has been cut.
It is a *bad omen.*
Gord Cantrell knew the value of an ill portent, but he didn't need one to tell him trouble lay ahead.
The uneasy feeling in his bread basket was all the warning he could stand.
And his guts had been churning for weeks.
There's something going on over there, all right.
Lots of activity.
No sign of the others, though.
Let's see what your little friends have learned.

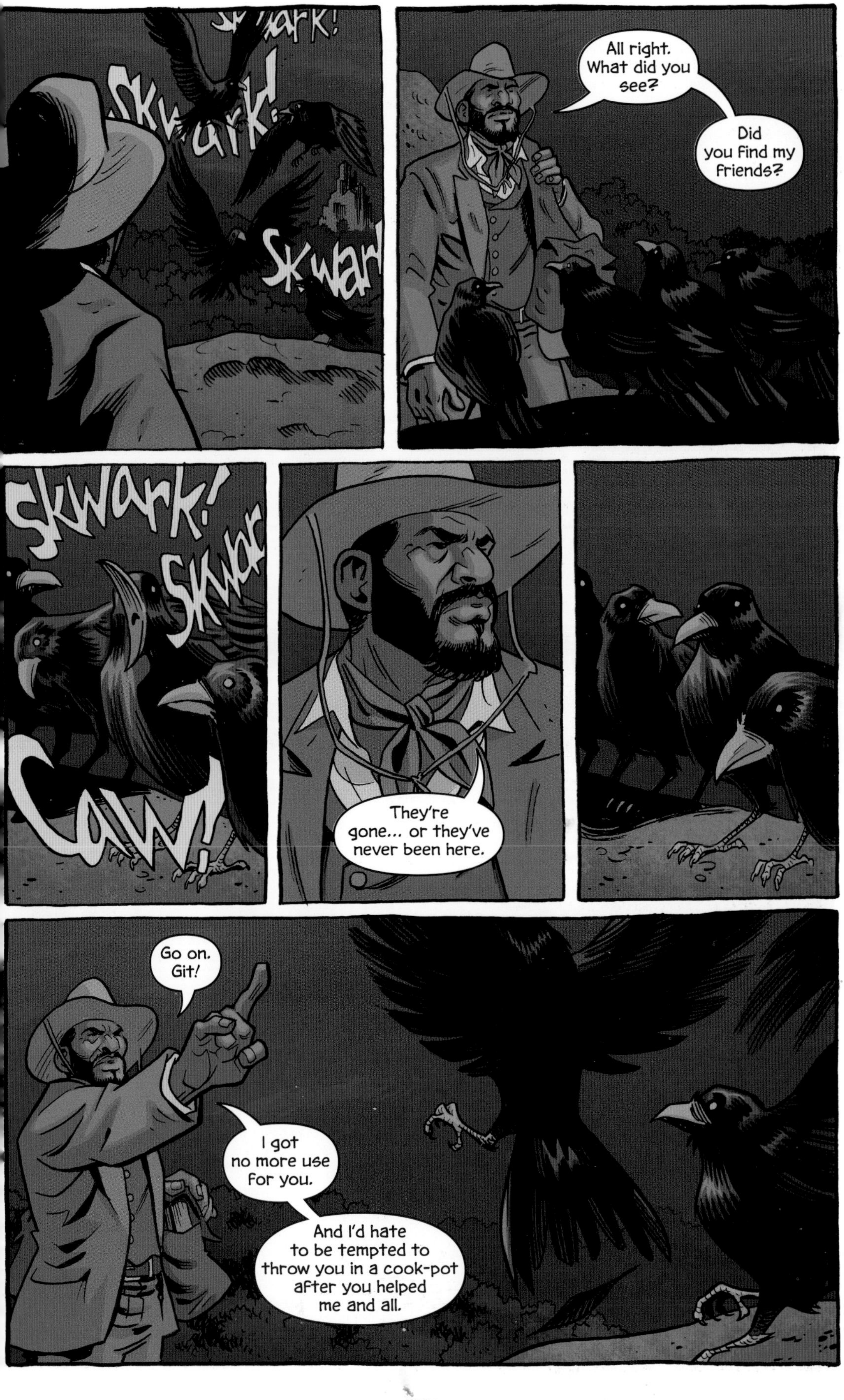
Skwark!
Skwark!
Skwar
All right. What did you see?
Did you find my friends?
Skwark!
Skwar
Caw!
They're gone... or they've never been here.
Go on. Git!
I got no more use for you.
And I'd hate to be tempted to throw you in a cook-pot after you helped me and all.

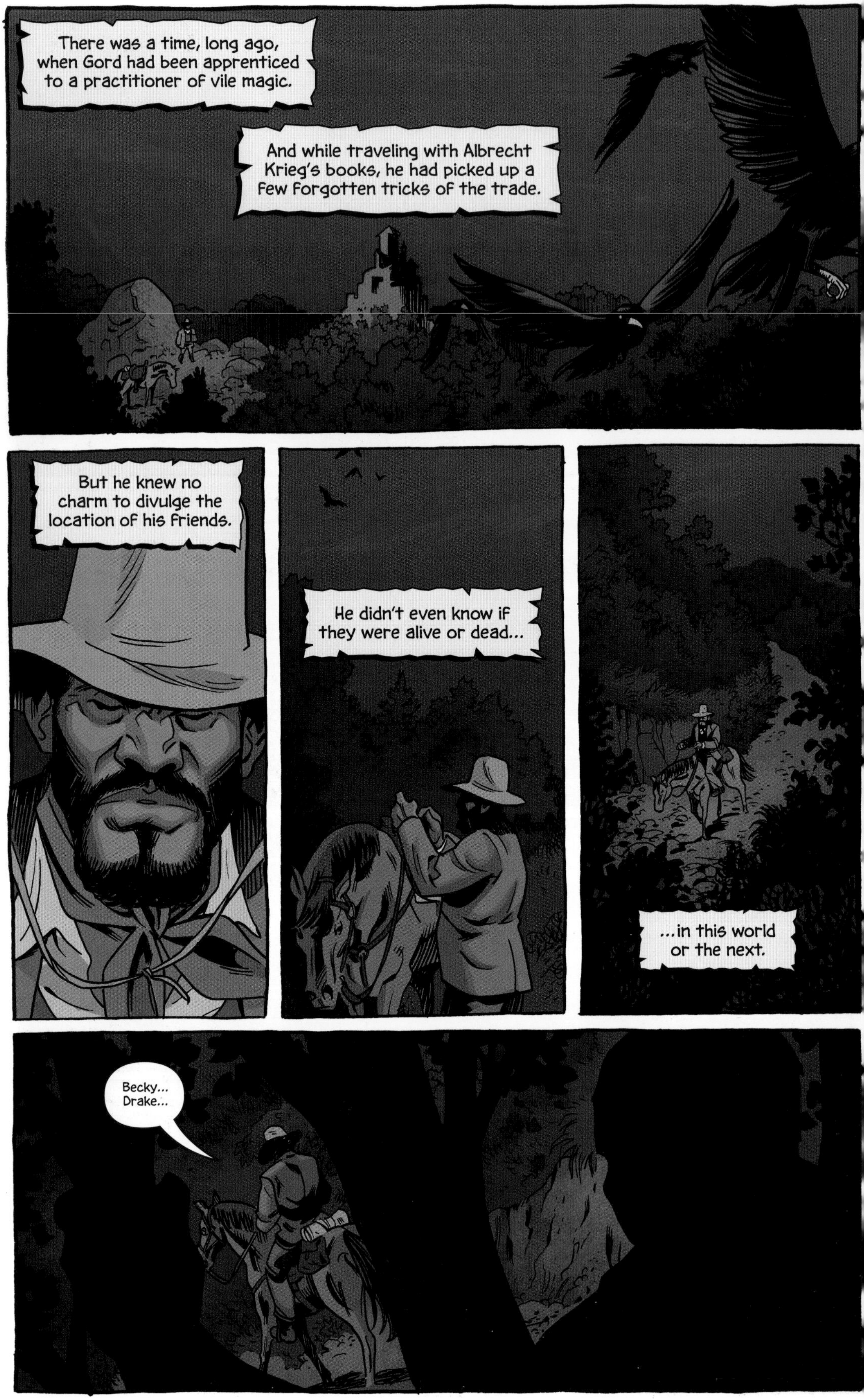
There was a time, long ago, when Gord had been apprenticed to a practitioner of vile magic.
And while traveling with Albrecht Krieg's books, he had picked up a few forgotten tricks of the trade.
But he knew no charm to divulge the location of his friends.
He didn't even know if they were alive or dead...
...in this world or the next.
Becky... Drake...

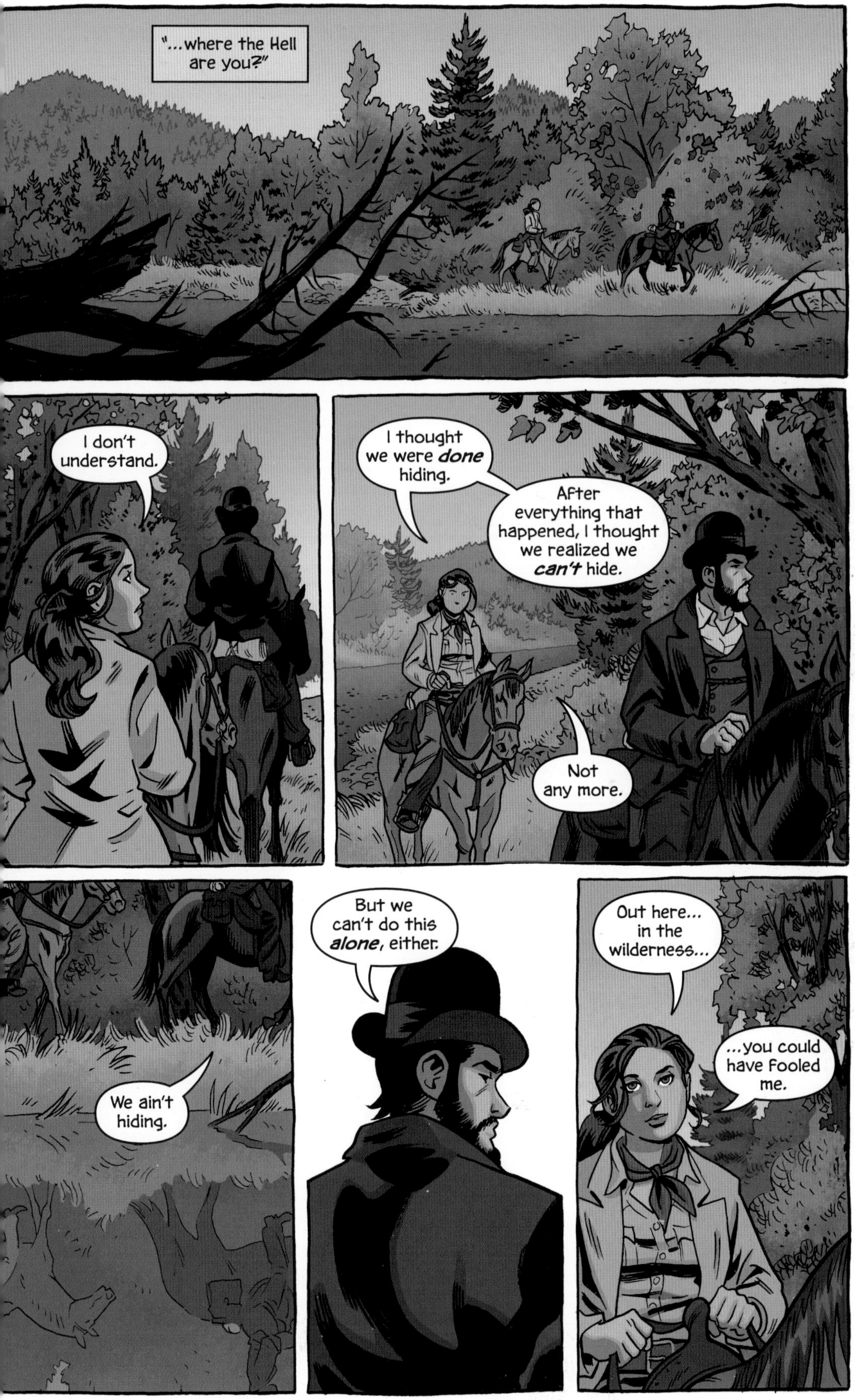
"...where the Hell are you?"
I don't understand.
I thought we were *done* hiding.
After everything that happened, I thought we realized we *can't* hide.
Not any more.
We ain't hiding.
But we can't do this *alone*, either.
Out here... in the wilderness...
...you could have fooled me.

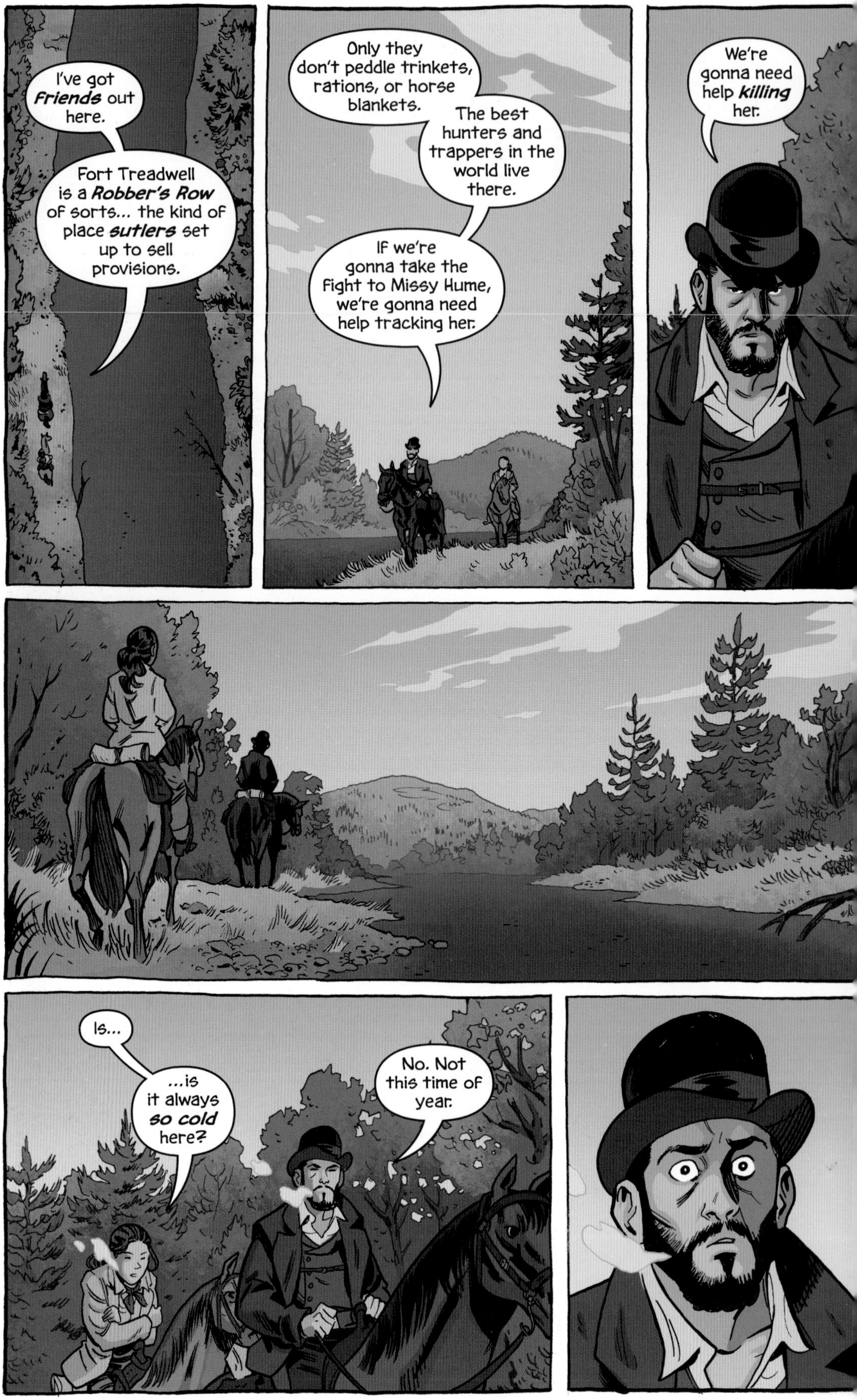
I've got *Friends* out here.
Fort Treadwell is a *Robber's Row* of sorts... the kind of place *sutlers* set up to sell provisions.
Only they don't peddle trinkets, rations, or horse blankets.
The best hunters and trappers in the world live there.
If we're gonna take the fight to Missy Hume, we're gonna need help tracking her.
We're gonna need help *killing* her.
Is...
...is it always *so cold* here?
No. Not this time of year.

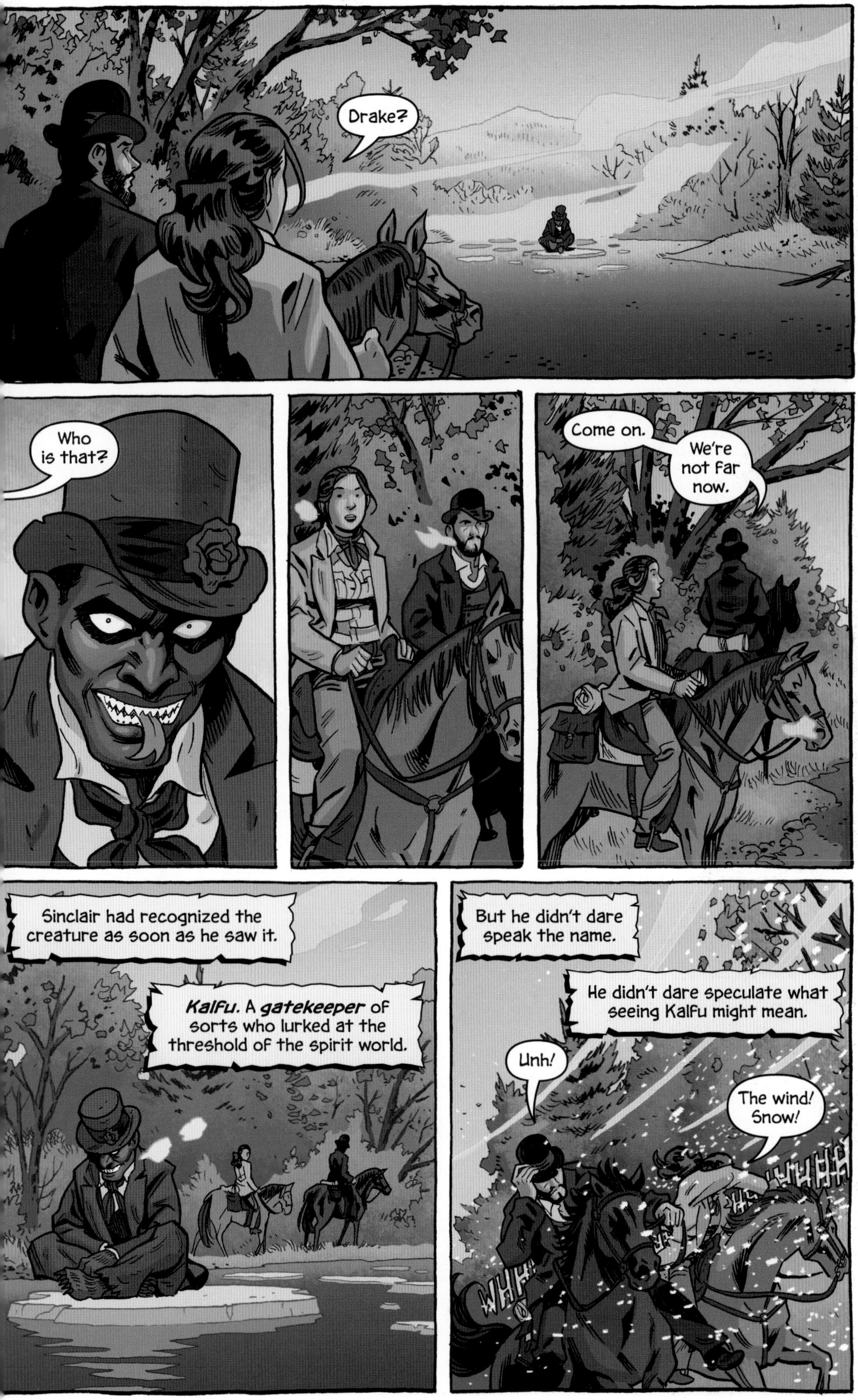

Drake?
Who is that?
Come on.
We're not far now.
Sinclair had recognized the creature as soon as he saw it.
Kalfu. A *gatekeeper* of sorts who lurked at the threshold of the spirit world.
But he didn't dare speak the name.
He didn't dare speculate what seeing Kalfu might mean.
Unh!
The wind! Snow!

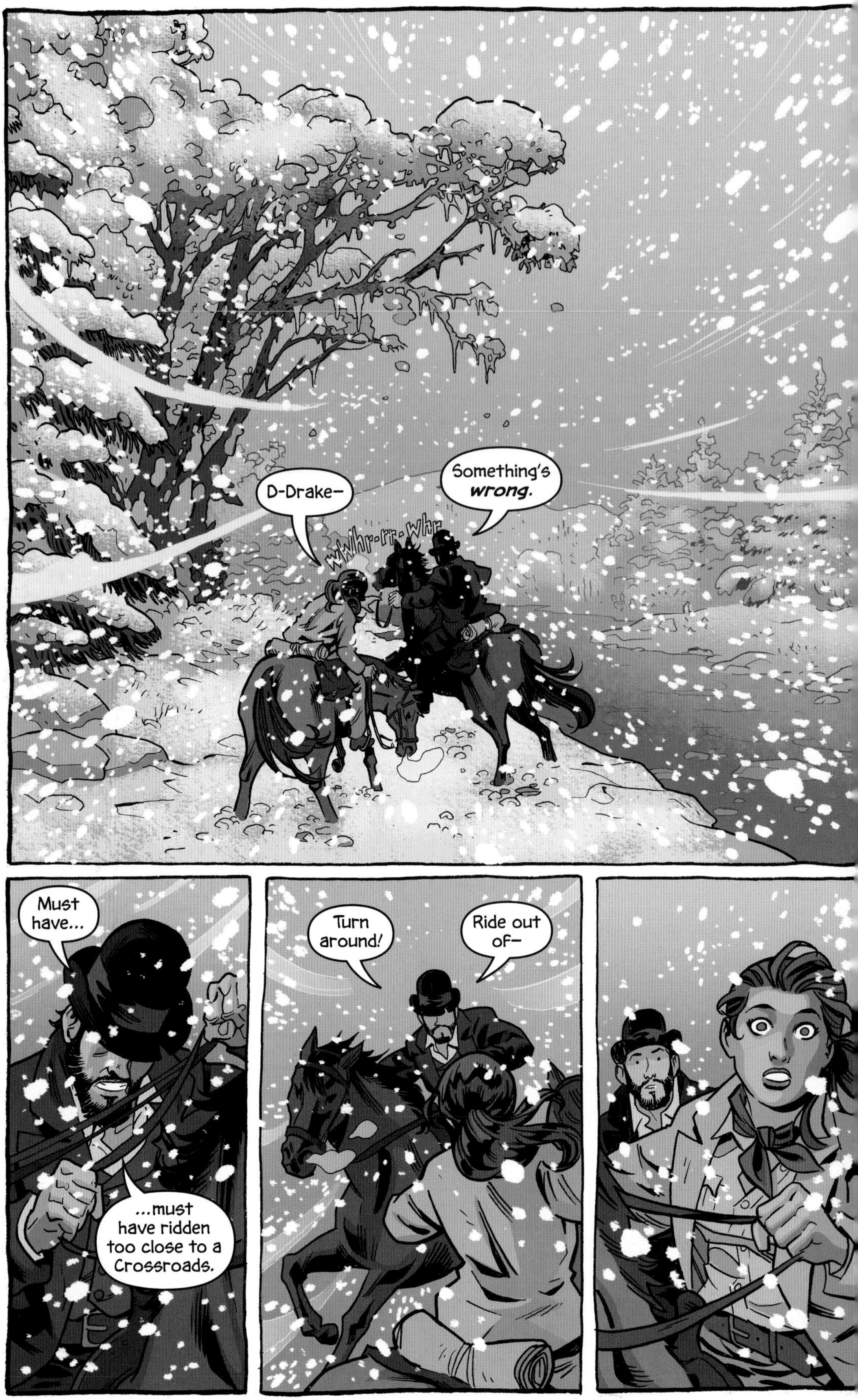
D-Drake–
Something's *wrong.*
wwhr-rr-whr
Must have...
...must have ridden too close to a Crossroads.
Turn around!
Ride out of–

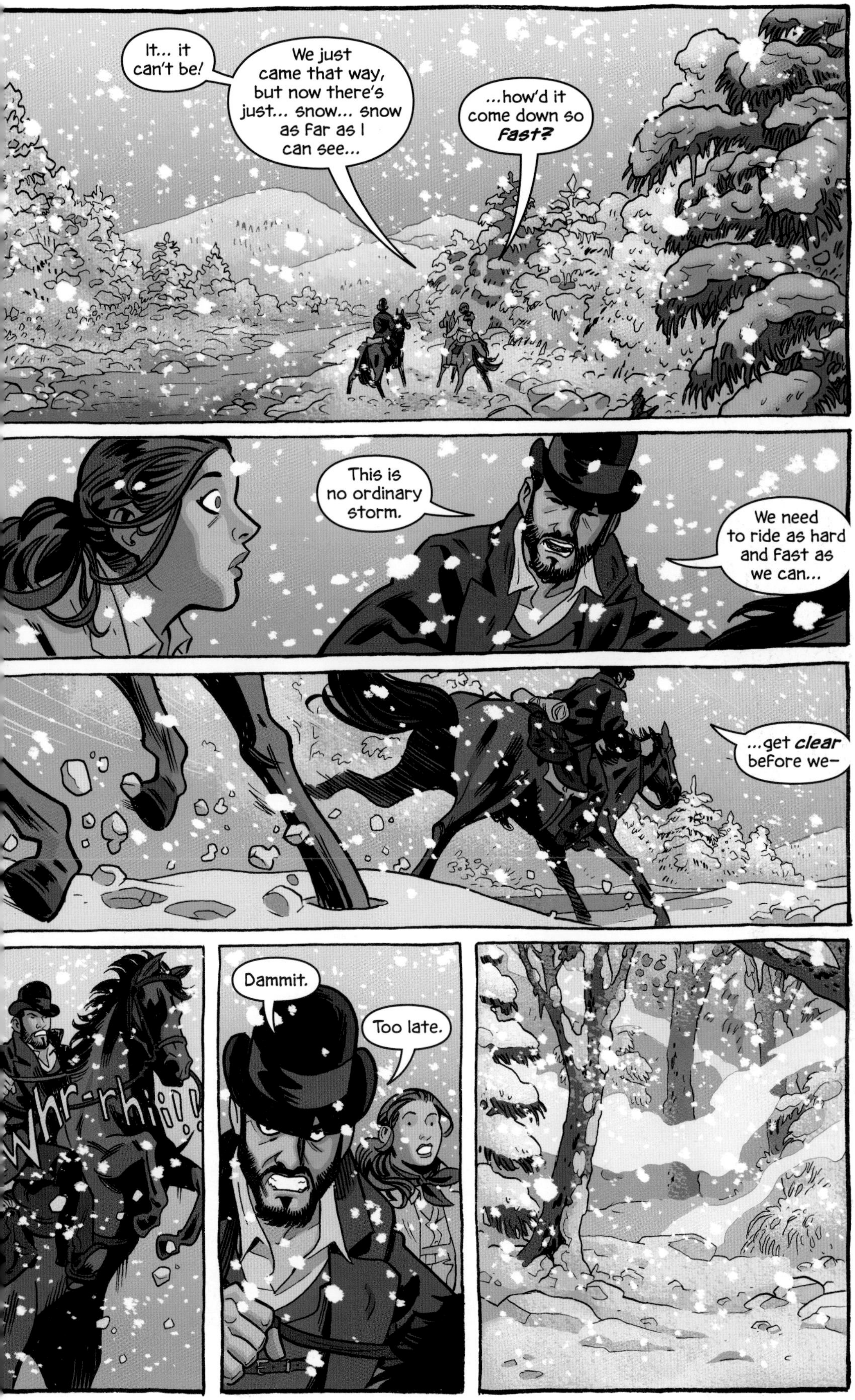
It... it can't be!
We just came that way, but now there's just... snow... snow as far as I can see...
...how'd it come down so *fast?*
This is no ordinary storm.
We need to ride as hard and fast as we can...
...get *clear* before we–
Whr-rhiii!!
Dammit.
Too late.

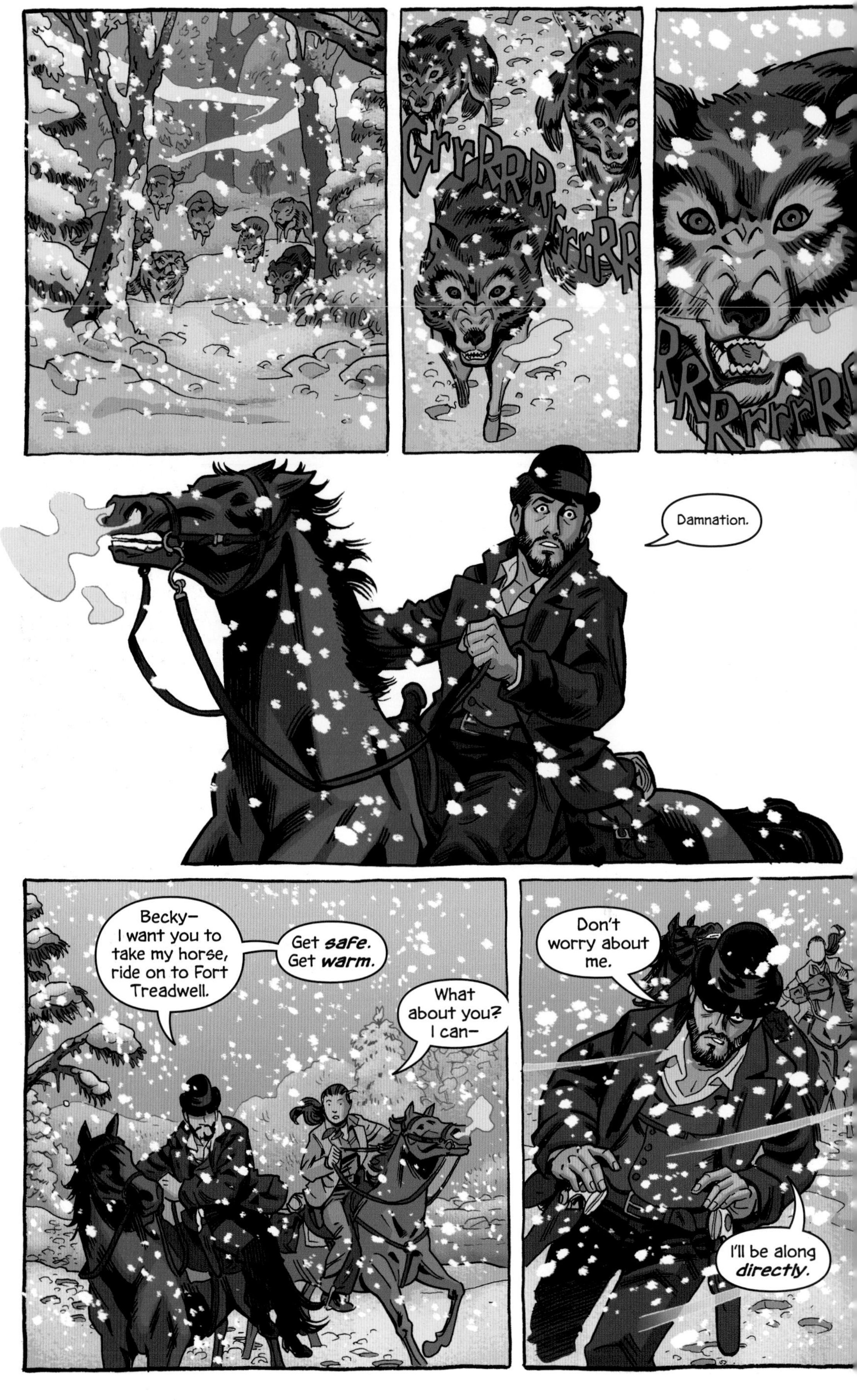
GrrRRRRrrrRR
RRRRrrrrR
Damnation.
Becky— I want you to take my horse, ride on to Fort Treadwell.
Get *safe*. Get *warm*.
What about you? I can—
Don't worry about me.
I'll be along *directly*.

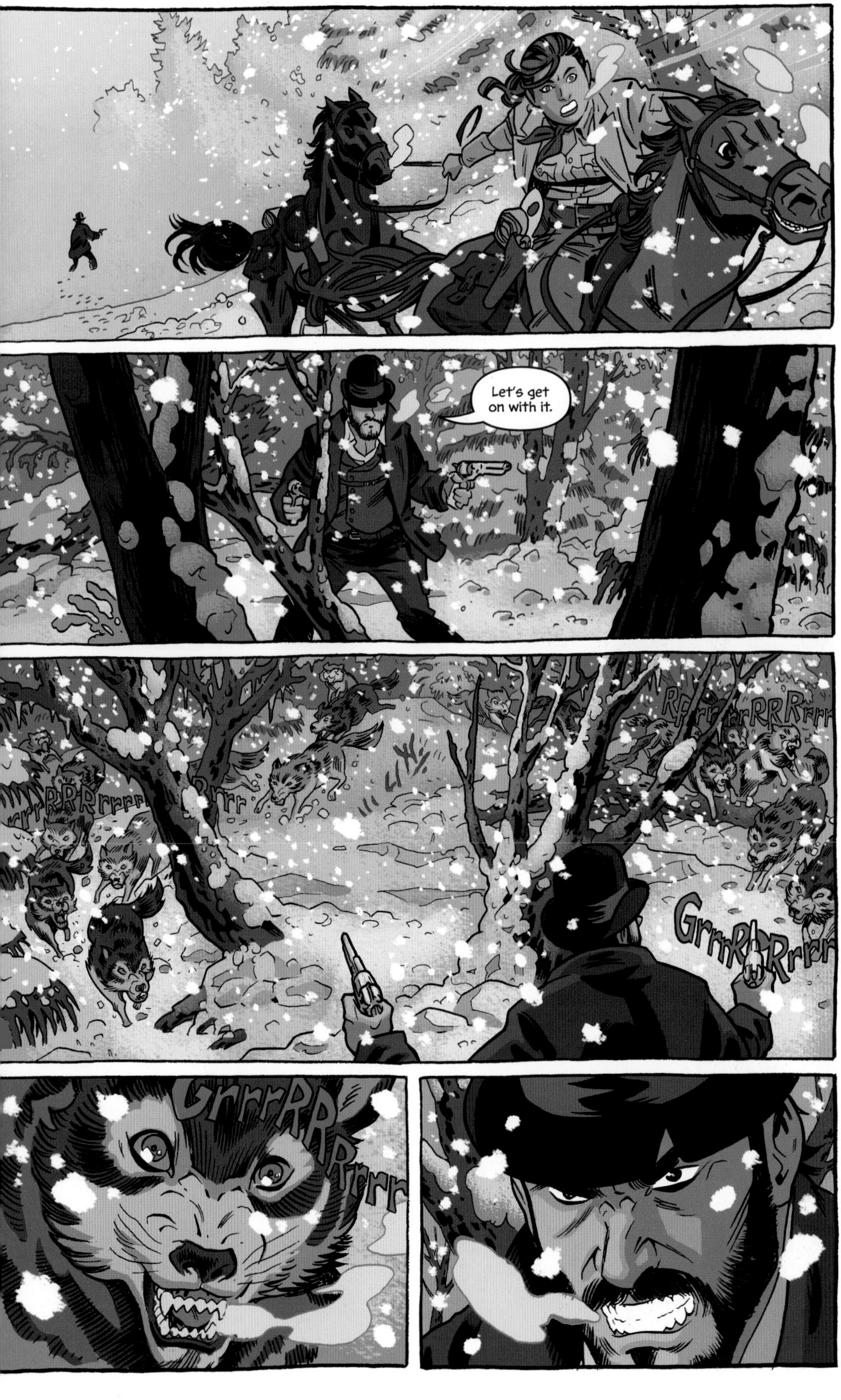
Let's get on with it.
RRrrrrrrRRRrrrr
rrrRRRrrrrrrr
Rrrr
GrrrRRRrrr
GrrrRRRrrrr

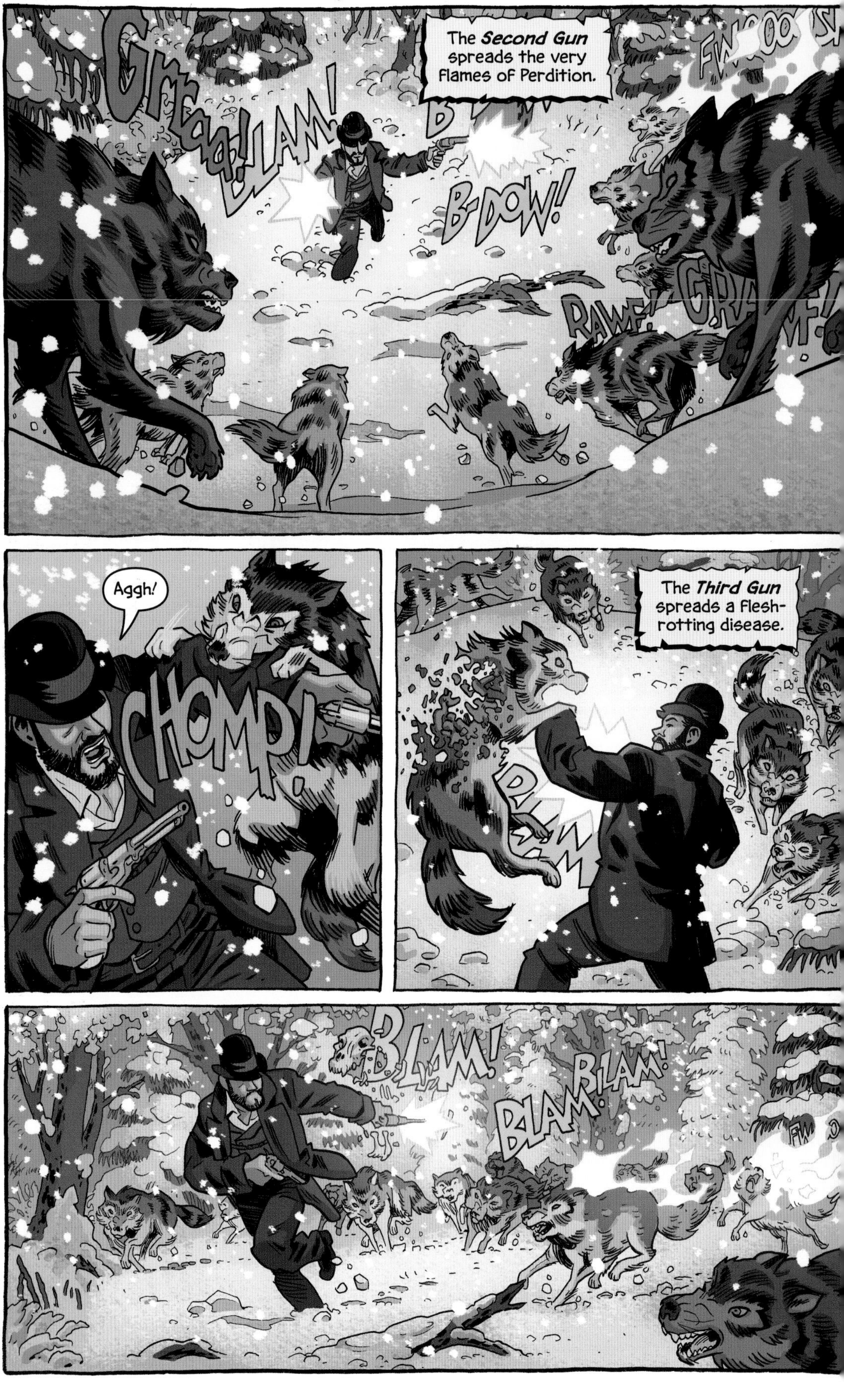
The *Second Gun* spreads the very flames of Perdition.
Grraaa!
BLAM!
B-DOW!
RAWF!
Aggh!
CHOMP!
The *Third Gun* spreads a flesh-rotting disease.
BLAM!
BLAM!
BLAM!

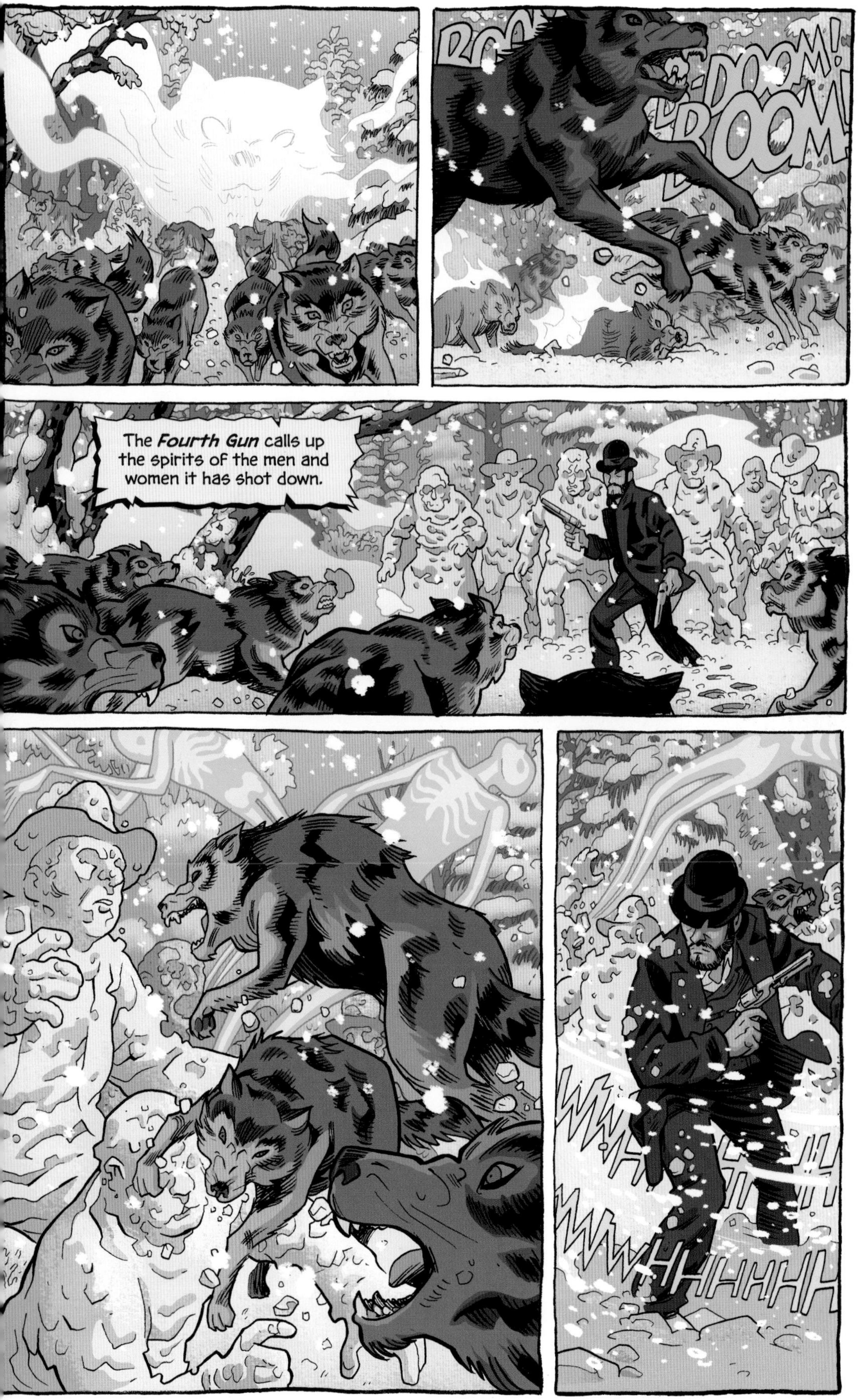

BOOM!
DOOM!
BOOM!
The Fourth Gun calls up the spirits of the men and women it has shot down.

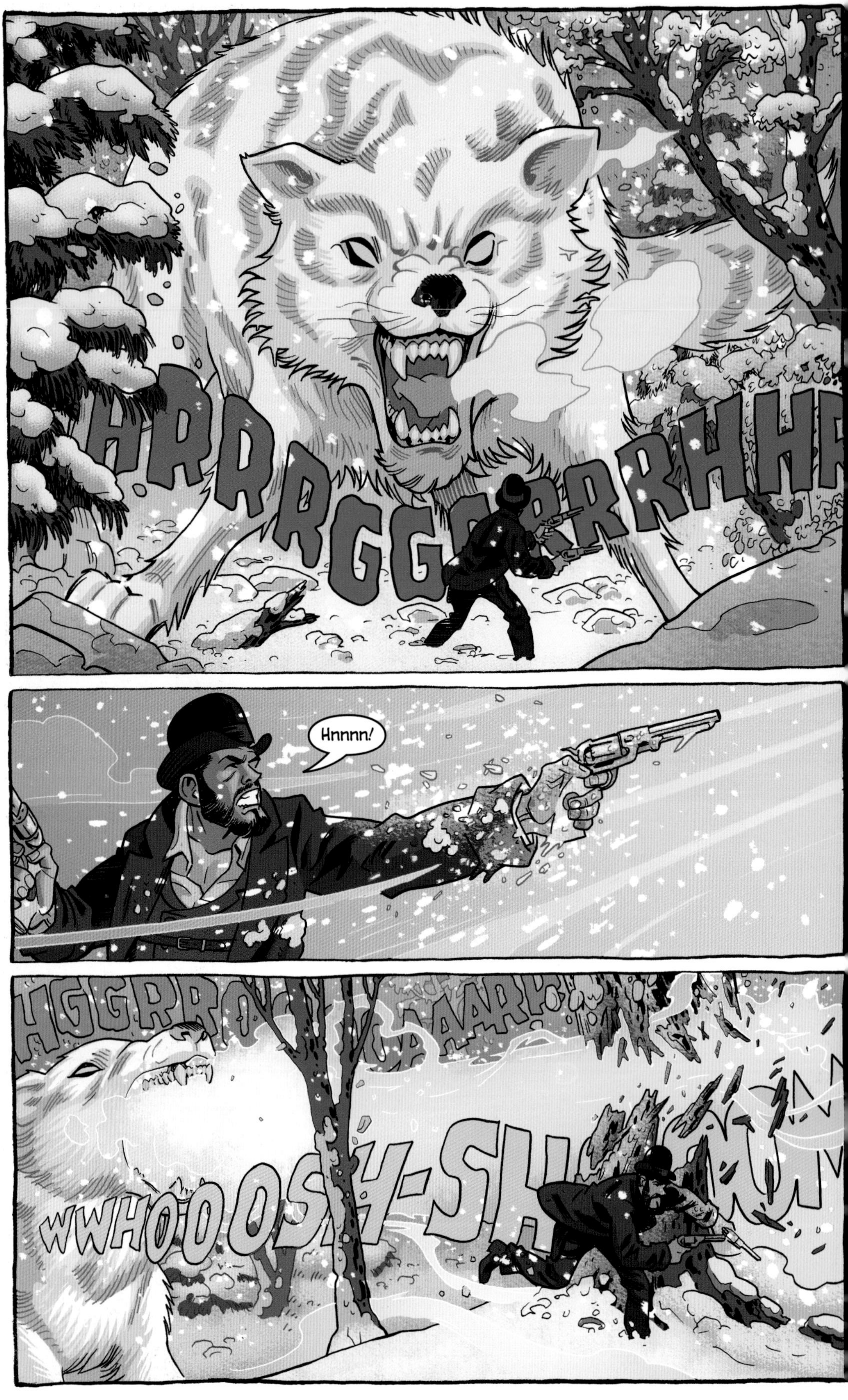
HRRRGG
RRRRHHR
Hnnnn!
HGGRRO
AAR
WWHOOOSH-SH

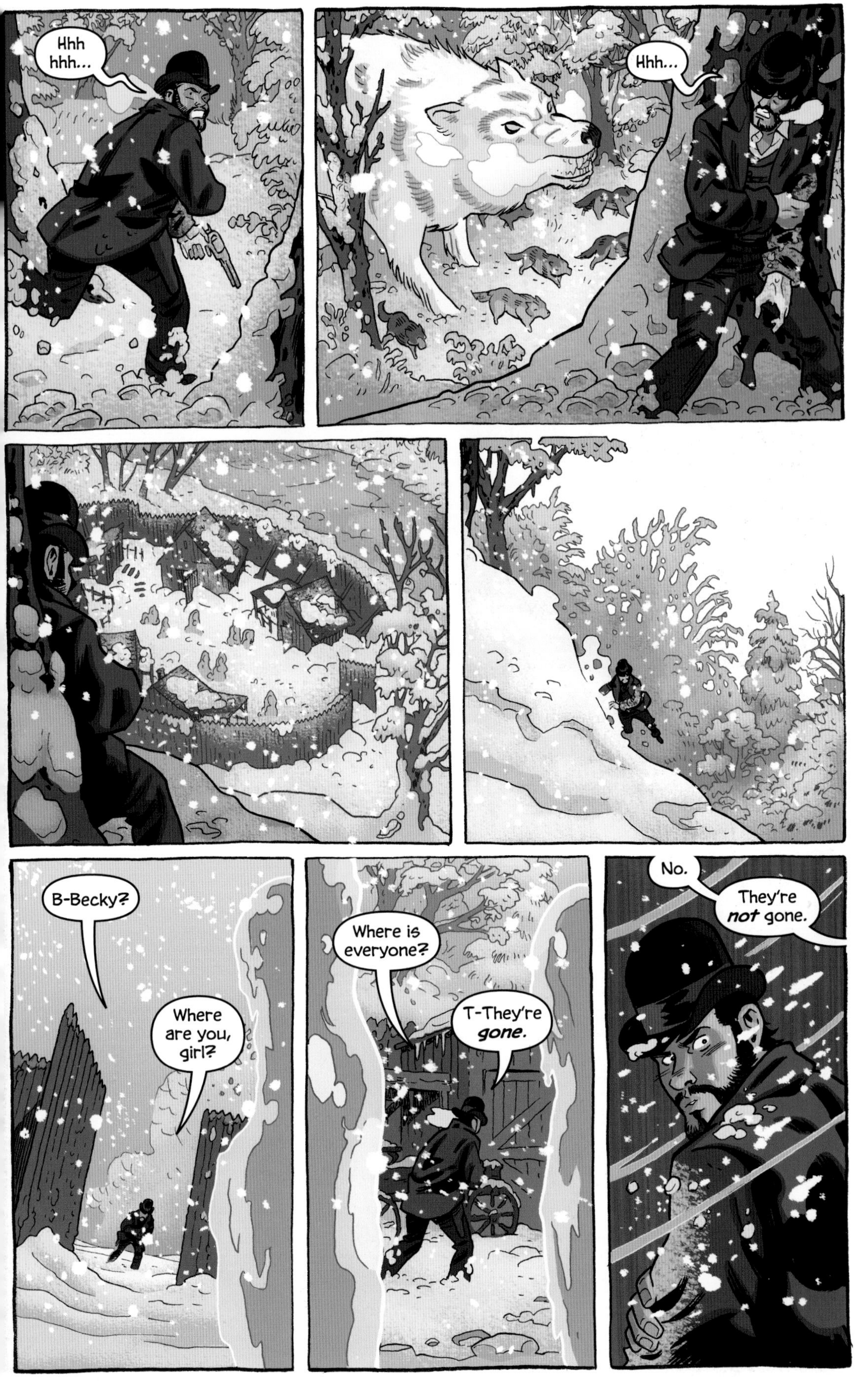
Hhh
hhh...
Hhh...
B-Becky?
Where are you, girl?
Where is everyone?
T-They're *gone.*
No.
They're *not* gone.

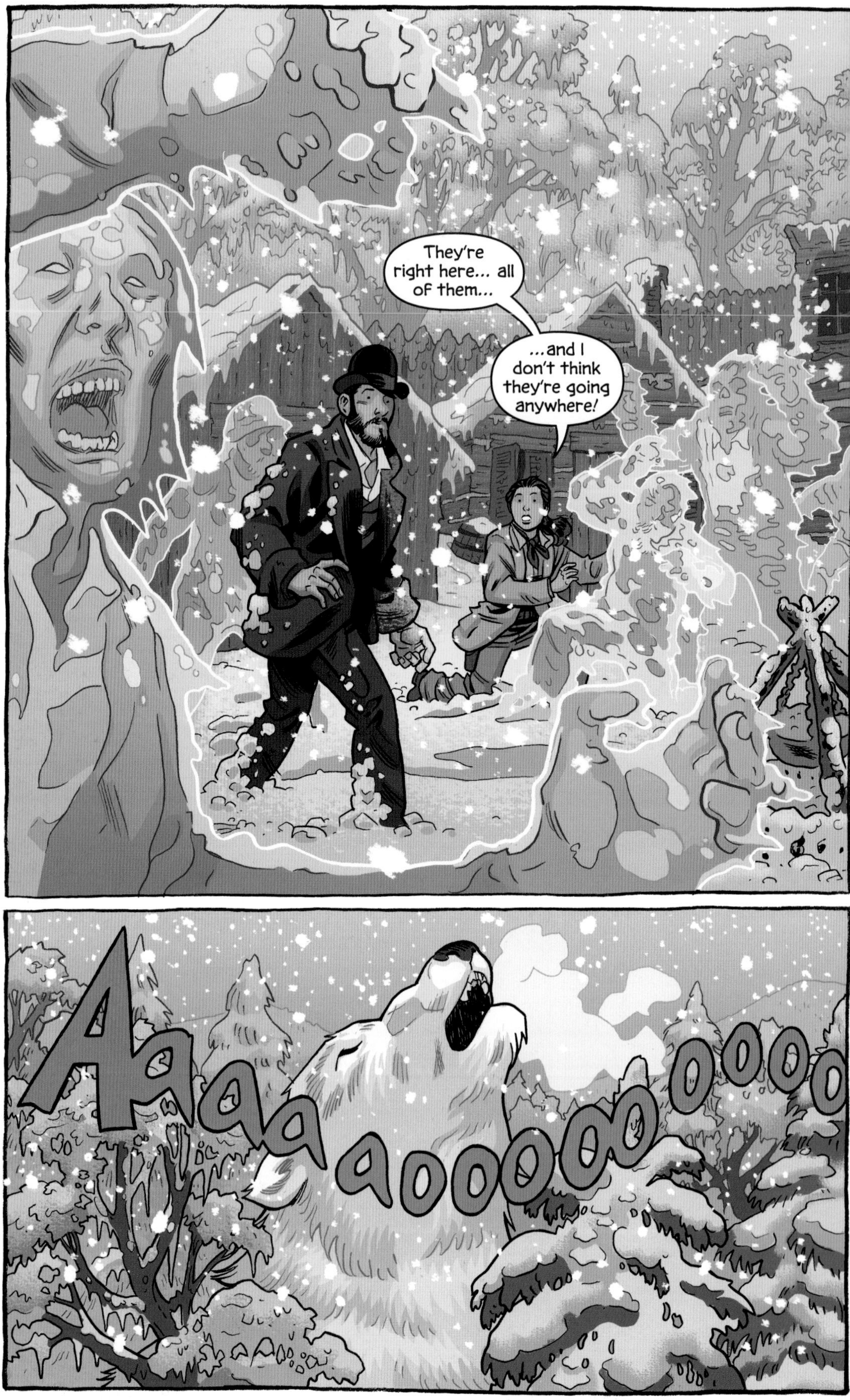
They're right here... all of them...
...and I don't think they're going anywhere!
Aaaaaooooooooooo

CHAPTER
TWO

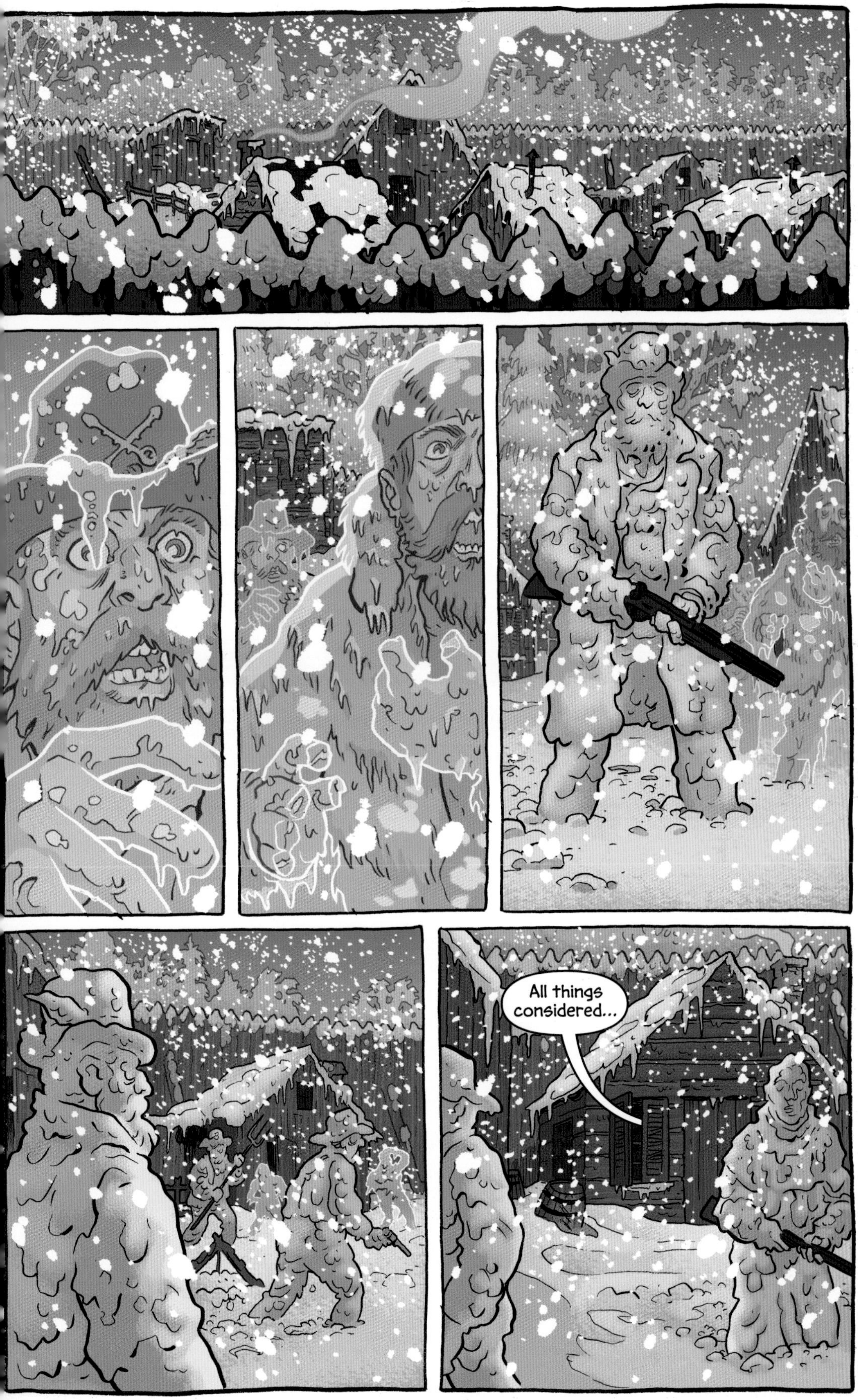
All things considered...

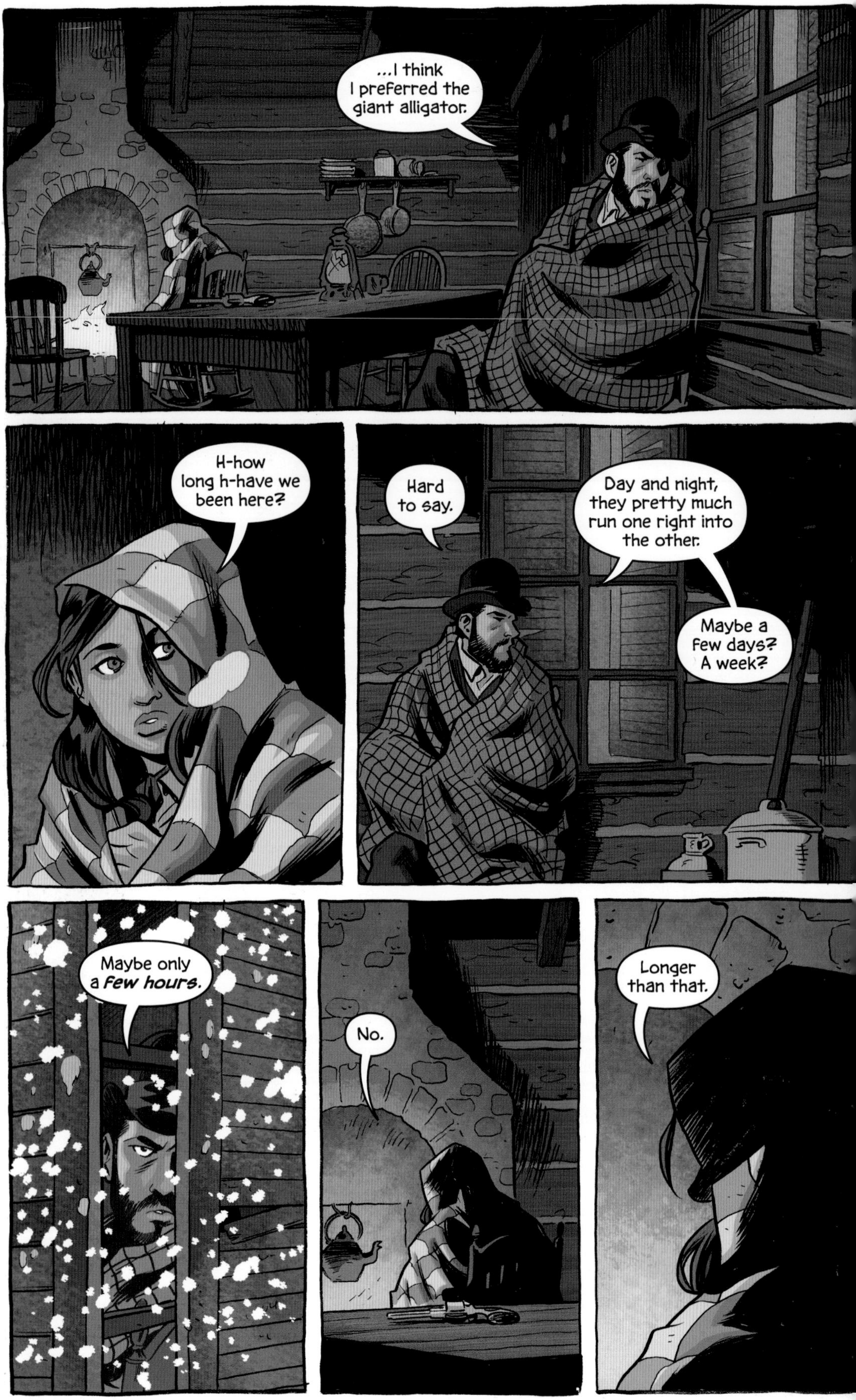
...I think I preferred the giant alligator.
H-how long h-have we been here?
Hard to say.
Day and night, they pretty much run one right into the other.
Maybe a few days? A week?
Maybe only a *few hours.*
No.
Longer than that.

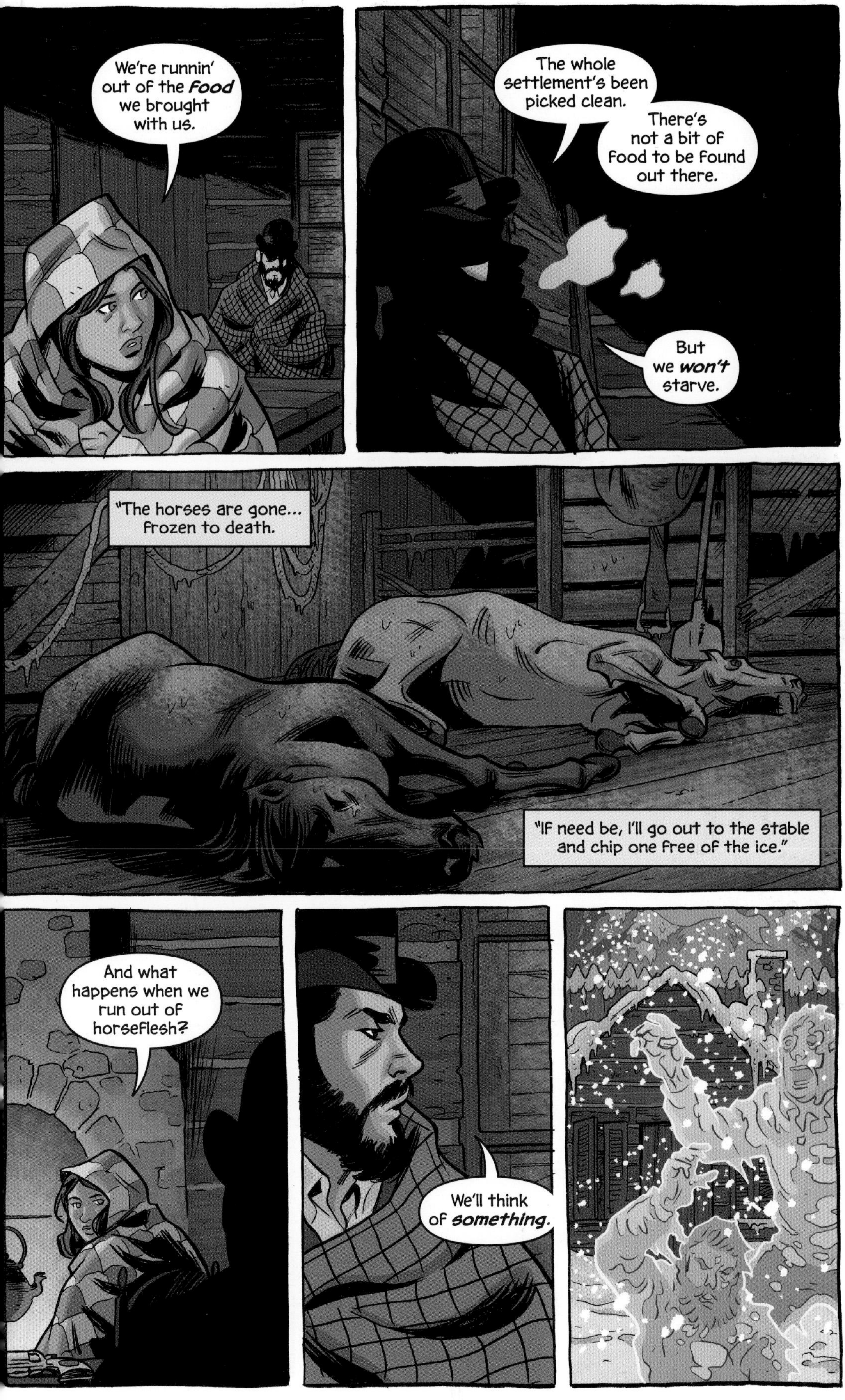
We're runnin' out of the *food* we brought with us.
The whole settlement's been picked clean.
There's not a bit of food to be found out there.
But we *won't* starve.
"The horses are gone... frozen to death.
"If need be, I'll go out to the stable and chip one free of the ice."
And what happens when we run out of horseflesh?
We'll think of *something*.

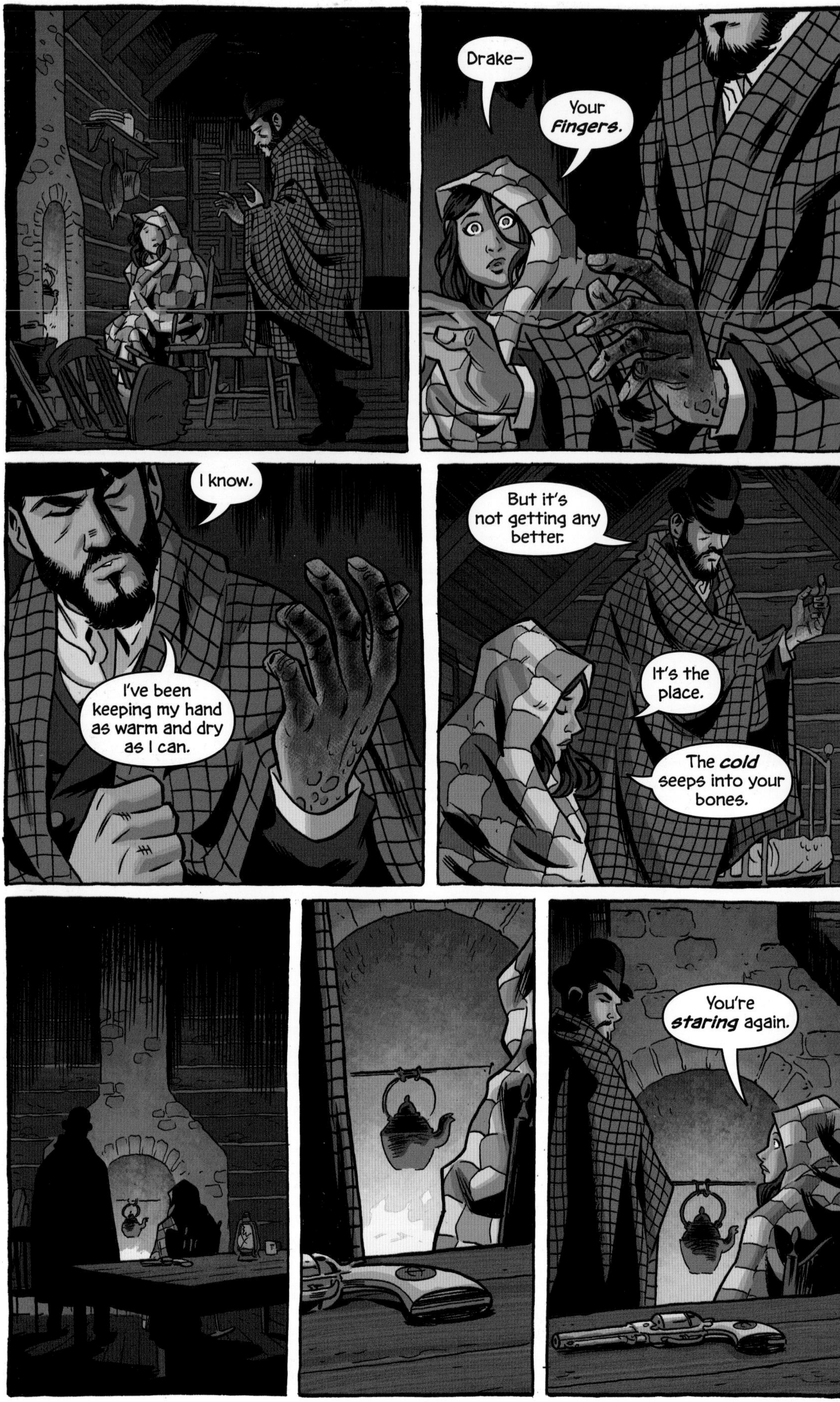

Drake–
Your *fingers*.
I know.
I've been keeping my hand as warm and dry as I can.
But it's not getting any better.
It's the place.
The *cold* seeps into your bones.
You're *staring* again.

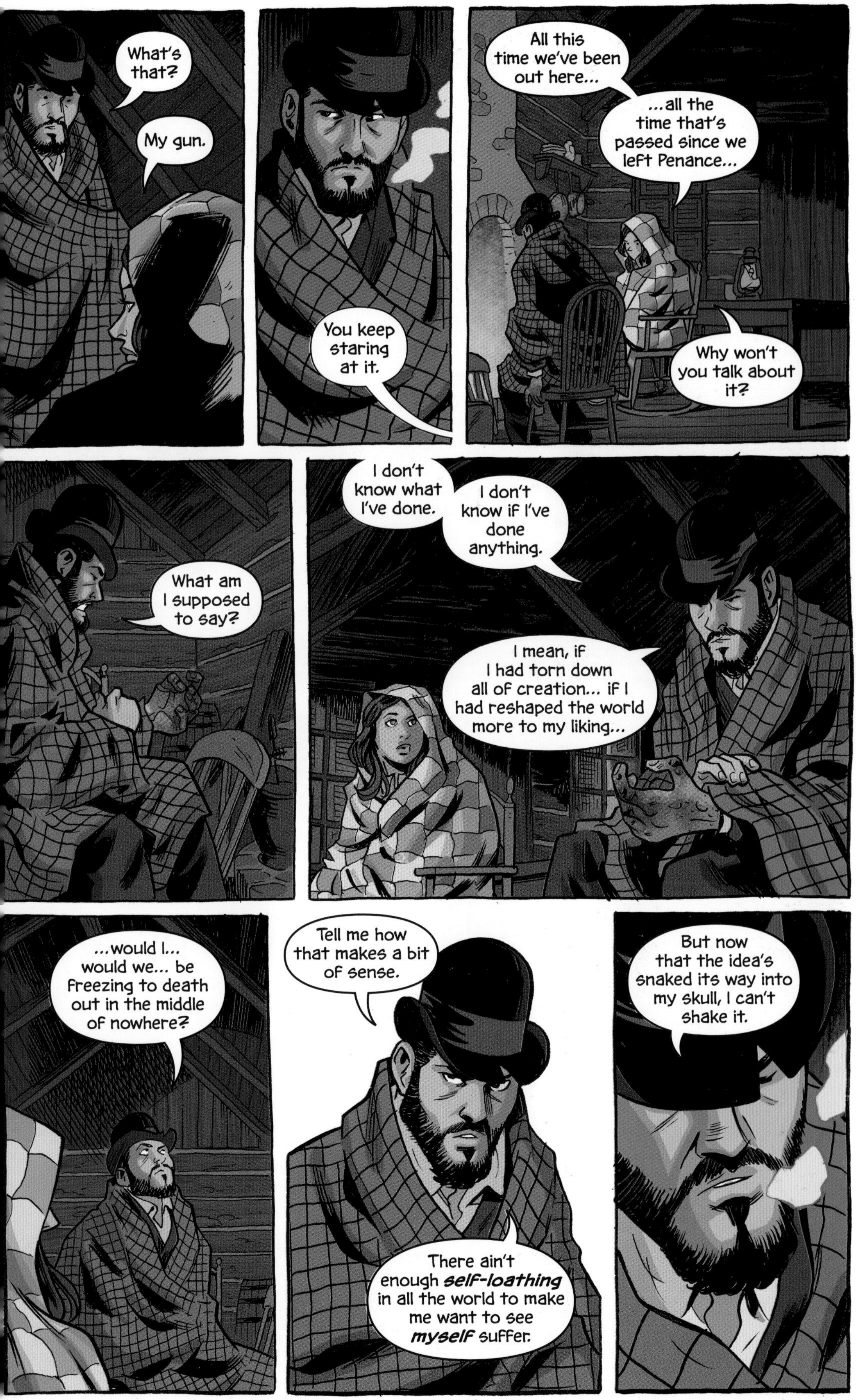
What's that?
My gun.
You keep staring at it.
All this time we've been out here...
...all the time that's passed since we left Penance...
Why won't you talk about it?
What am I supposed to say?
I don't know what I've done.
I don't know if I've done anything.
I mean, if I had torn down all of creation... if I had reshaped the world more to my liking...
...would I... would we... be freezing to death out in the middle of nowhere?
Tell me how that makes a bit of sense.
There ain't enough *self-loathing* in all the world to make me want to see *myself* suffer.
But now that the idea's snaked its way into my skull, I can't shake it.

"It's like this *nightmare*... always lurking on the outskirts of everything I know to be rational."

"And I can't help but think that it's coming for me... that it's going to swallow me whole."

I've tried to use the gun... tried to see a way for us to escape.

But I can't see past the blizzard.

It's like the storm is as big as the world.

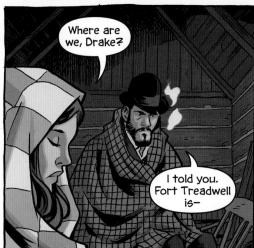

Where are we, Drake?

I told you. Fort Treadwell is—

No.

"Where are we *really?*"

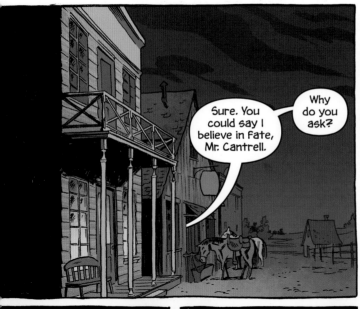

Why do you ask?

Sure. You could say I believe in Fate, Mr. Cantrell.

You gonna read my *Fortune?*

A man who believes in destiny shouldn't worry over a fortune-teller.

But you and me... it seems we have a shared fate of sorts.

Mister, I ain't even sure we're gonna share this table for more than a few more seconds.

What makes you think—

A fortnight past, I came across a... man.

Rather, *he* found *me.*

Seems he has a *knack* for that.

For finding folks.

It was this man who led me to you.

To what end?

If you're still *raw* about what happened in New Orleans—

We want the same thing, you and me.

Is that a fact?

And what might that be?

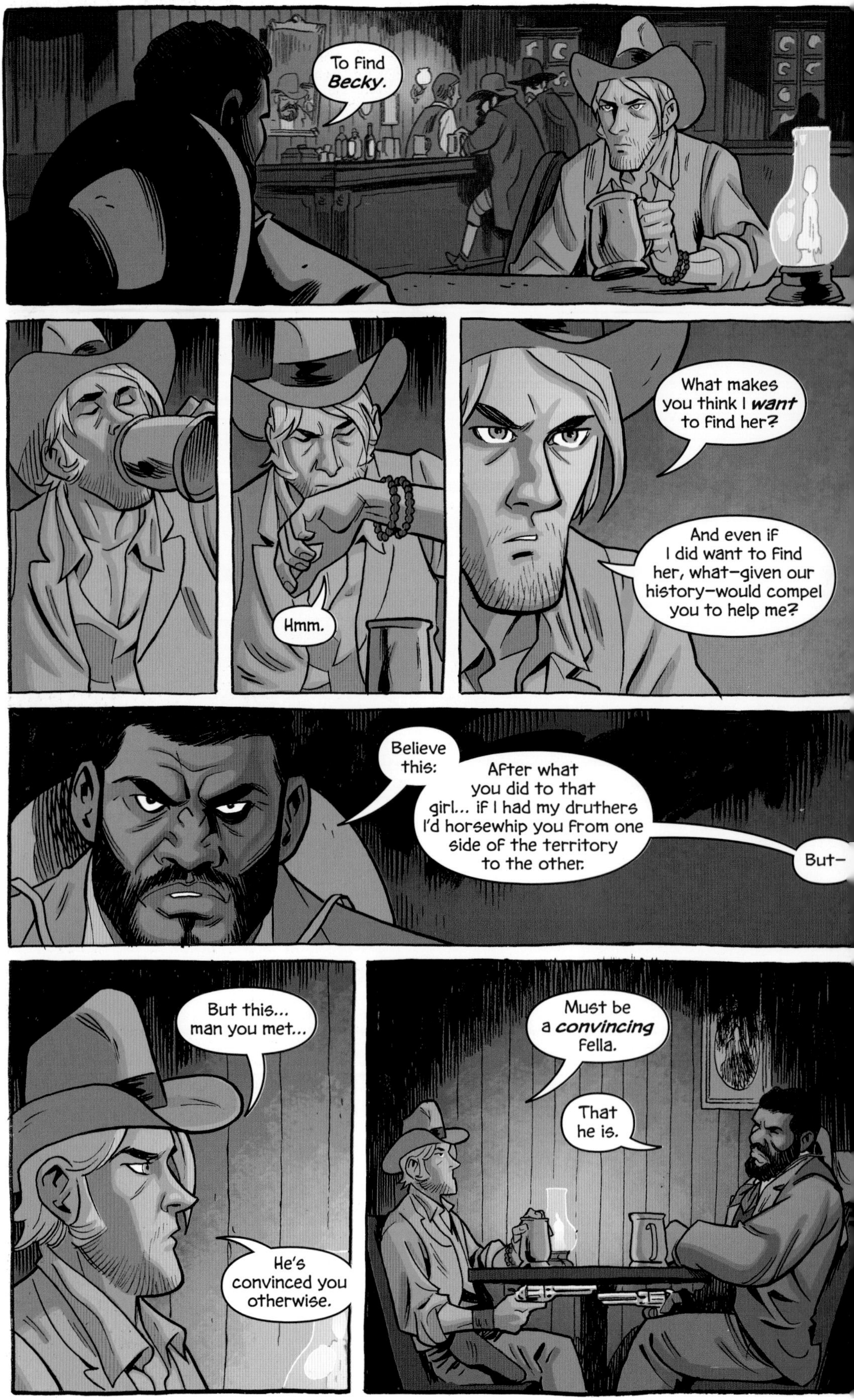
To find Becky.
Hmm.
What makes you think I want to find her?
And even if I did want to find her, what—given our history—would compel you to help me?
Believe this:
After what you did to that girl... if I had my druthers I'd horsewhip you from one side of the territory to the other.
But—
But this... man you met...
He's convinced you otherwise.
Must be a convincing fella.
That he is.

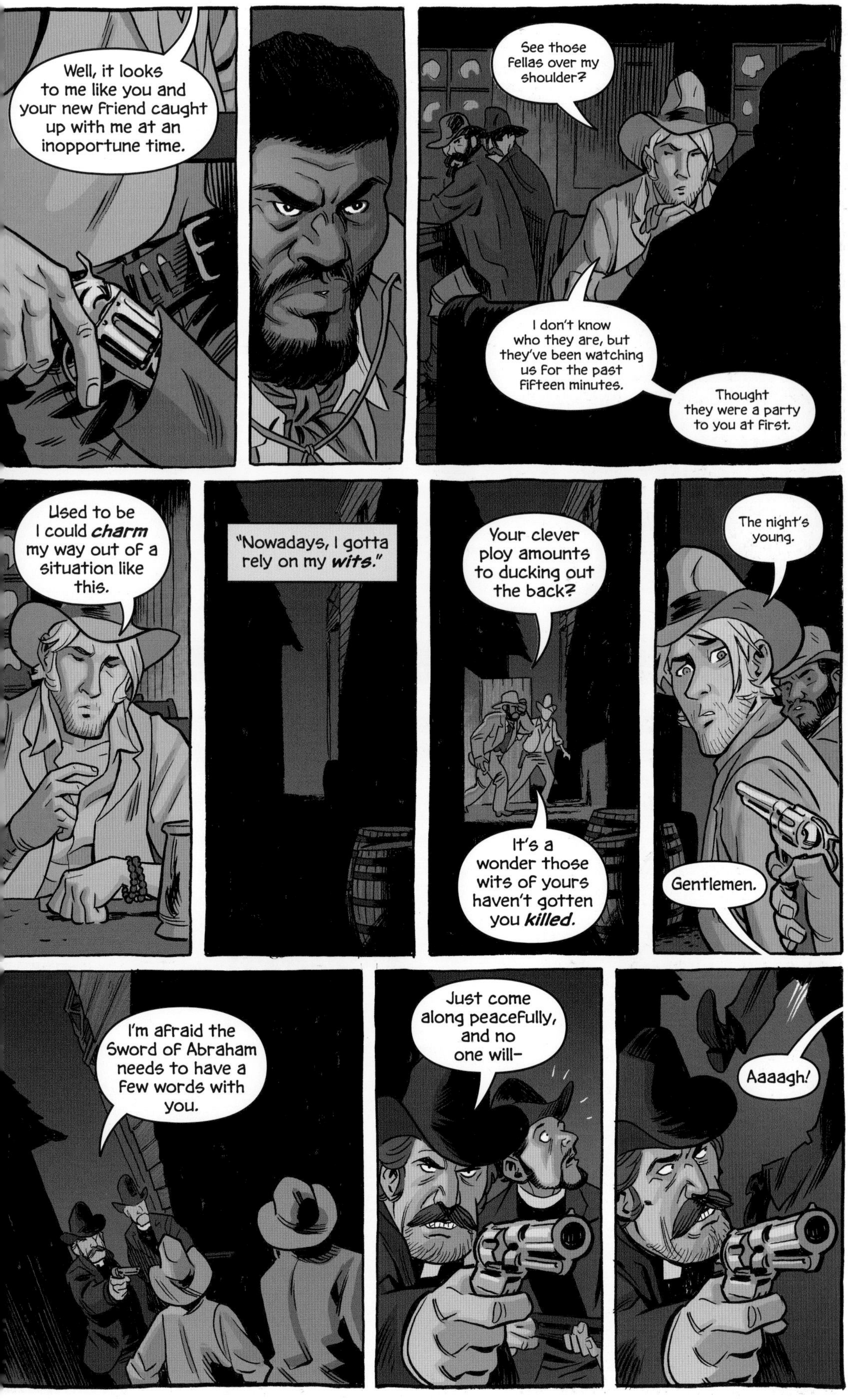
Well, it looks to me like you and your new friend caught up with me at an inopportune time.
See those fellas over my shoulder?
I don't know who they are, but they've been watching us for the past fifteen minutes.
Thought they were a party to you at first.
Used to be I could *charm* my way out of a situation like this.
"Nowadays, I gotta rely on my *wits*."
Your clever ploy amounts to ducking out the back?
It's a wonder those wits of yours haven't gotten you *killed*.
The night's young.
Gentlemen.
I'm afraid the Sword of Abraham needs to have a few words with you.
Just come along peacefully, and no one will–
Aaaagh!

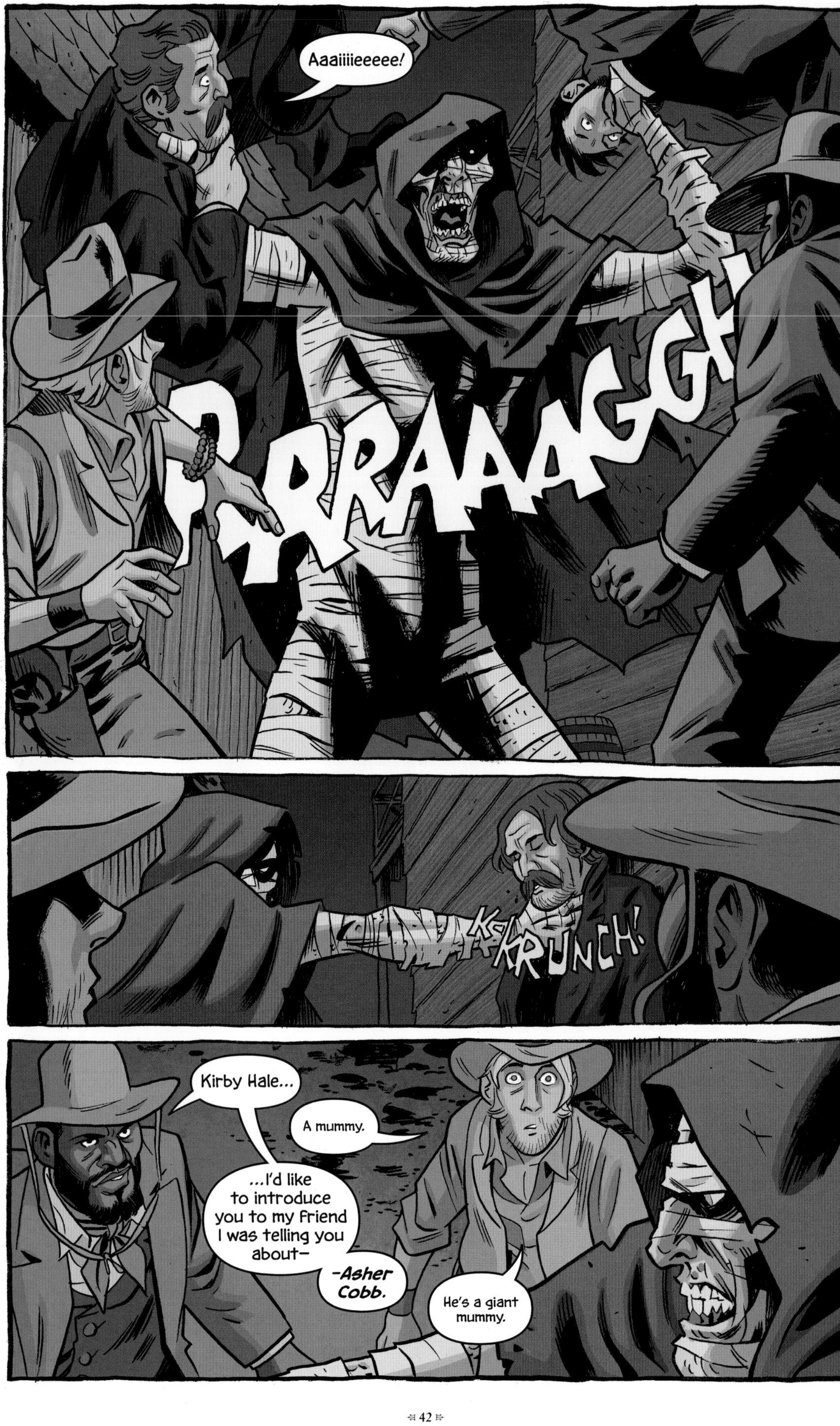
Aaaiiiieeeee!
BRRAAAAGGH
K-KRUNCH!
Kirby Hale...
A mummy.
...I'd like to introduce you to my friend I was telling you about—
—Asher Cobb.
He's a giant mummy.

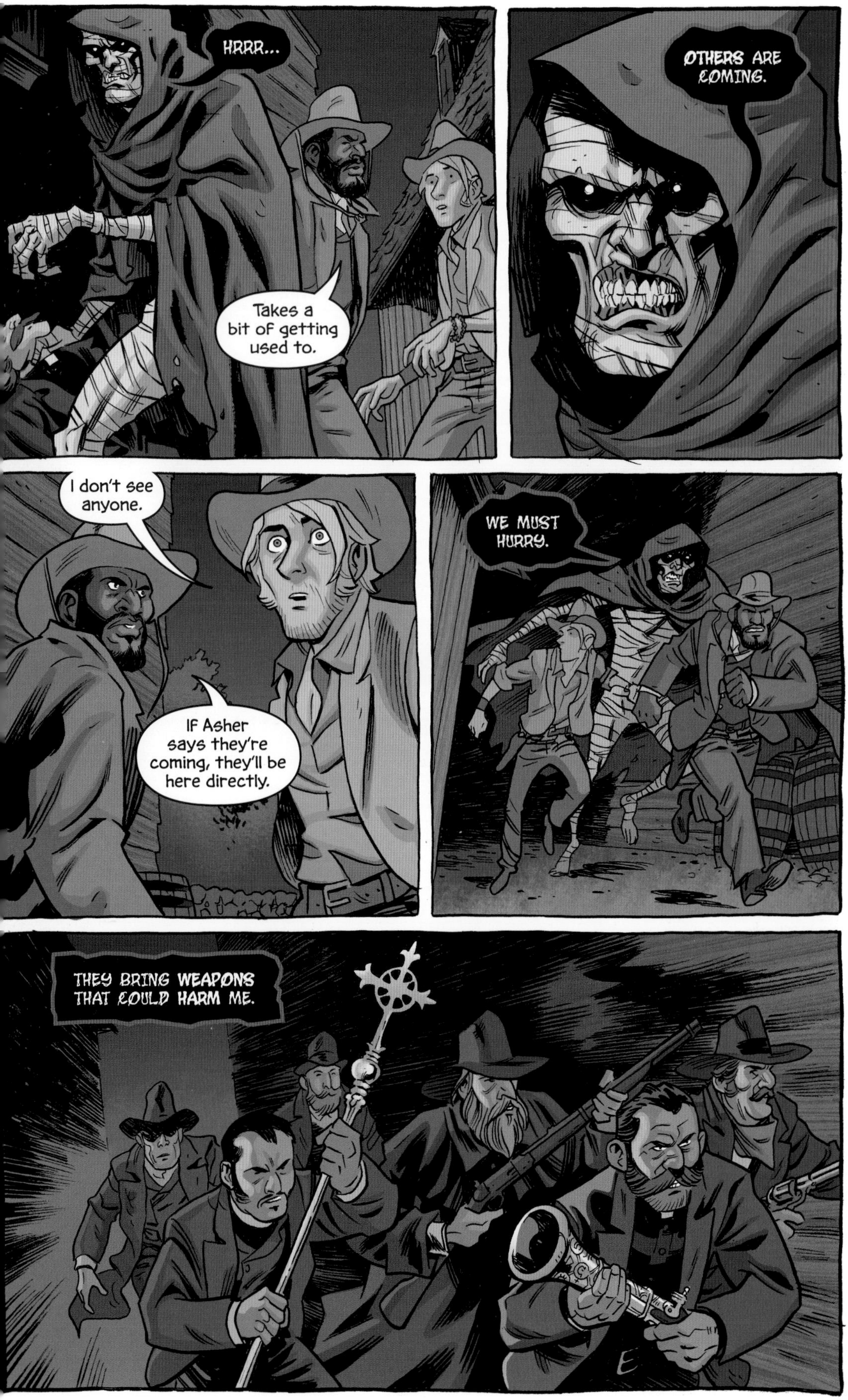
HRRR...
Takes a bit of getting used to.
OTHERS ARE COMING.
I don't see anyone.
If Asher says they're coming, they'll be here directly.
WE MUST HURRY.
THEY BRING WEAPONS THAT COULD HARM ME.

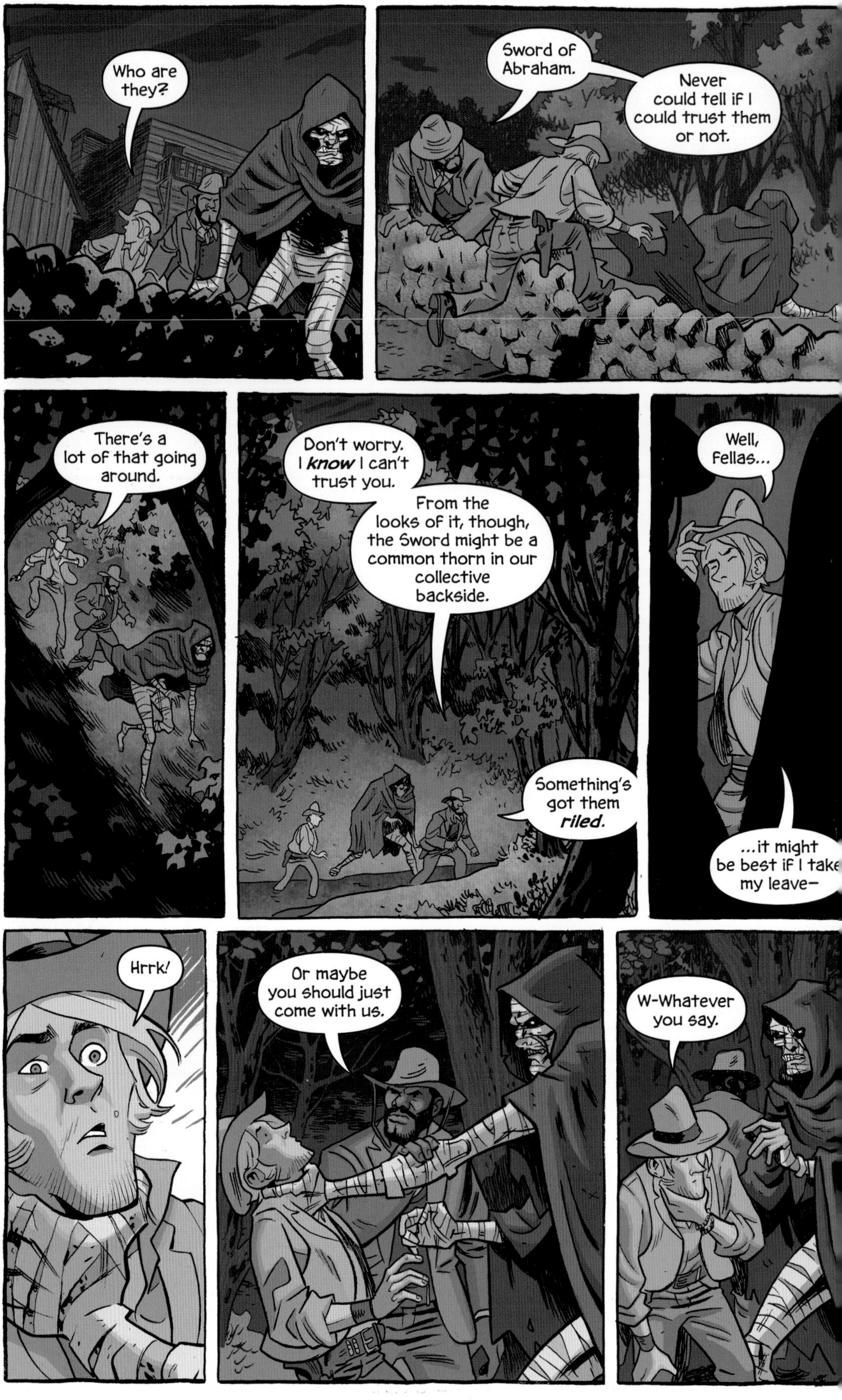
Who are they?
Sword of Abraham.
Never could tell if I could trust them or not.
There's a lot of that going around.
Don't worry. I *know* I can't trust you.
From the looks of it, though, the Sword might be a common thorn in our collective backside.
Something's got them *riled*.
Well, fellas...
...it might be best if I take my leave—
Hrrk!
Or maybe you should just come with us.
W-Whatever you say.

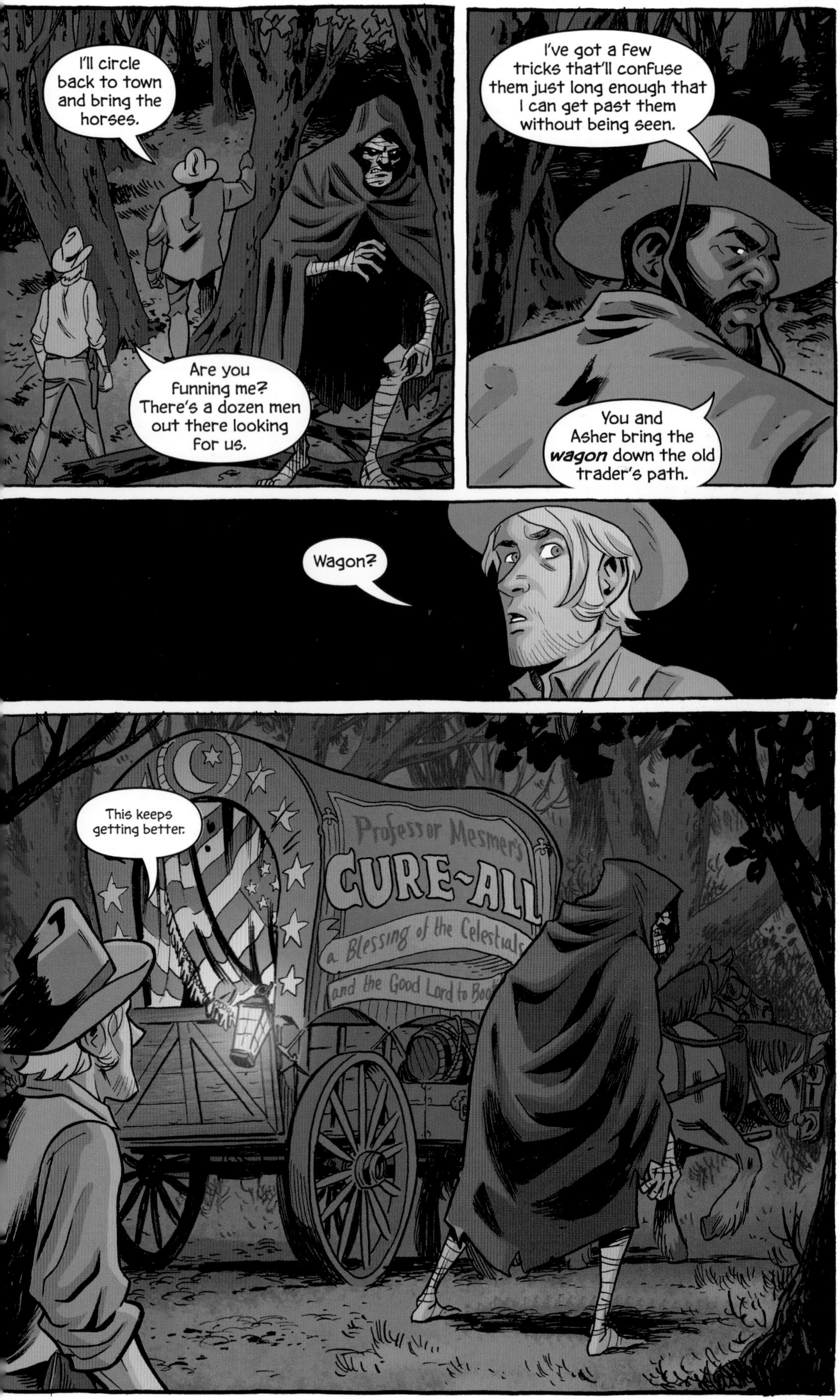
I'll circle back to town and bring the horses.
Are you funning me? There's a dozen men out there looking for us.
I've got a few tricks that'll confuse them just long enough that I can get past them without being seen.
You and Asher bring the *wagon* down the old trader's path.
Wagon?
This keeps getting better.
Professor Mesmer's
CURE~ALL
a Blessing of the Celestials
and the Good Lord to Boot

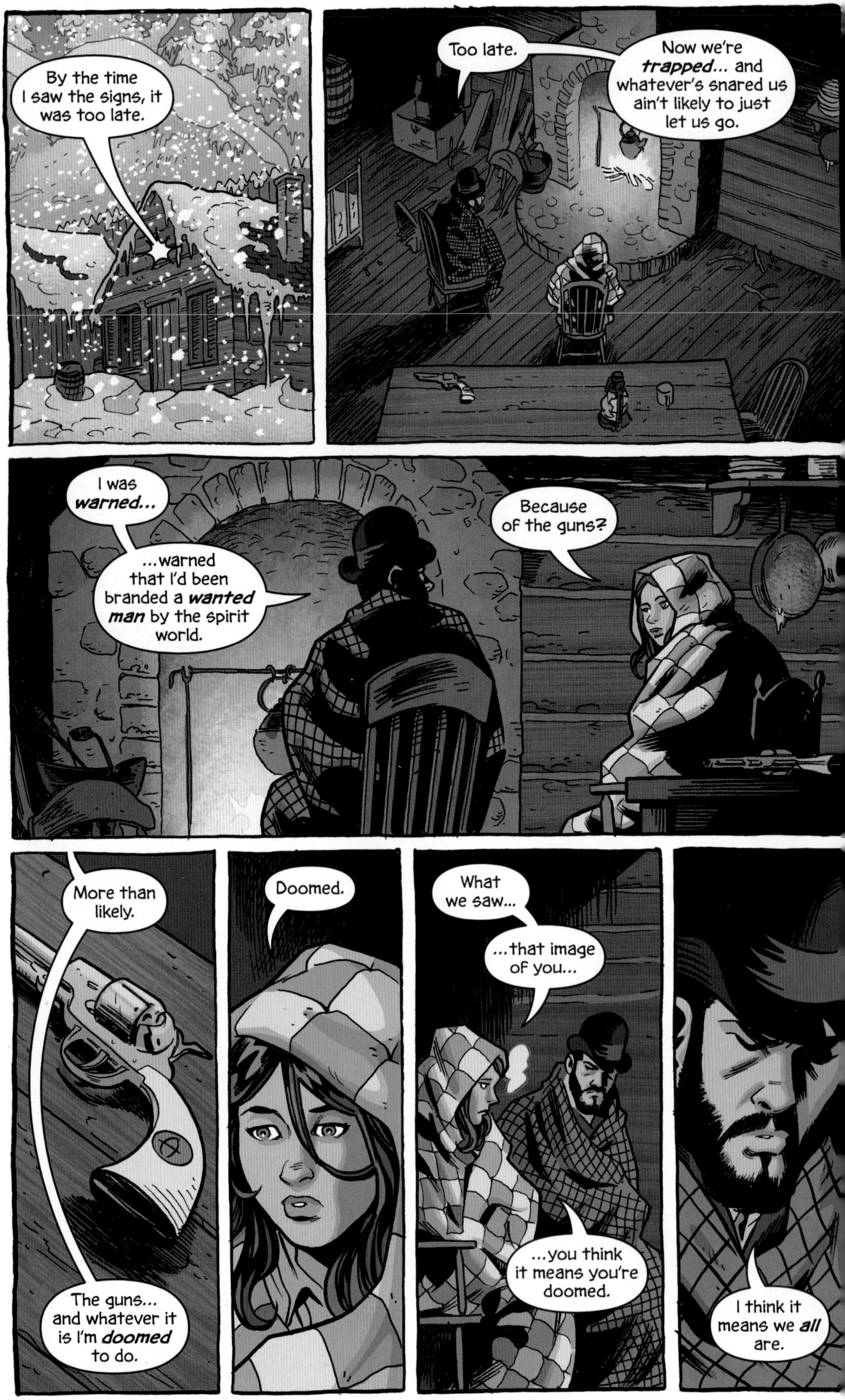
By the time I saw the signs, it was too late.
Too late.
Now we're *trapped*... and whatever's snared us ain't likely to just let us go.
I was *warned...*
...warned that I'd been branded a *wanted man* by the spirit world.
Because of the guns?
More than likely.
The guns... and whatever it is I'm *doomed* to do.
Doomed.
What we saw...
...that image of you...
...you think it means you're doomed.
I think it means we *all* are.

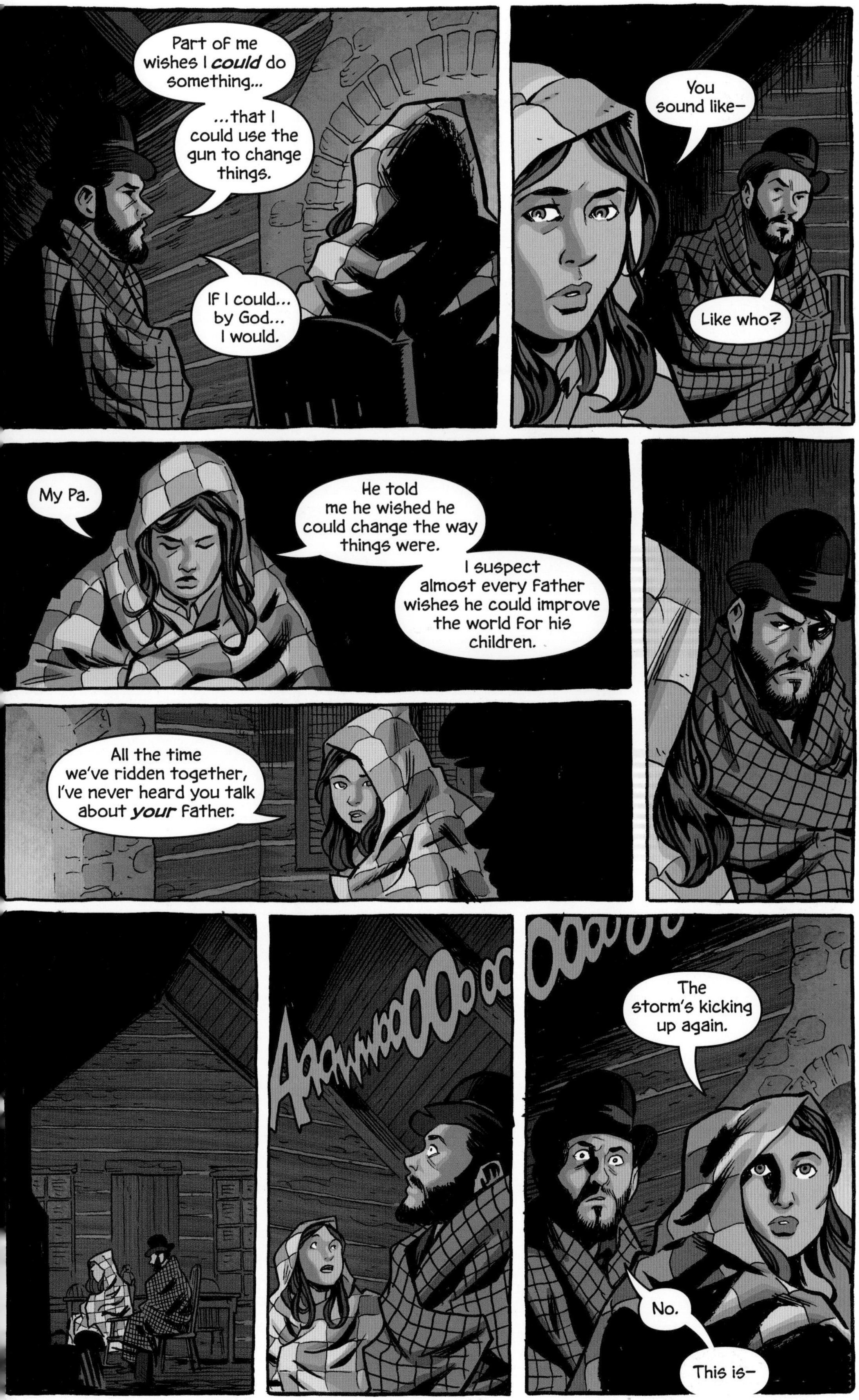
Part of me wishes I *could* do something...
...that I could use the gun to change things.
If I could... by God... I would.
You sound like–
Like who?
My Pa.
He told me he wished he could change the way things were.
I suspect almost every father wishes he could improve the world for his children.
All the time we've ridden together, I've never heard you talk about *your* father.
AAAWWOOOOoooOOOOO
The storm's kicking up again.
No.
This is–

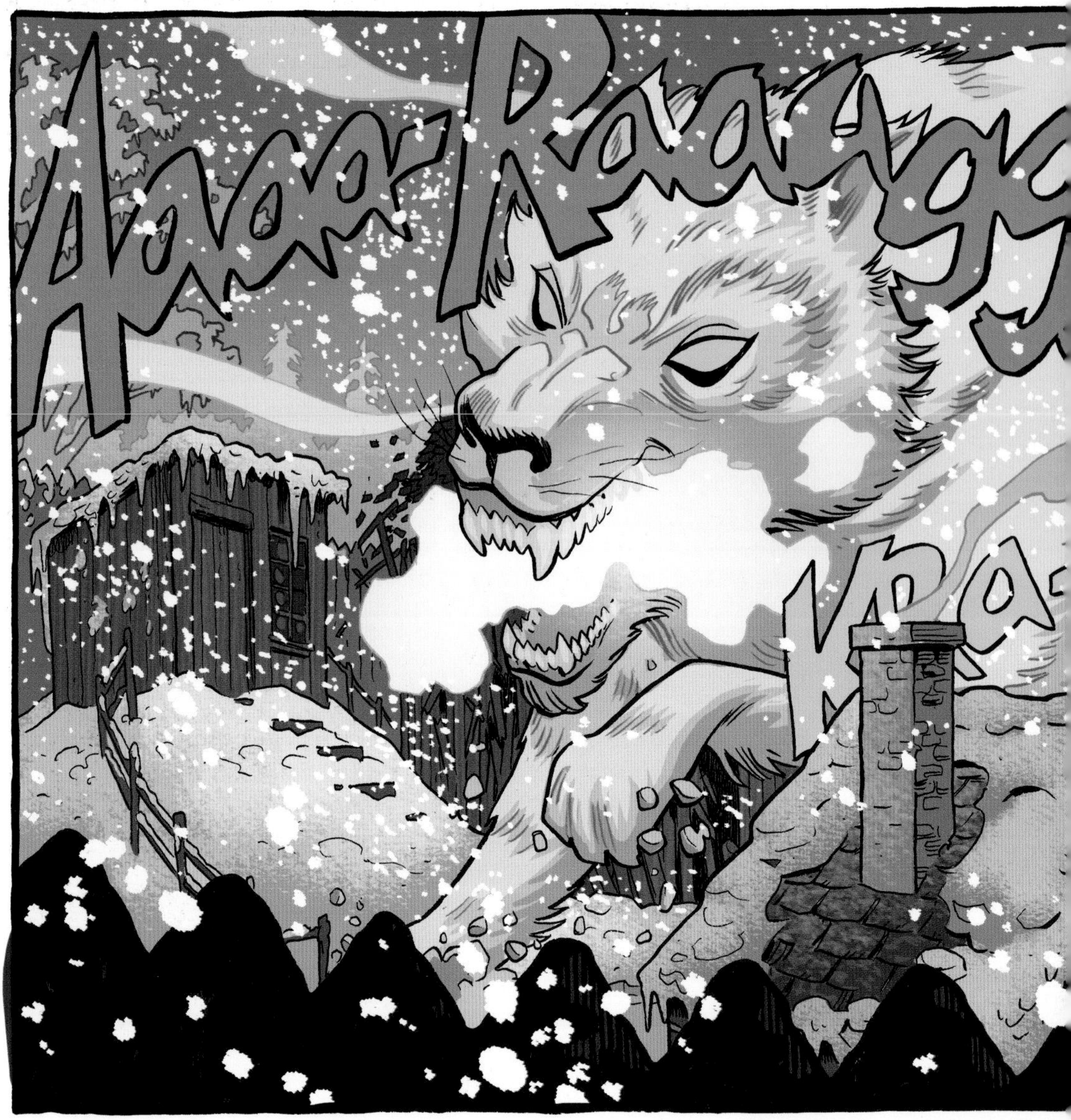
Aaaa Raaag
KRA-

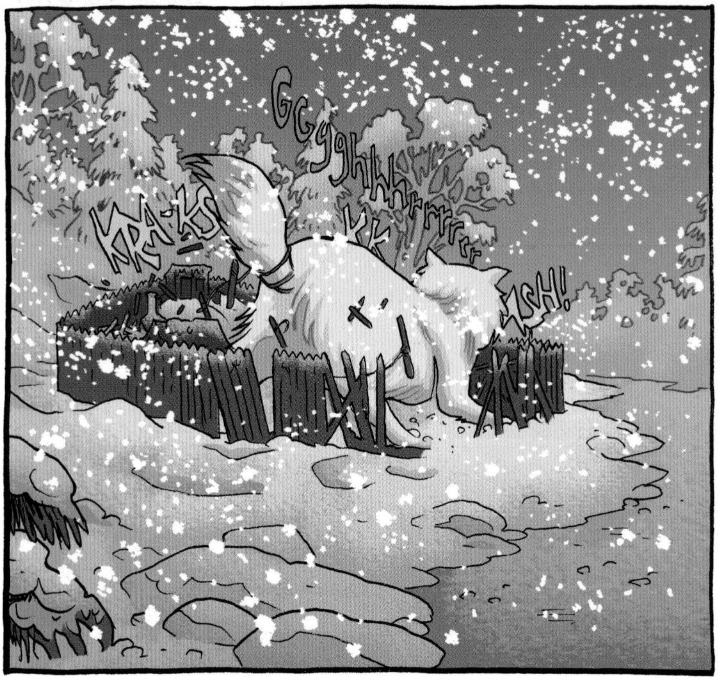
KRAKS
Gggghhhhrrrrrr
KK
SH!

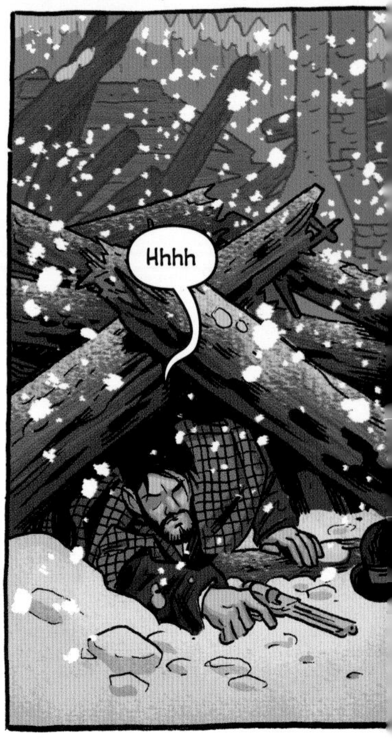
Hhhh

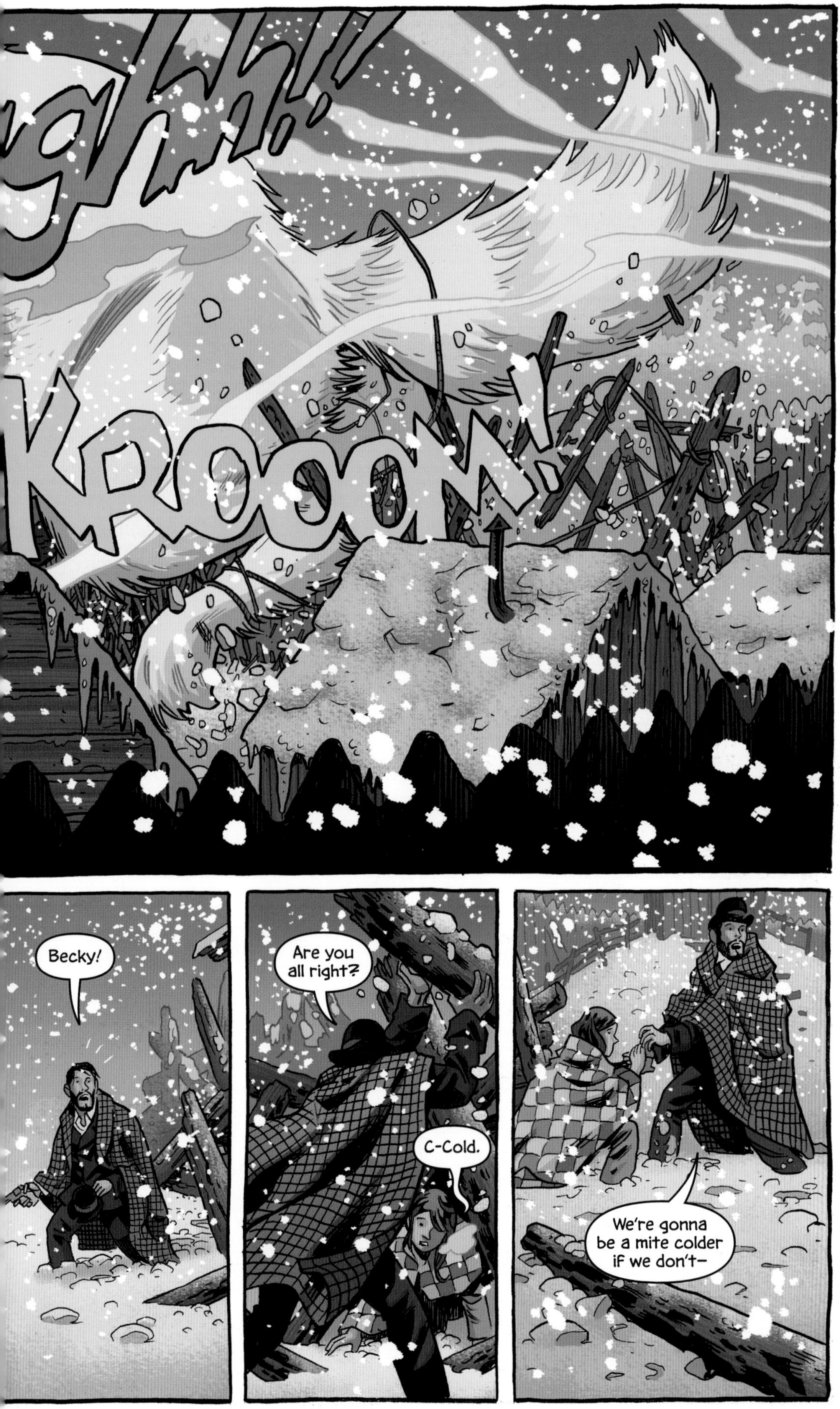
...ghhh!!
KROOOM!
Becky!
Are you all right?
C-Cold.
We're gonna be a mite colder if we don't–

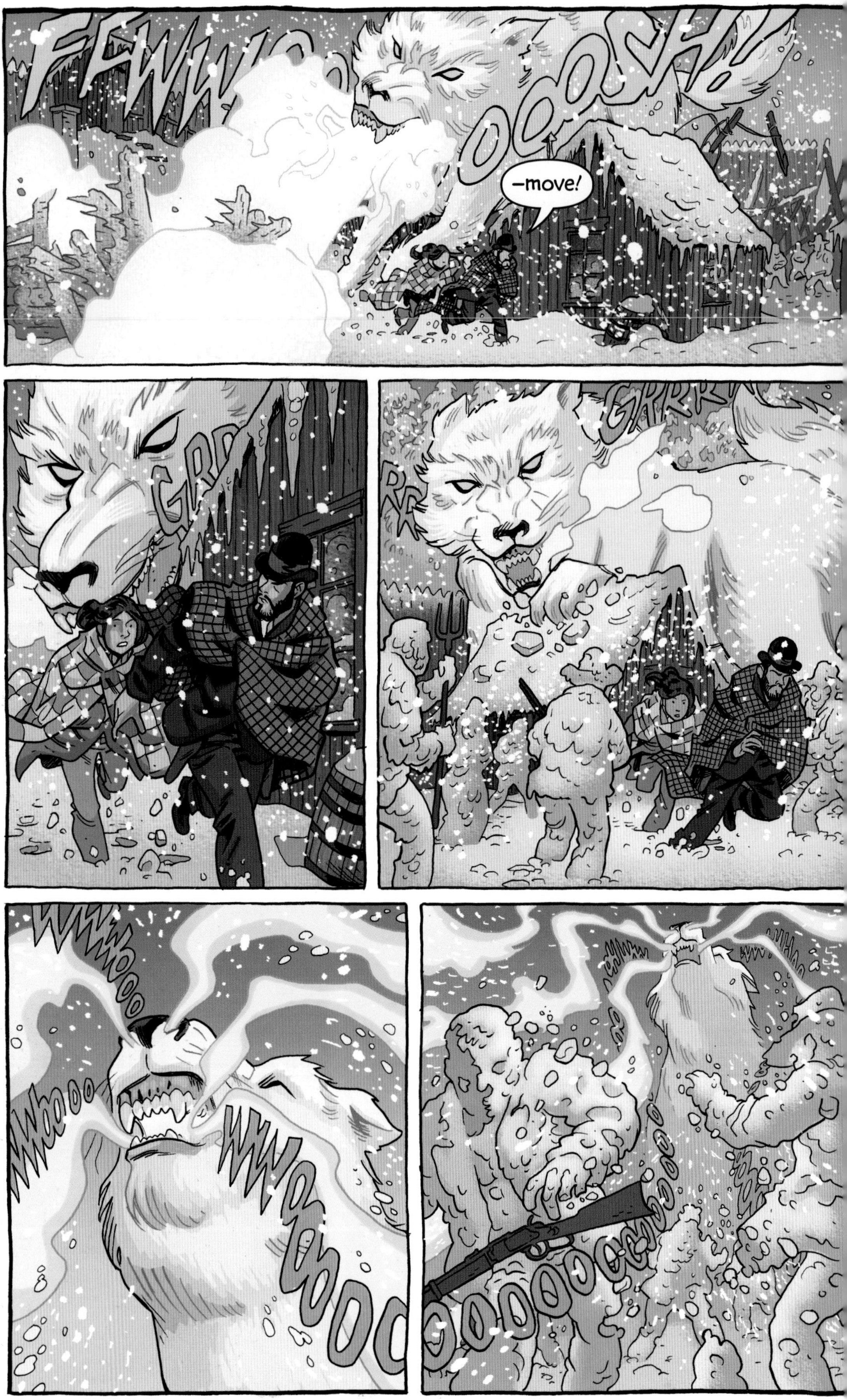
–move!

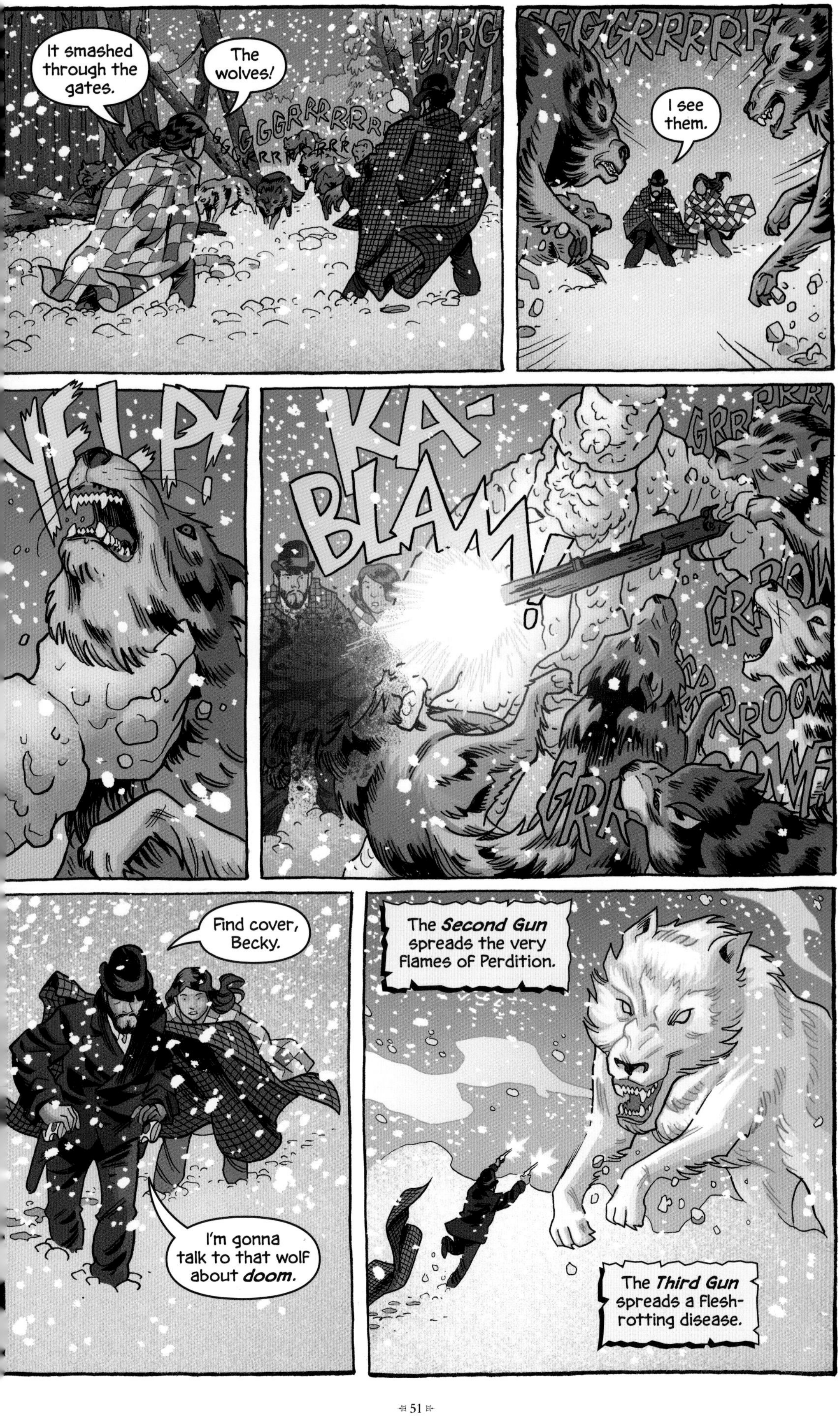
It smashed through the gates.
The wolves!
GRRG
GGGRRRRRR
GGGGRRRRRR
GGGRRRRRR
I see them.
YELP!
KA-BLAM!
GRRR
GROW
Find cover, Becky.
I'm gonna talk to that wolf about *doom.*
The ***Second Gun*** spreads the very flames of Perdition.
The ***Third Gun*** spreads a flesh-rotting disease.

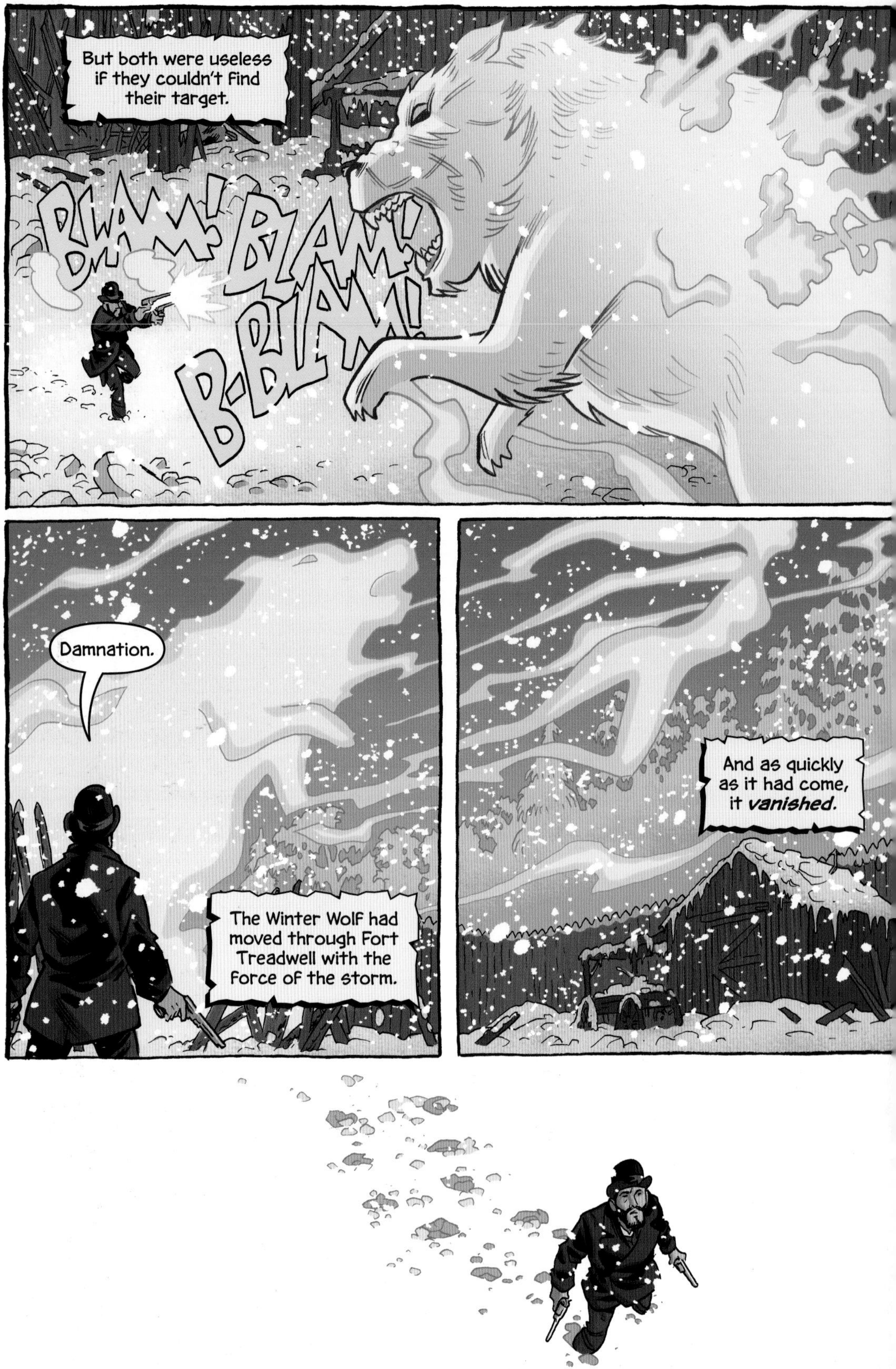
But both were useless if they couldn't find their target.
BLAM! BLAM! B-BLAM!
Damnation.
The Winter Wolf had moved through Fort Treadwell with the force of the storm.
And as quickly as it had come, it *vanished.*

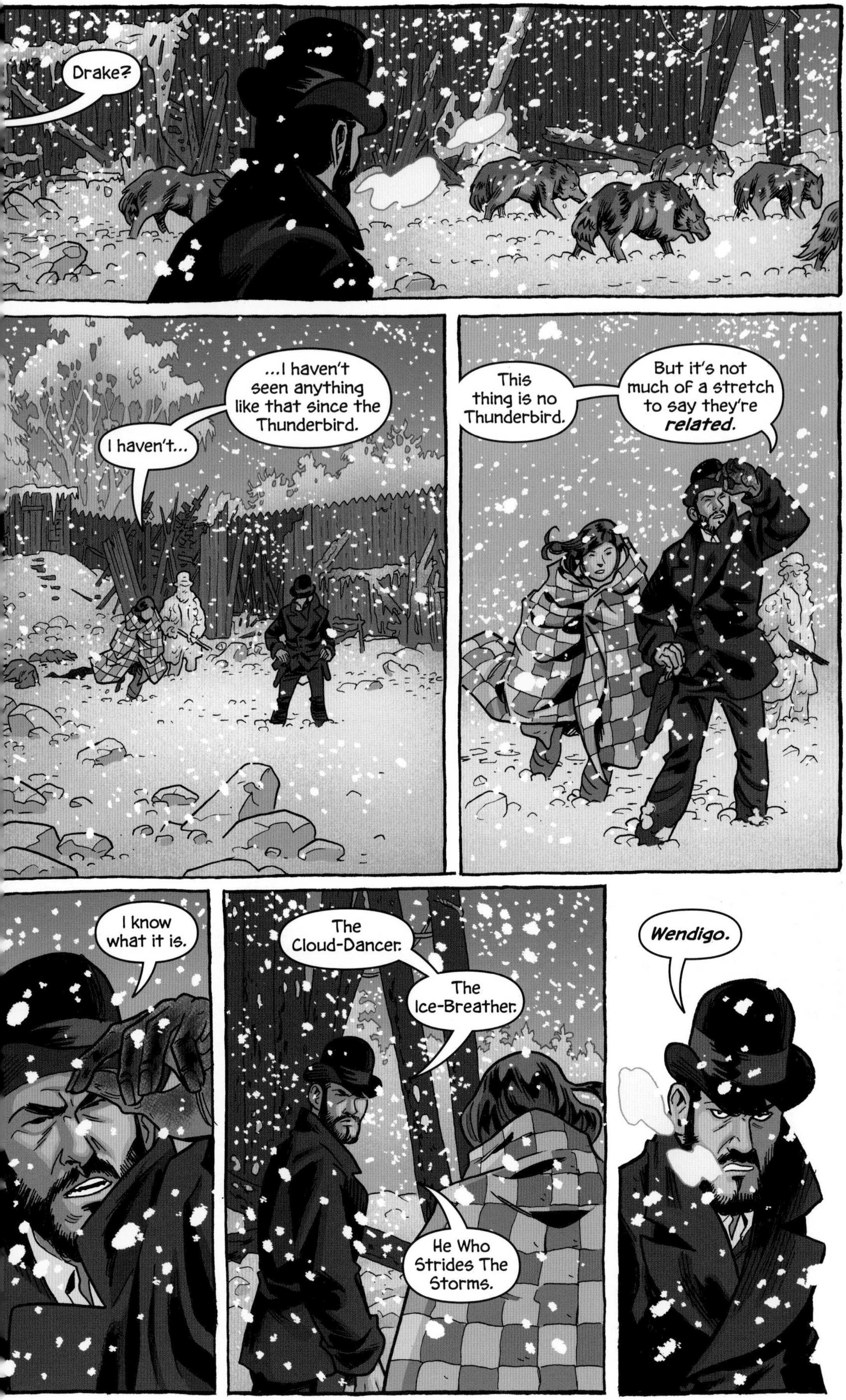
Drake?
I haven't...
...I haven't seen anything like that since the Thunderbird.
This thing is no Thunderbird.
But it's not much of a stretch to say they're *related*.
I know what it is.
The Cloud-Dancer.
The Ice-Breather.
He Who Strides The Storms.
Wendigo.

I know what that thing is.

And I know how to *kill* it.

I suspect that's what we ought to do.

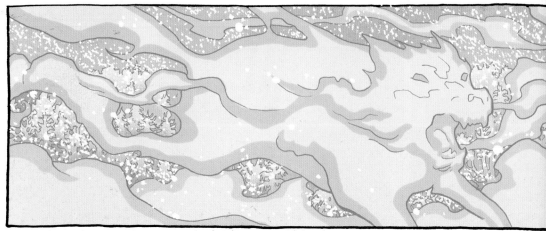

CHAPTER THREE

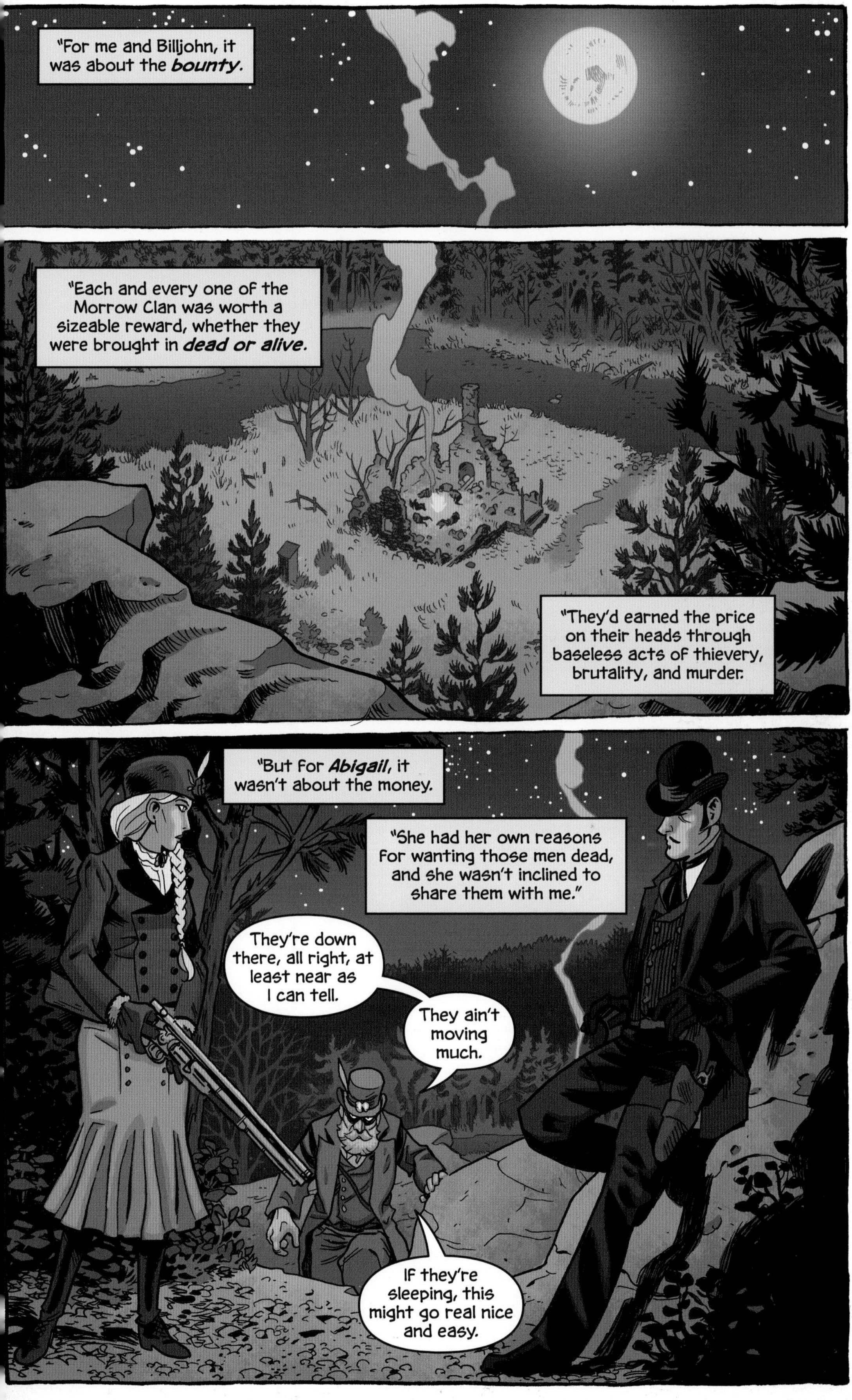

"For me and Billjohn, it was about the *bounty*.
"Each and every one of the Morrow Clan was worth a sizeable reward, whether they were brought in *dead or alive*.
"They'd earned the price on their heads through baseless acts of thievery, brutality, and murder.
"But for *Abigail*, it wasn't about the money.
"She had her own reasons for wanting those men dead, and she wasn't inclined to share them with me."
They're down there, all right, at least near as I can tell.
They ain't moving much.
If they're sleeping, this might go real nice and easy.

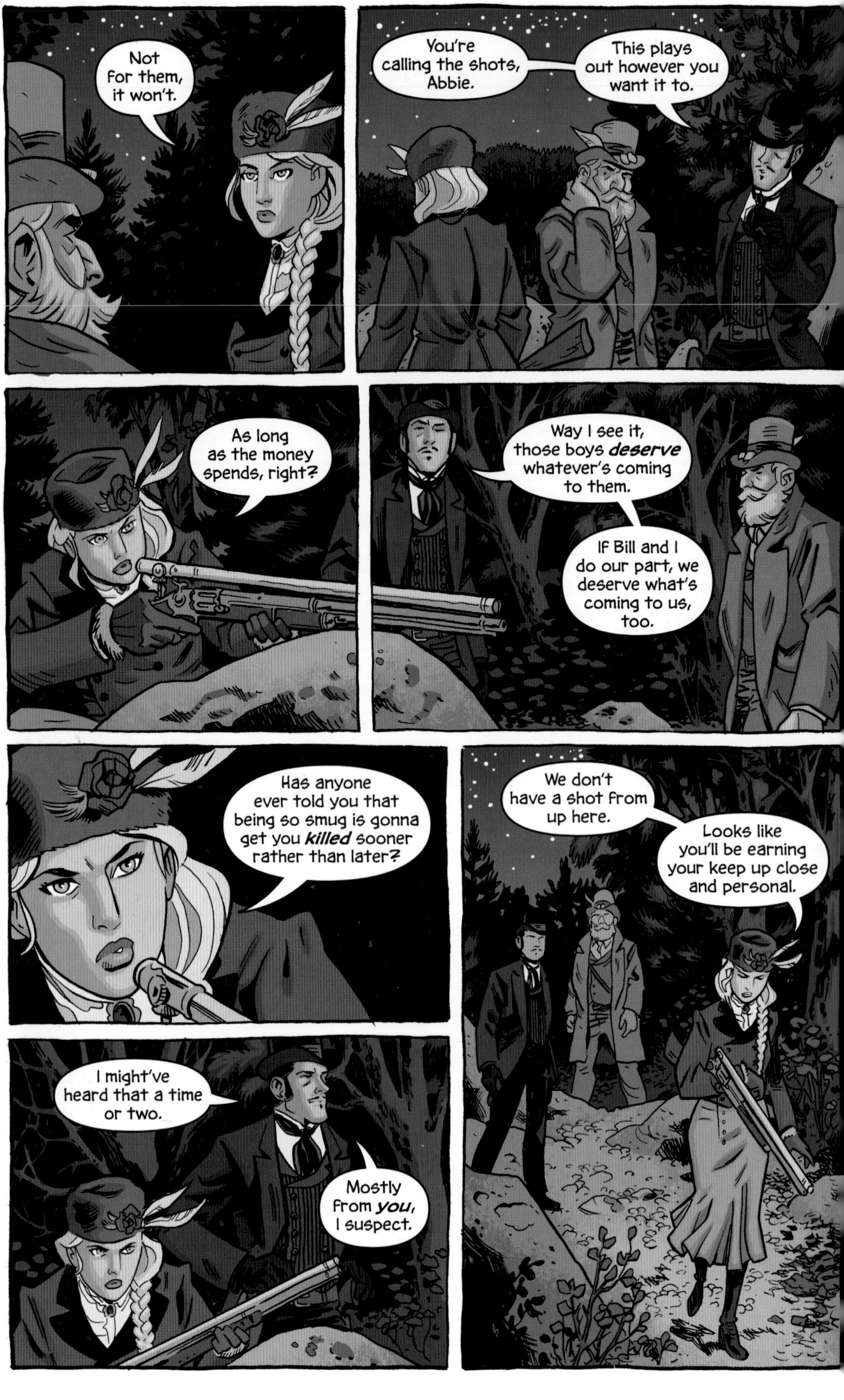
Not for them, it won't.
You're calling the shots, Abbie.
This plays out however you want it to.
As long as the money spends, right?
Way I see it, those boys ***deserve*** whatever's coming to them.
If Bill and I do our part, we deserve what's coming to us, too.
Has anyone ever told you that being so smug is gonna get you ***killed*** sooner rather than later?
I might've heard that a time or two.
Mostly from ***you***, I suspect.
We don't have a shot from up here.
Looks like you'll be earning your keep up close and personal.

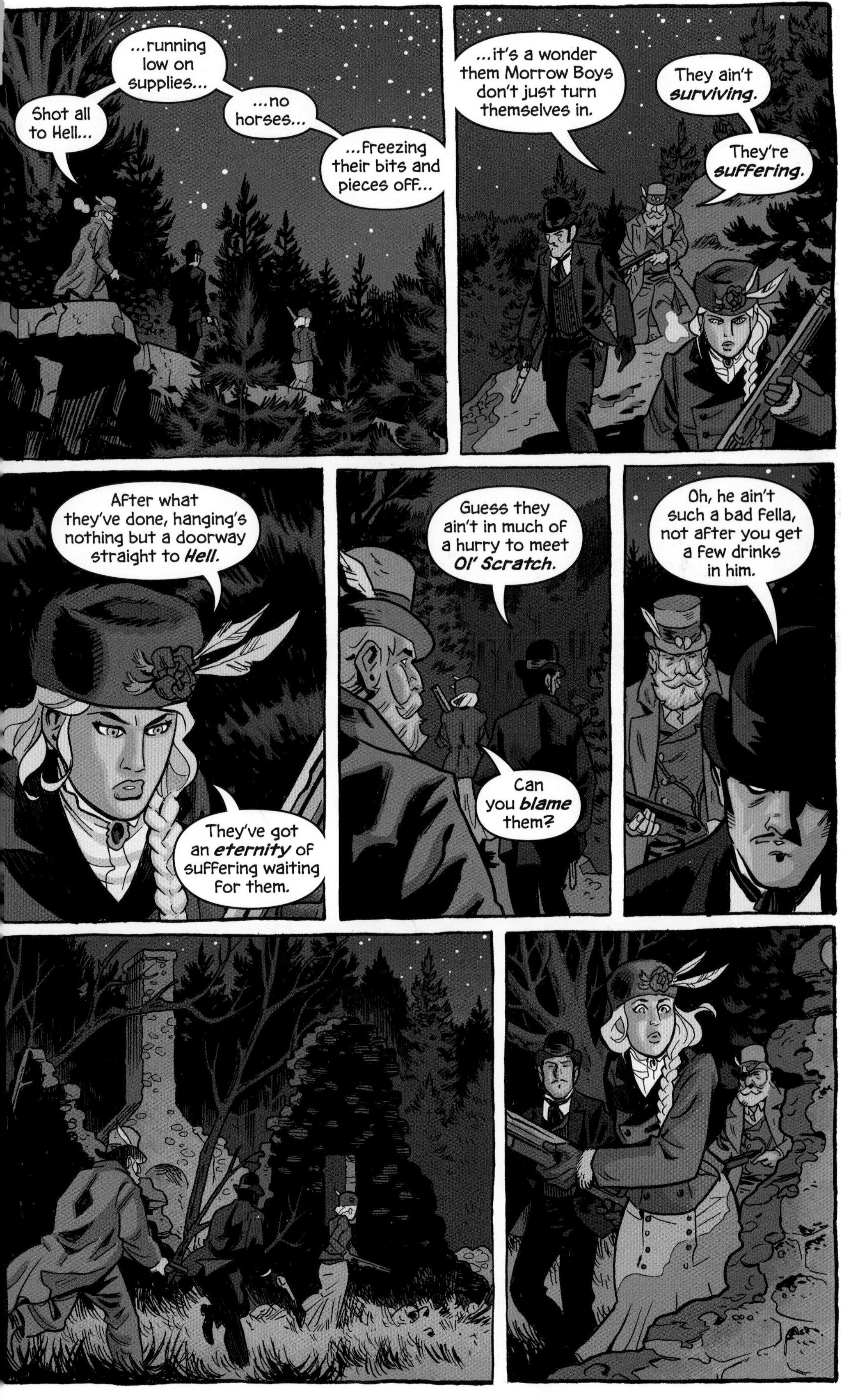
Shot all to Hell...
...running low on supplies...
...no horses...
...freezing their bits and pieces off...
...it's a wonder them Morrow Boys don't just turn themselves in.
They ain't surviving.
They're suffering.
After what they've done, hanging's nothing but a doorway straight to Hell.
They've got an eternity of suffering waiting for them.
Guess they ain't in much of a hurry to meet Ol' Scratch.
Can you blame them?
Oh, he ain't such a bad fella, not after you get a few drinks in him.

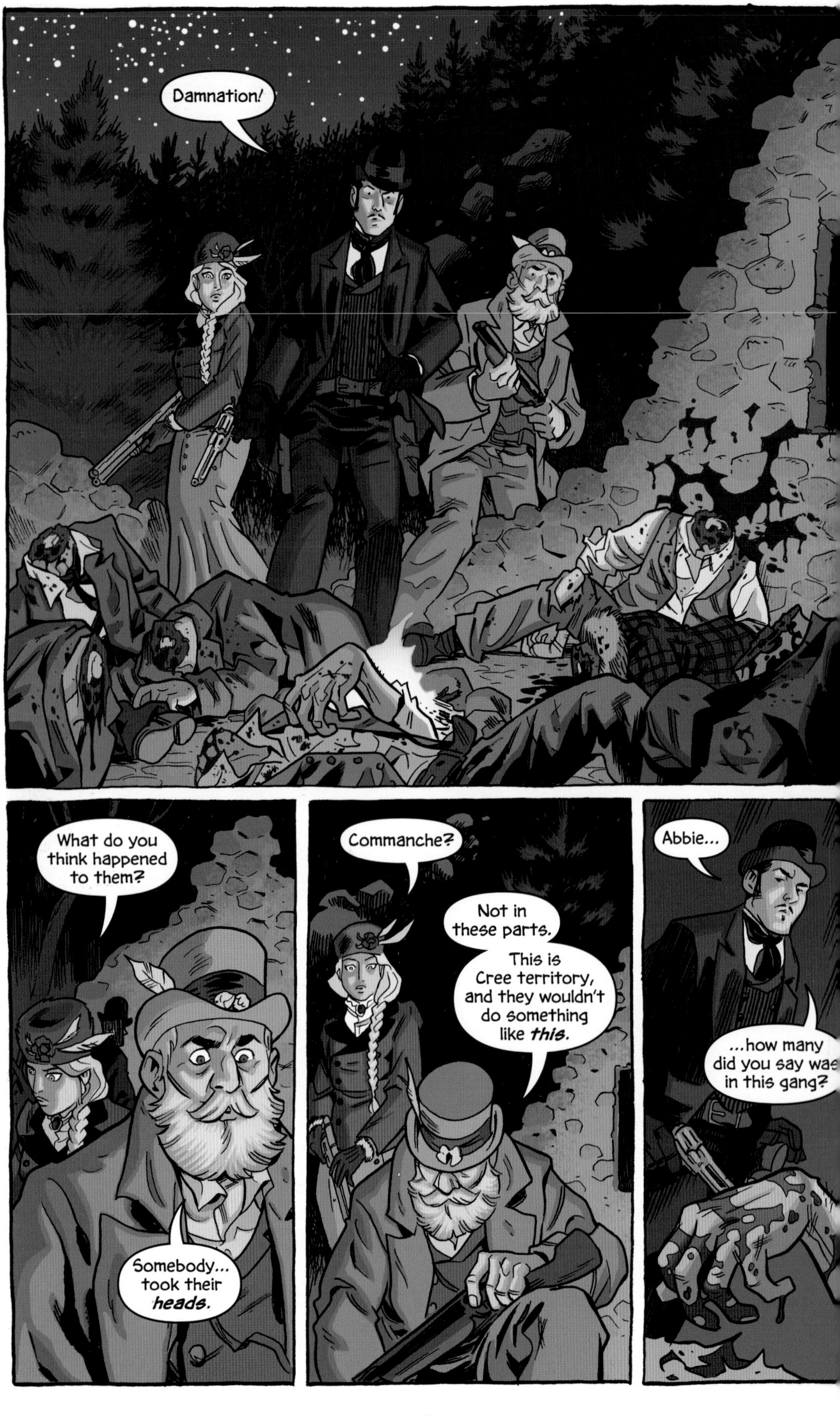
Damnation!
What do you think happened to them?
Somebody... took their *heads.*
Commanche?
Not in these parts.
This is Cree territory, and they wouldn't do something like *this.*
Abbie...
...how many did you say was in this gang?

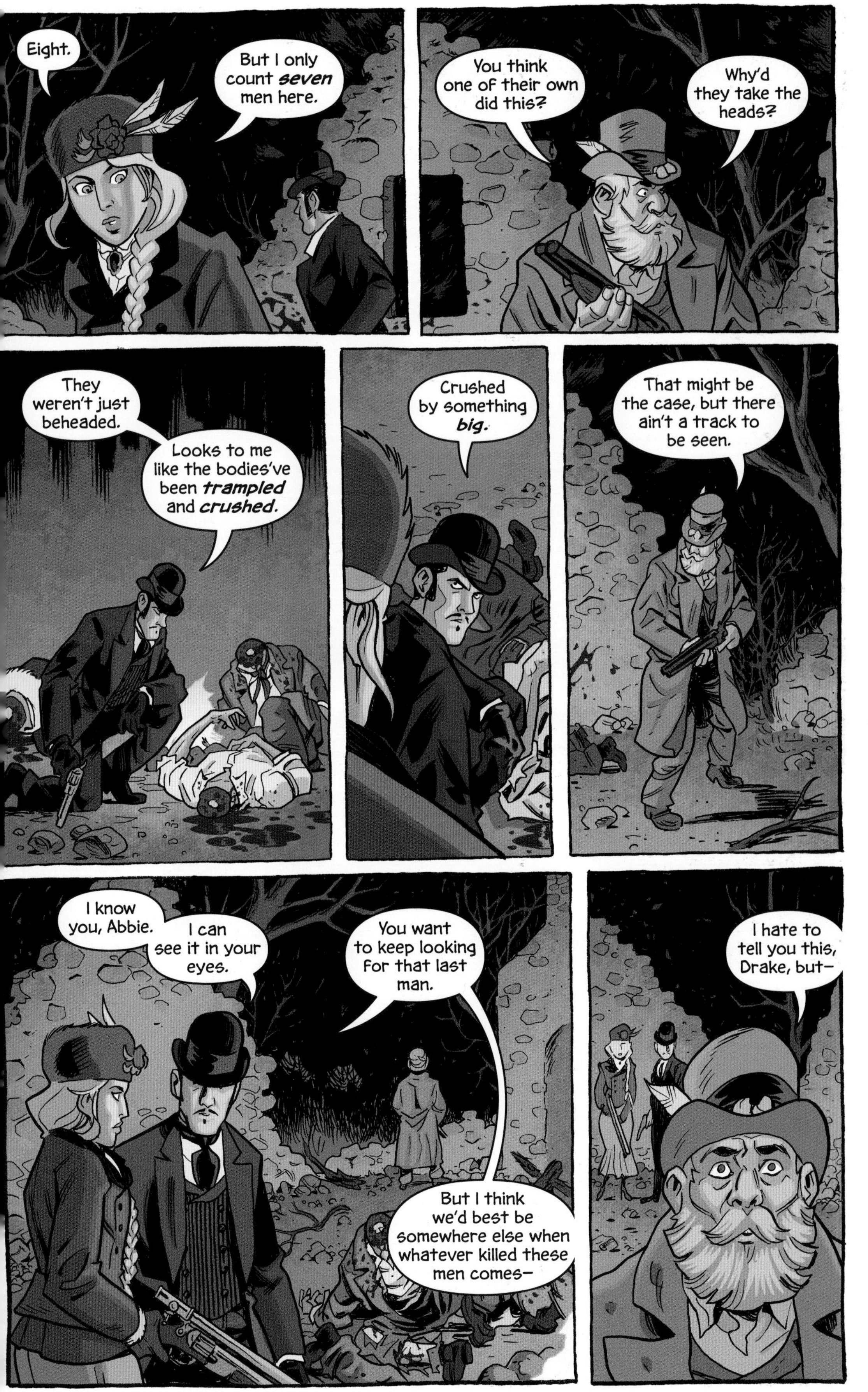
Eight.
But I only count *seven* men here.
You think one of their own did this?
Why'd they take the heads?
They weren't just beheaded.
Looks to me like the bodies've been *trampled* and *crushed*.
Crushed by something *big*.
That might be the case, but there ain't a track to be seen.
I know you, Abbie.
I can see it in your eyes.
You want to keep looking for that last man.
But I think we'd best be somewhere else when whatever killed these men comes—
I hate to tell you this, Drake, but—

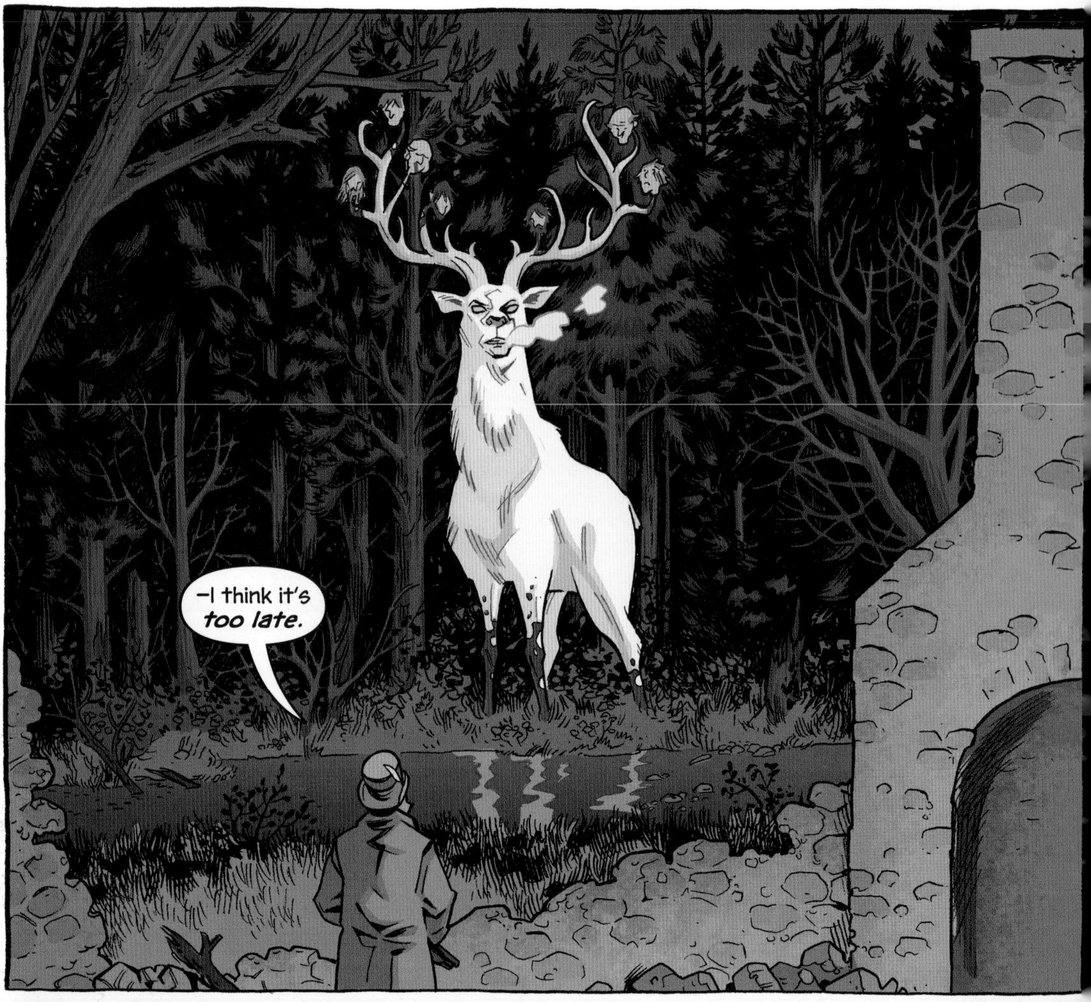
–I think it's *too late.*

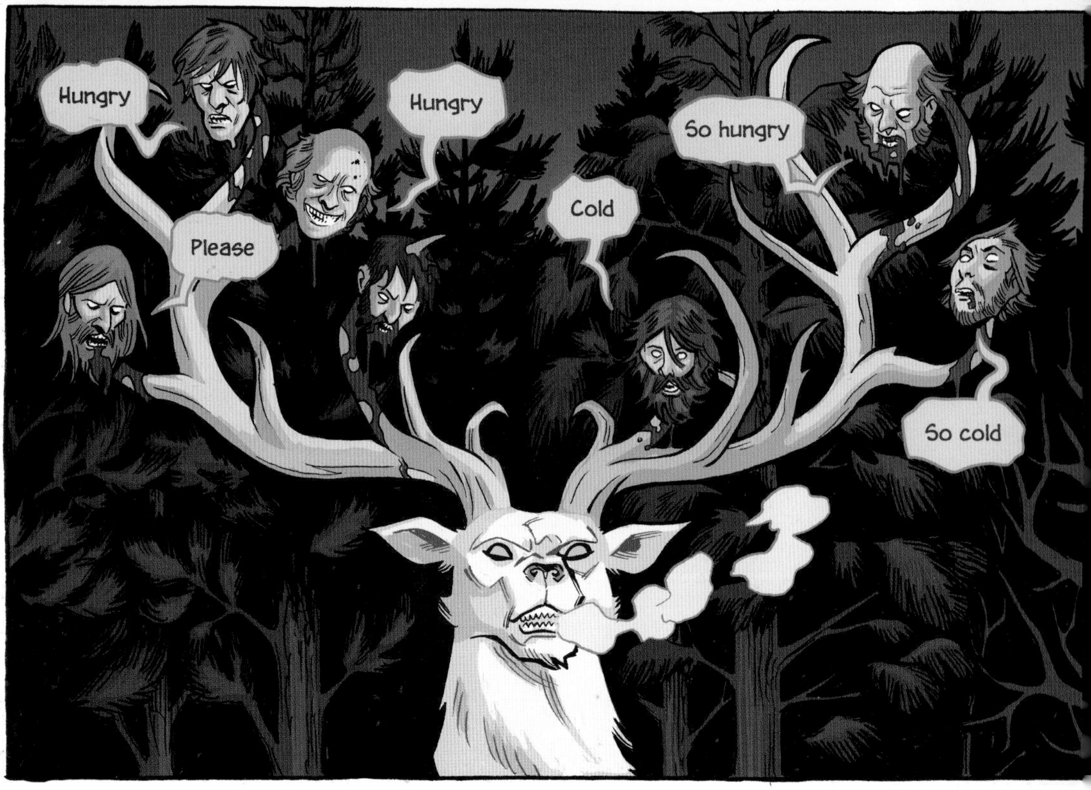
Hungry
Hungry
So hungry
Please
Cold
So cold

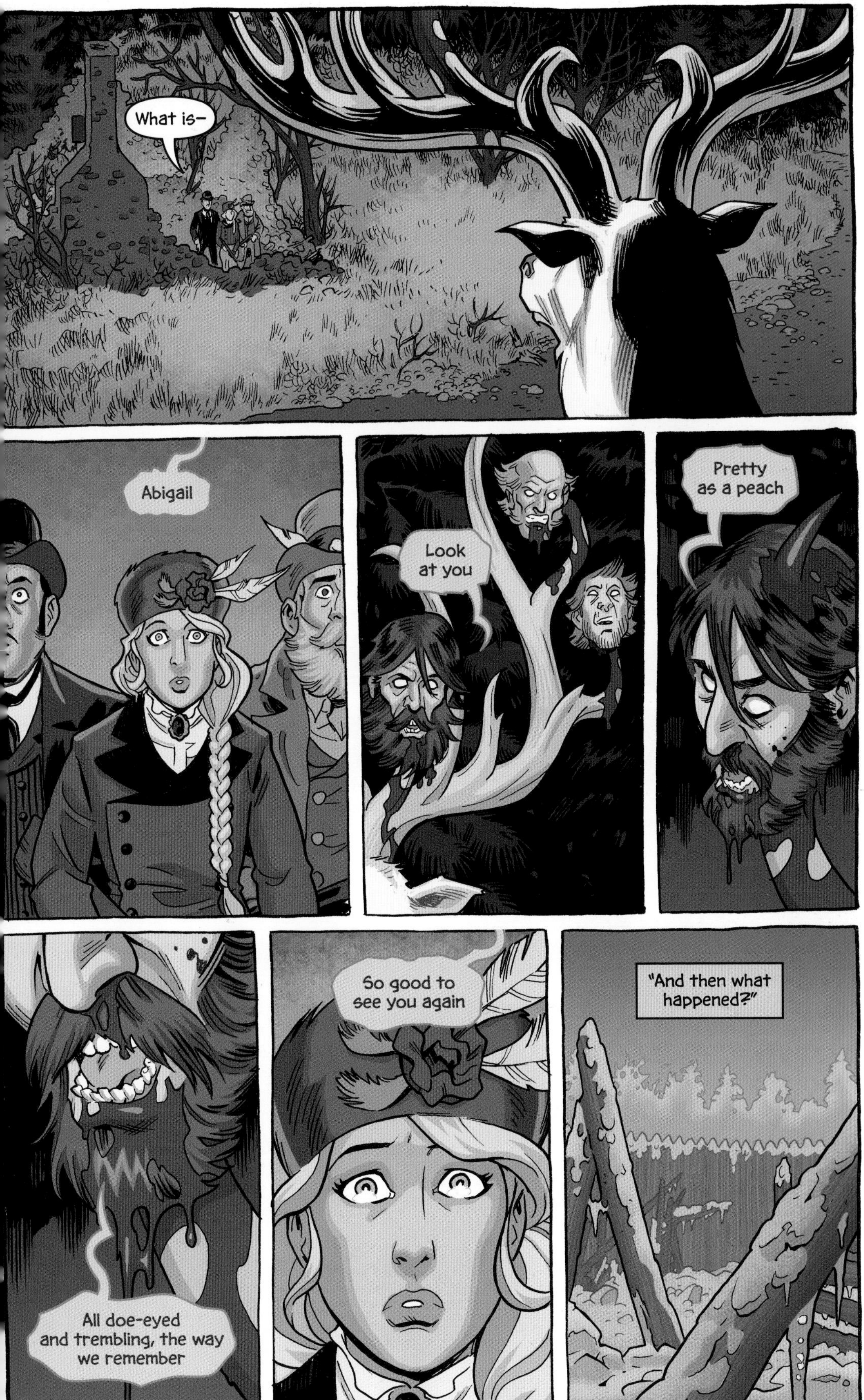
What is–
Abigail
Look at you
Pretty as a peach
All doe-eyed and trembling, the way we remember
So good to see you again
"And then what happened?"

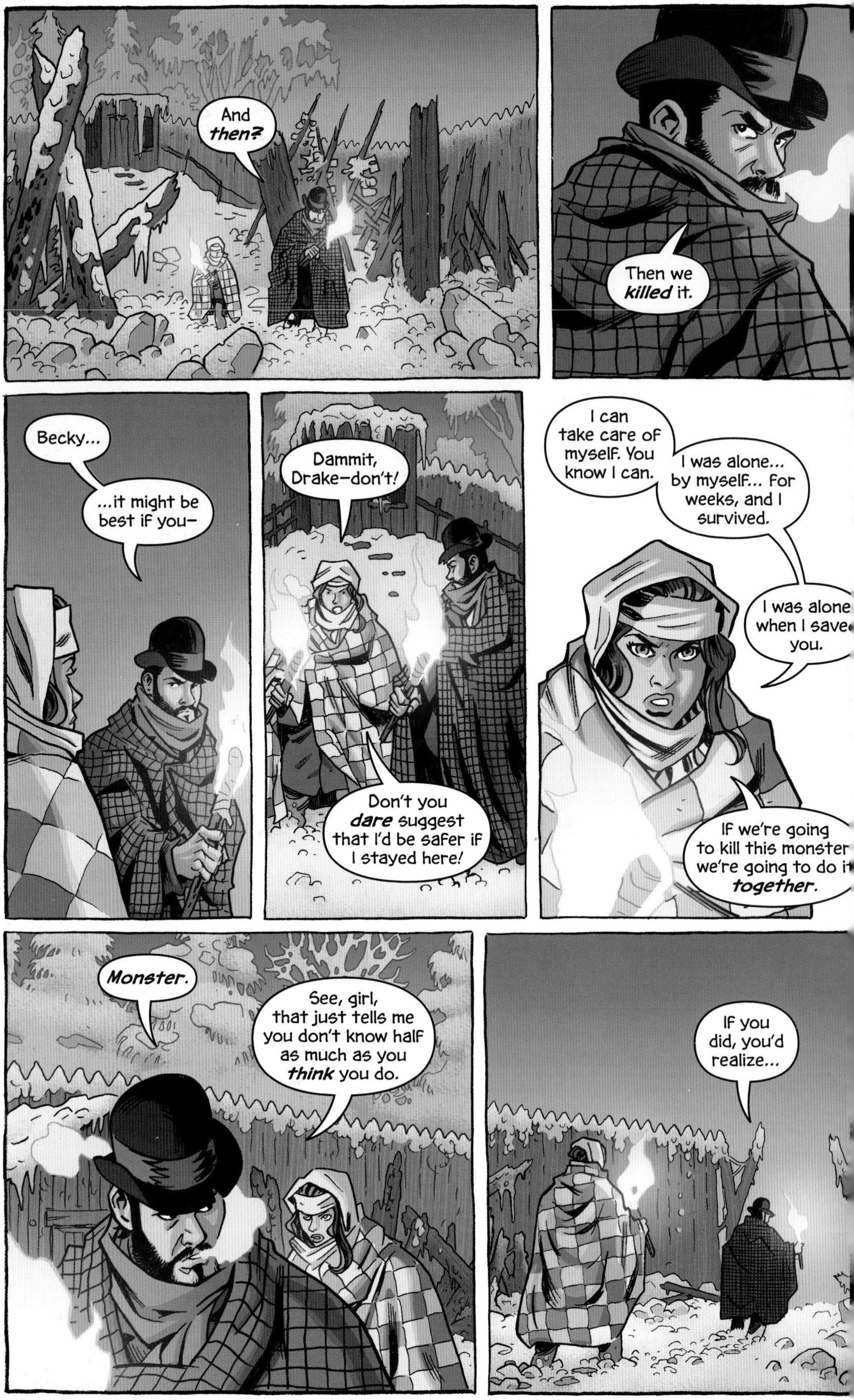

And *then?*
Then we *killed* it.
Becky...
...it might be best if you–
Dammit, Drake–don't!
Don't you *dare* suggest that I'd be safer if I stayed here!
I can take care of myself. You know I can.
I was alone... by myself... for weeks, and I survived.
I was alone when I save you.
If we're going to kill this monster we're going to do i *together*.
Monster.
See, girl, that just tells me you don't know half as much as you *think* you do.
If you did, you'd realize...

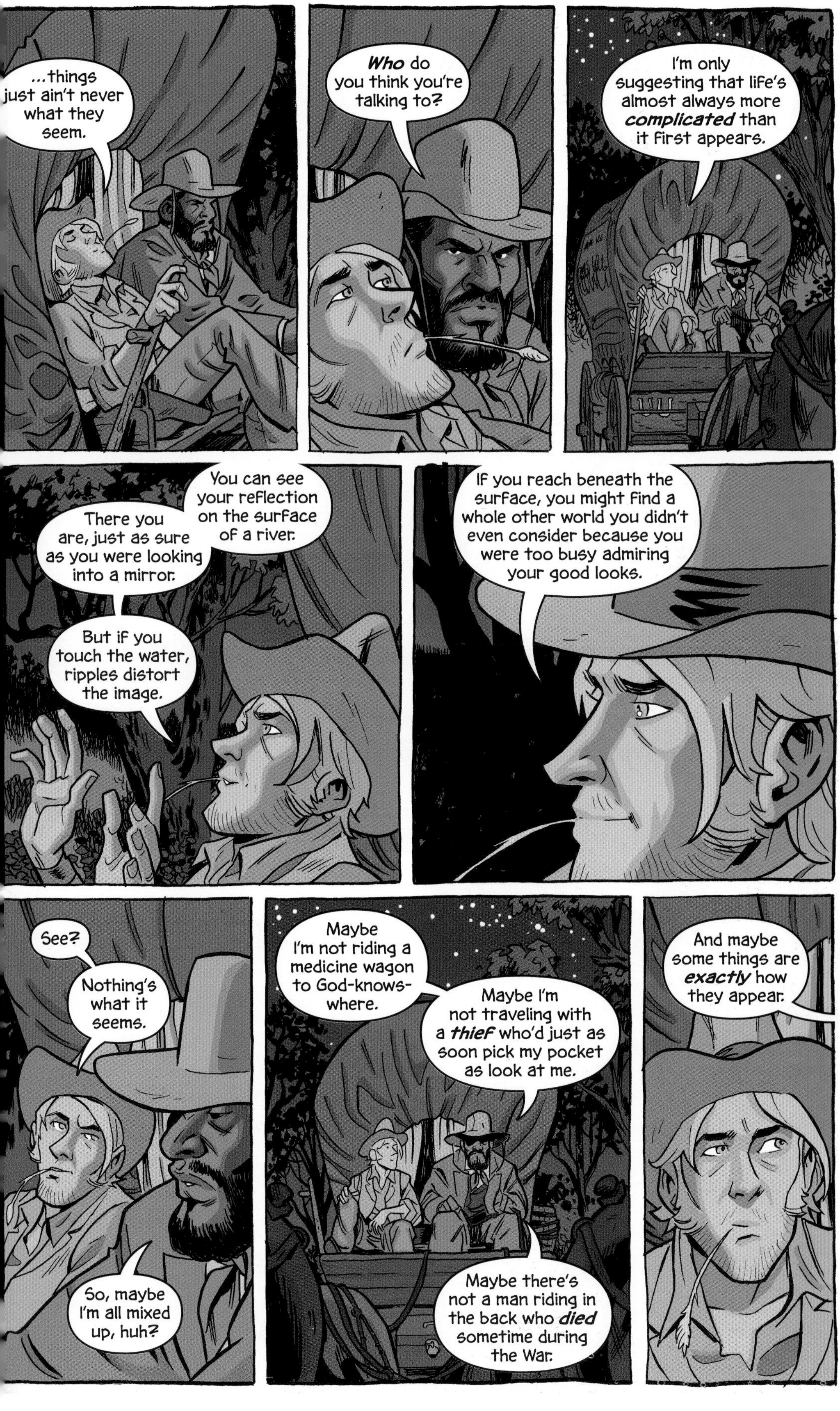
...things just ain't never what they seem.
Who do you think you're talking to?
I'm only suggesting that life's almost always more complicated than it first appears.
You can see your reflection on the surface of a river.
There you are, just as sure as you were looking into a mirror.
But if you touch the water, ripples distort the image.
If you reach beneath the surface, you might find a whole other world you didn't even consider because you were too busy admiring your good looks.
See?
Nothing's what it seems.
So, maybe I'm all mixed up, huh?
Maybe I'm not riding a medicine wagon to God-knows-where.
Maybe I'm not traveling with a thief who'd just as soon pick my pocket as look at me.
Maybe there's not a man riding in the back who died sometime during the War.
And maybe some things are exactly how they appear.

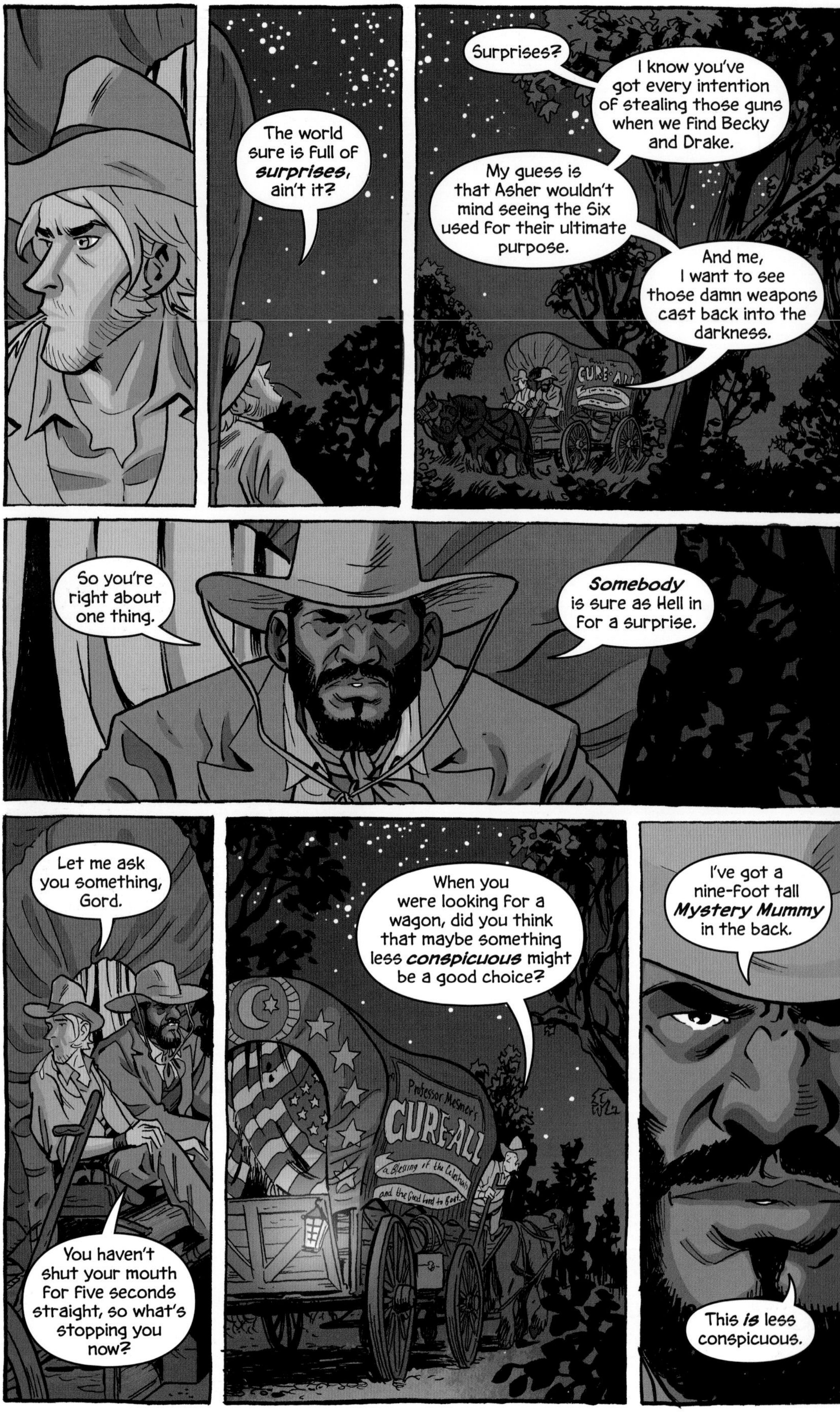
The world sure is full of *surprises*, ain't it?
Surprises?
I know you've got every intention of stealing those guns when we find Becky and Drake.
My guess is that Asher wouldn't mind seeing the Six used for their ultimate purpose.
And me, I want to see those damn weapons cast back into the darkness.
CURE-ALL
So you're right about one thing.
Somebody is sure as Hell in for a surprise.
Let me ask you something, Gord.
You haven't shut your mouth for five seconds straight, so what's stopping you now?
When you were looking for a wagon, did you think that maybe something less *conspicuous* might be a good choice?
Professor Mesmer's
CURE-ALL
a Blessing of the Celestials
and the Good Lord to Boot
I've got a nine-foot tall *Mystery Mummy* in the back.
This *is* less conspicuous.

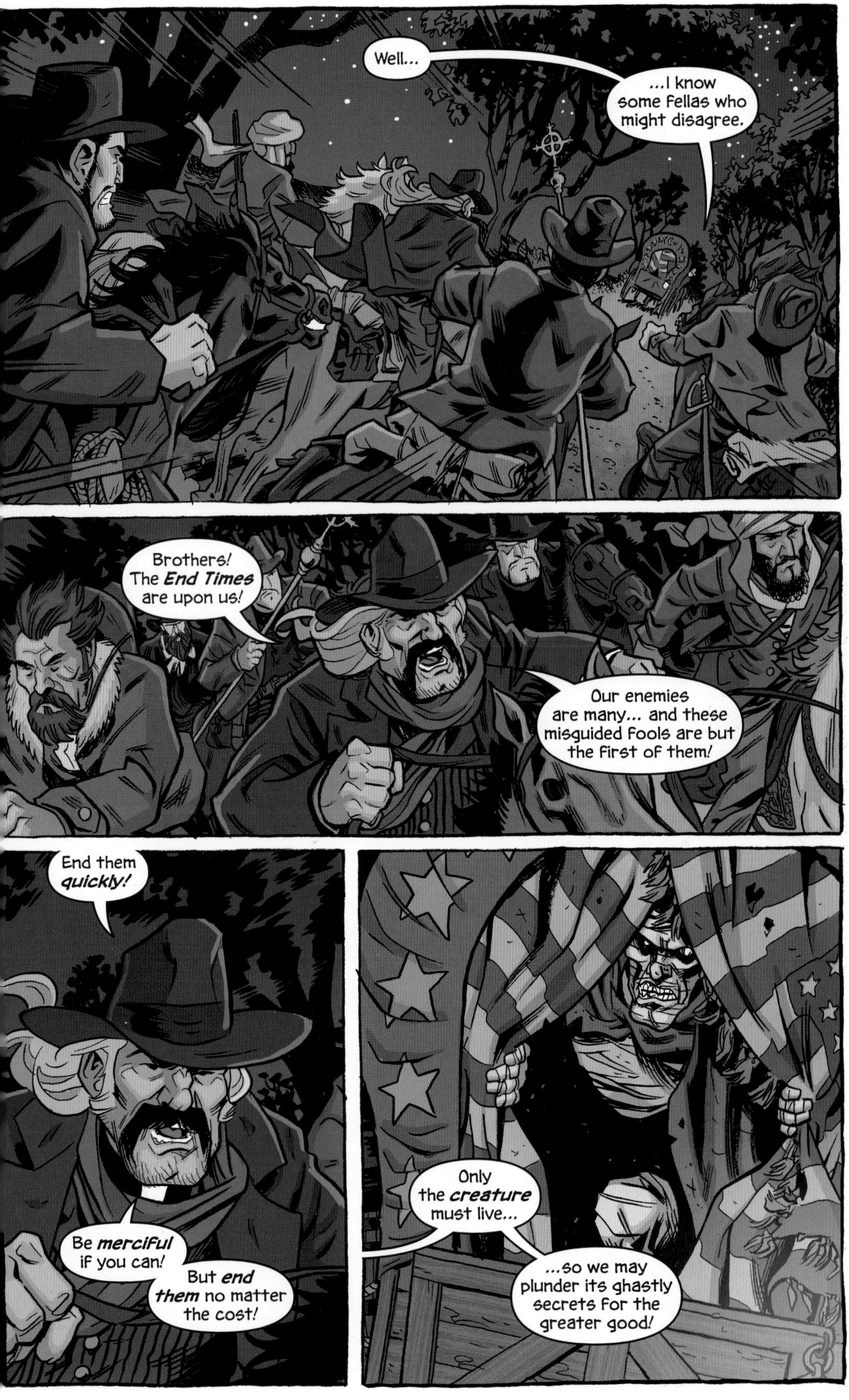
Well...
...I know some fellas who might disagree.
Brothers! The *End Times* are upon us!
Our enemies are many... and these misguided fools are but the first of them!
End them *quickly!*
Be *merciful* if you can!
But *end them* no matter the cost!
Only the *creature* must live...
...so we may plunder its ghastly secrets for the greater good!

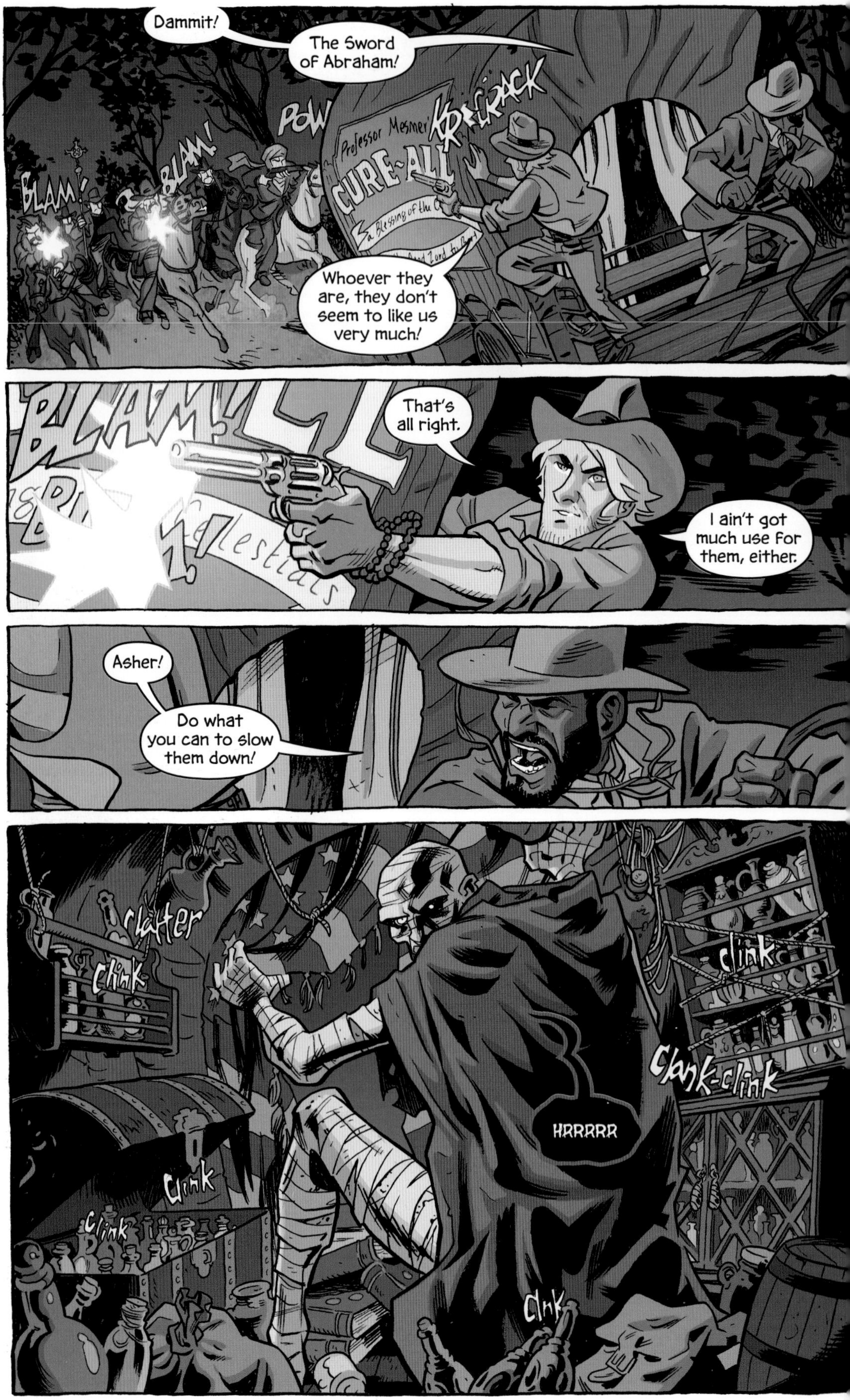
Dammit!
The Sword of Abraham!
POW
KRRACK
BLAM!
BLAM!
Professor Mesmer's
CURE-ALL
Whoever they are, they don't seem to like us very much!
BLAM!
That's all right.
I ain't got much use for them, either.
Asher!
Do what you can to slow them down!
clatter
clink
clink
clank-clink
HRRRRR
clink
clink
clink

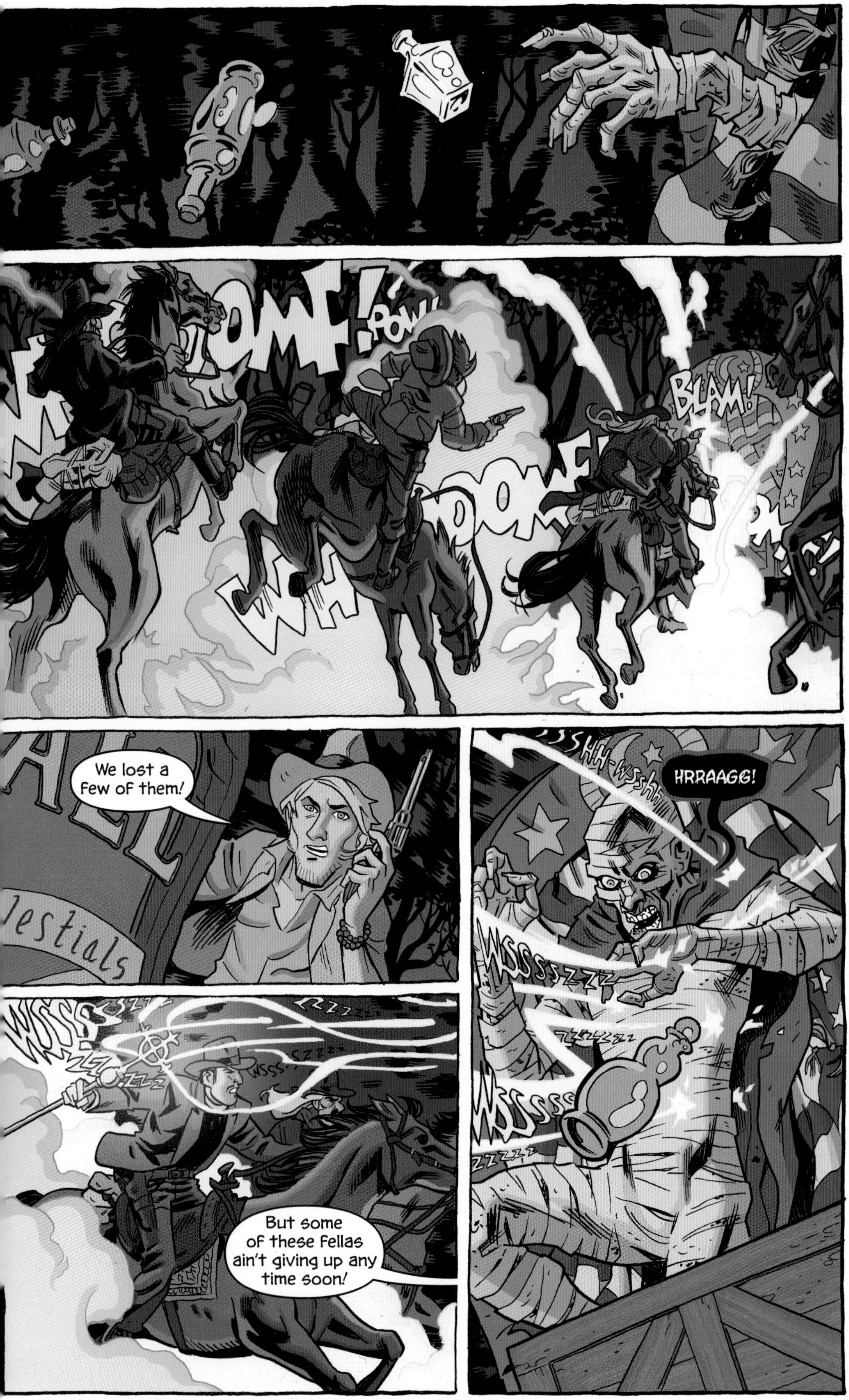
POW!
BLAM!
We lost a few of them!
HRRAAGG!
But some of these fellas ain't giving up any time soon!

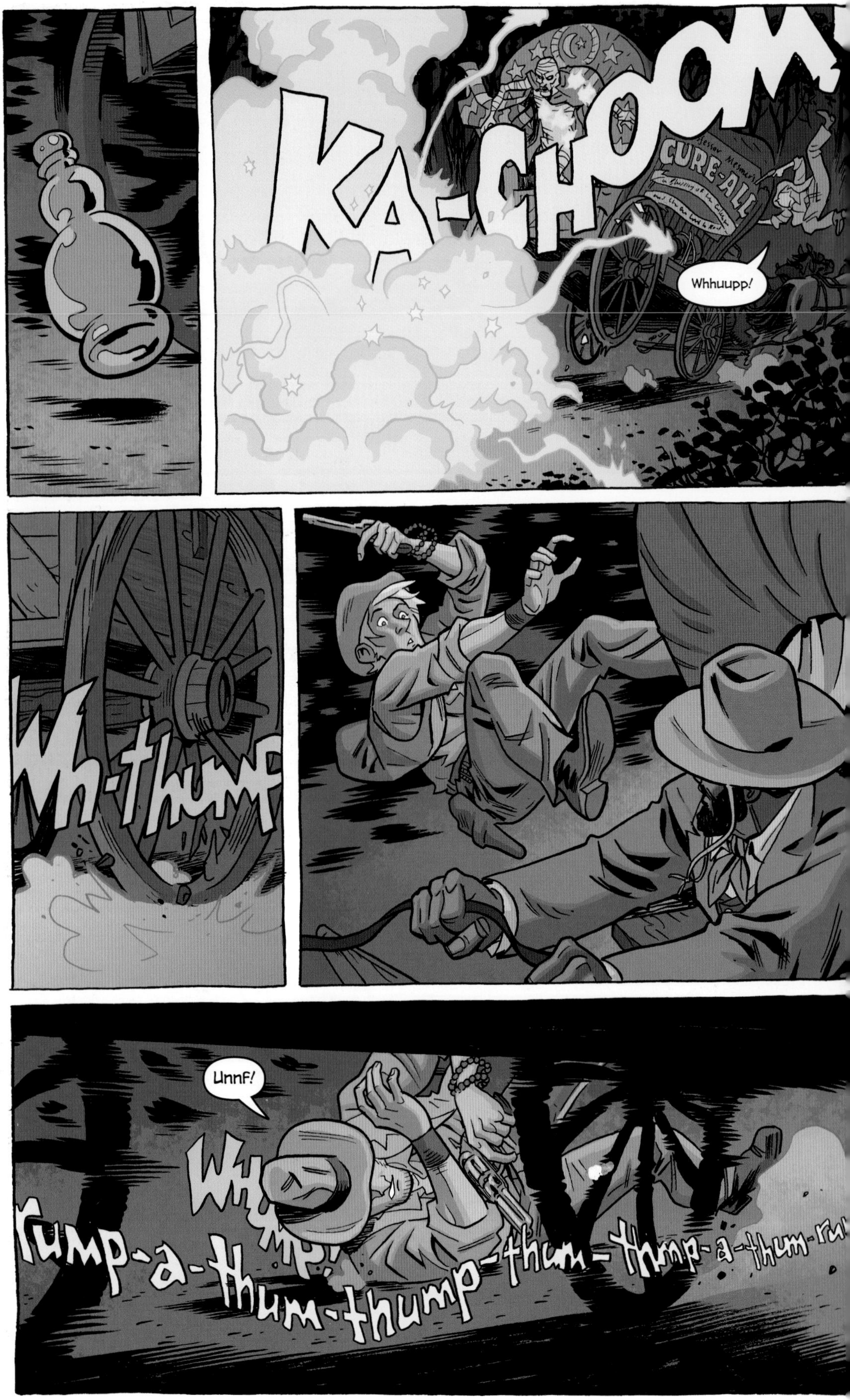
KA-CHOOM!
CURE-ALL
Whhuupp!
Wh-thump
Unnf!
WHUMP!
rump-a-thum-thump-thum-thmp-a-thum-ru

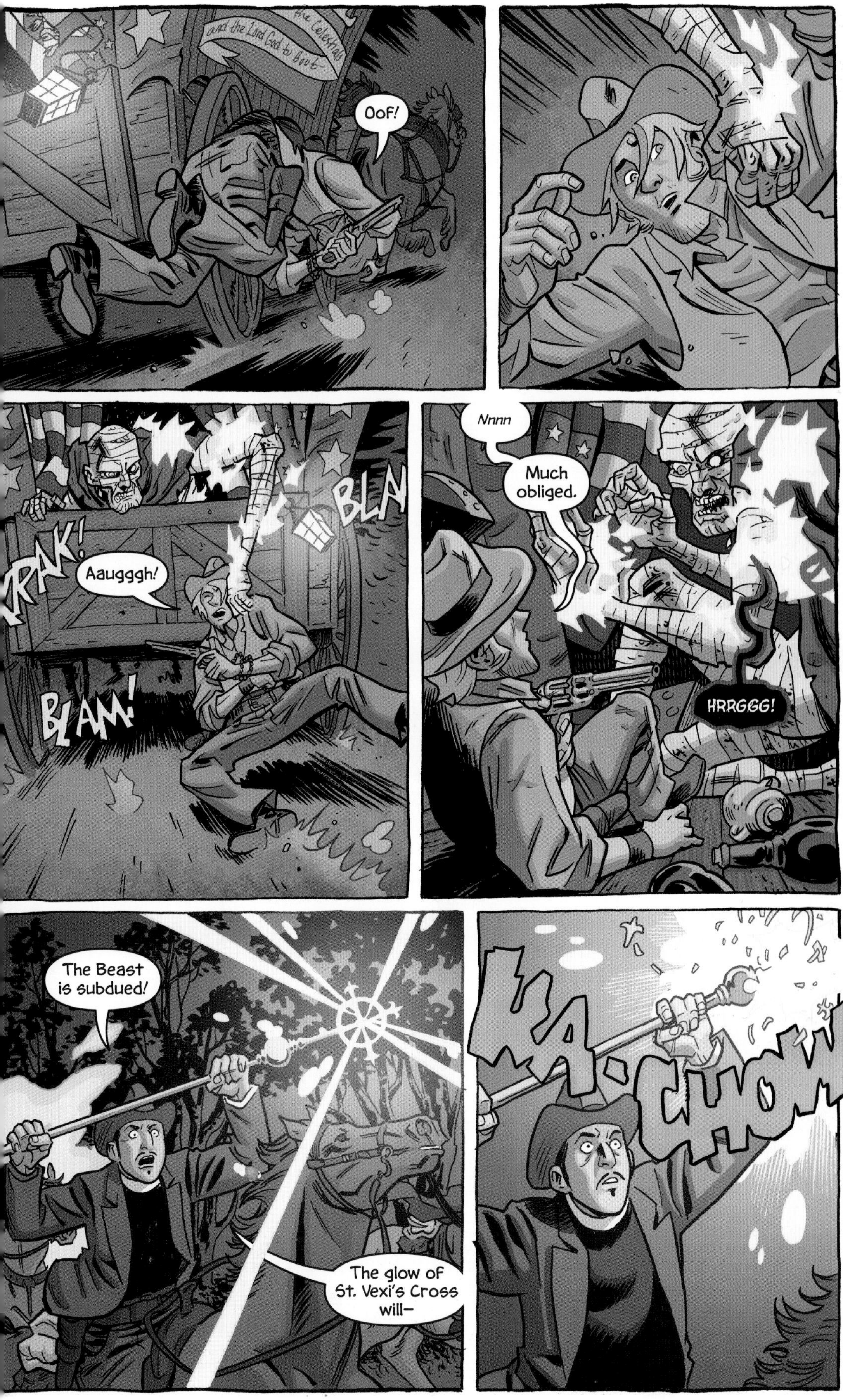
The Celestials
and the Lord God to boot
Oof!
RAK!
Aaugggh!
BLA
BLAM!
Nnnn
Much obliged.
HRRGGG!
The Beast is subdued!
The glow of St. Vexi's Cross will—
KA-CHOW

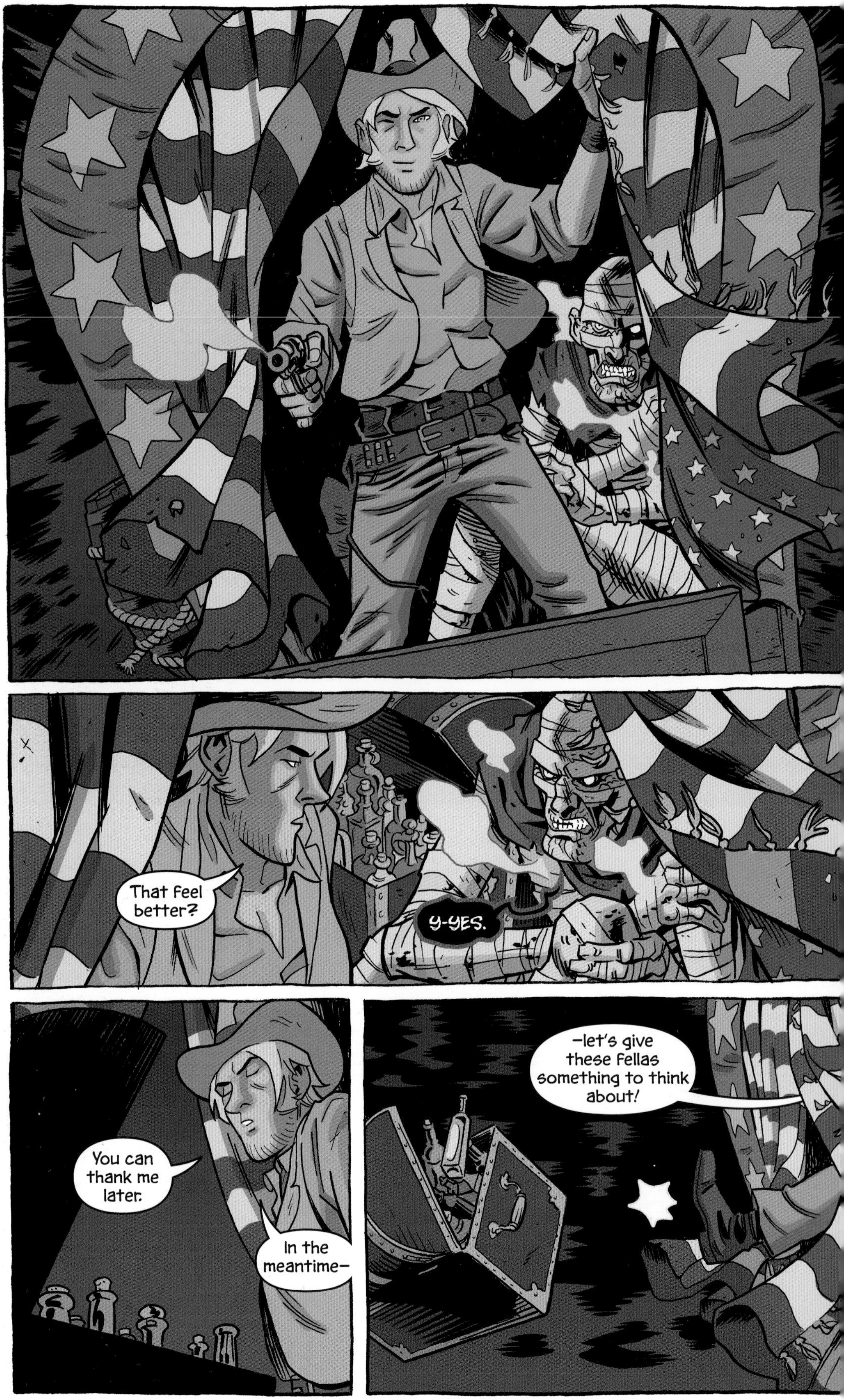

That feel better?
Y-YES.
You can thank me later.
In the meantime—
—let's give these fellas something to think about!

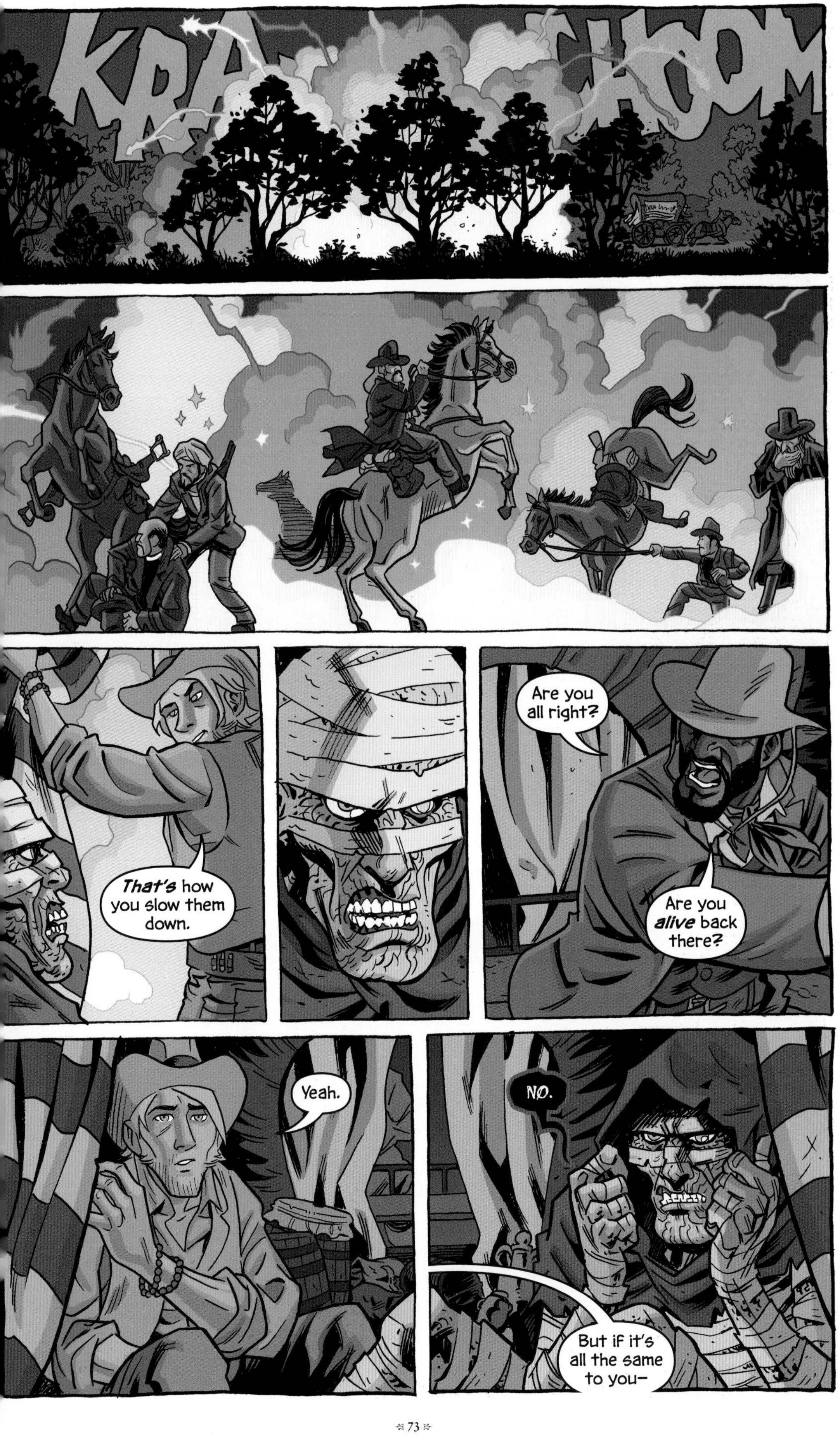
That's how you slow them down.
Are you all right?
Are you *alive* back there?
Yeah.
NO.
But if it's all the same to you—

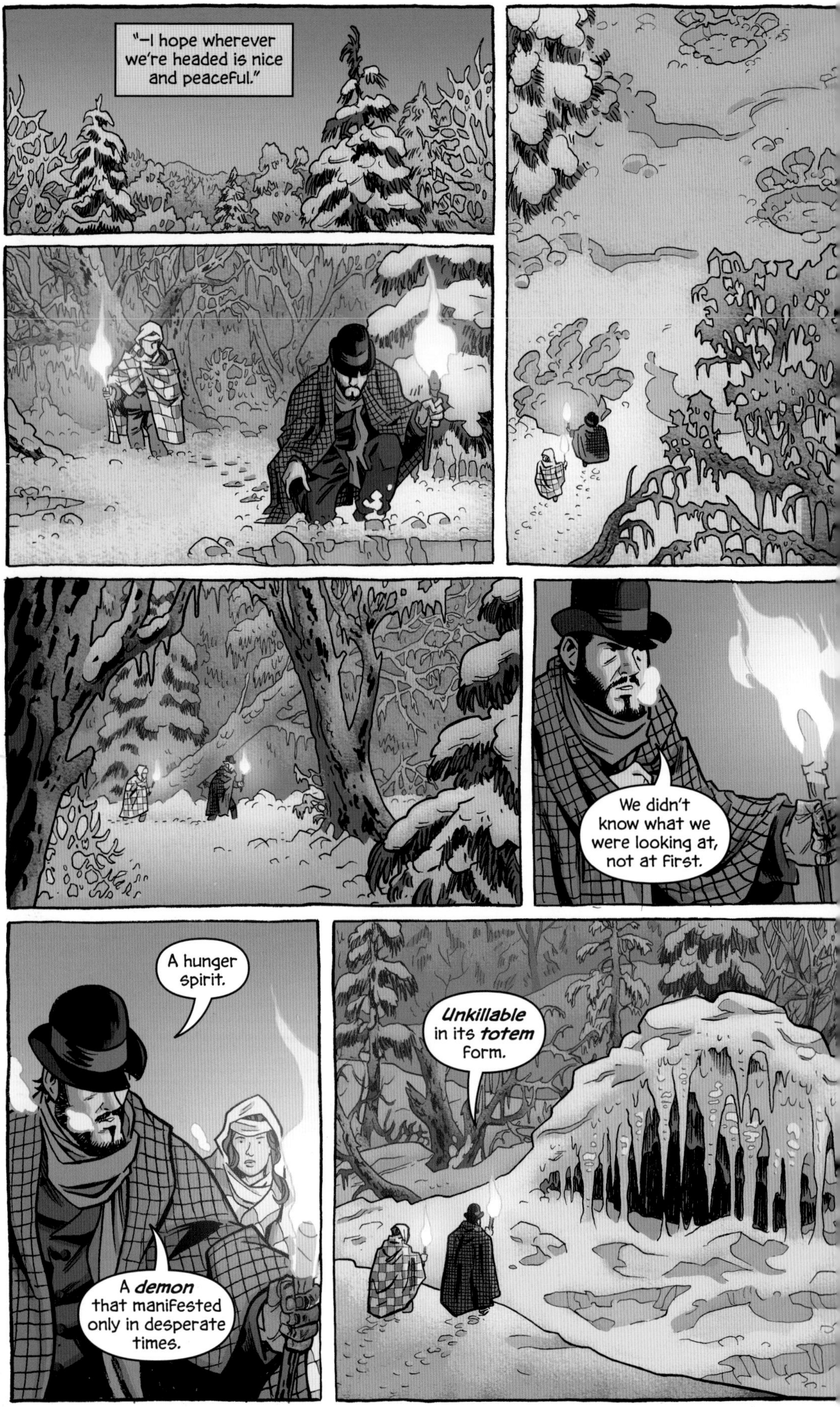
"—I hope wherever we're headed is nice and peaceful."
We didn't know what we were looking at, not at first.
A hunger spirit.
A *demon* that manifested only in desperate times.
Unkillable in its *totem* form.

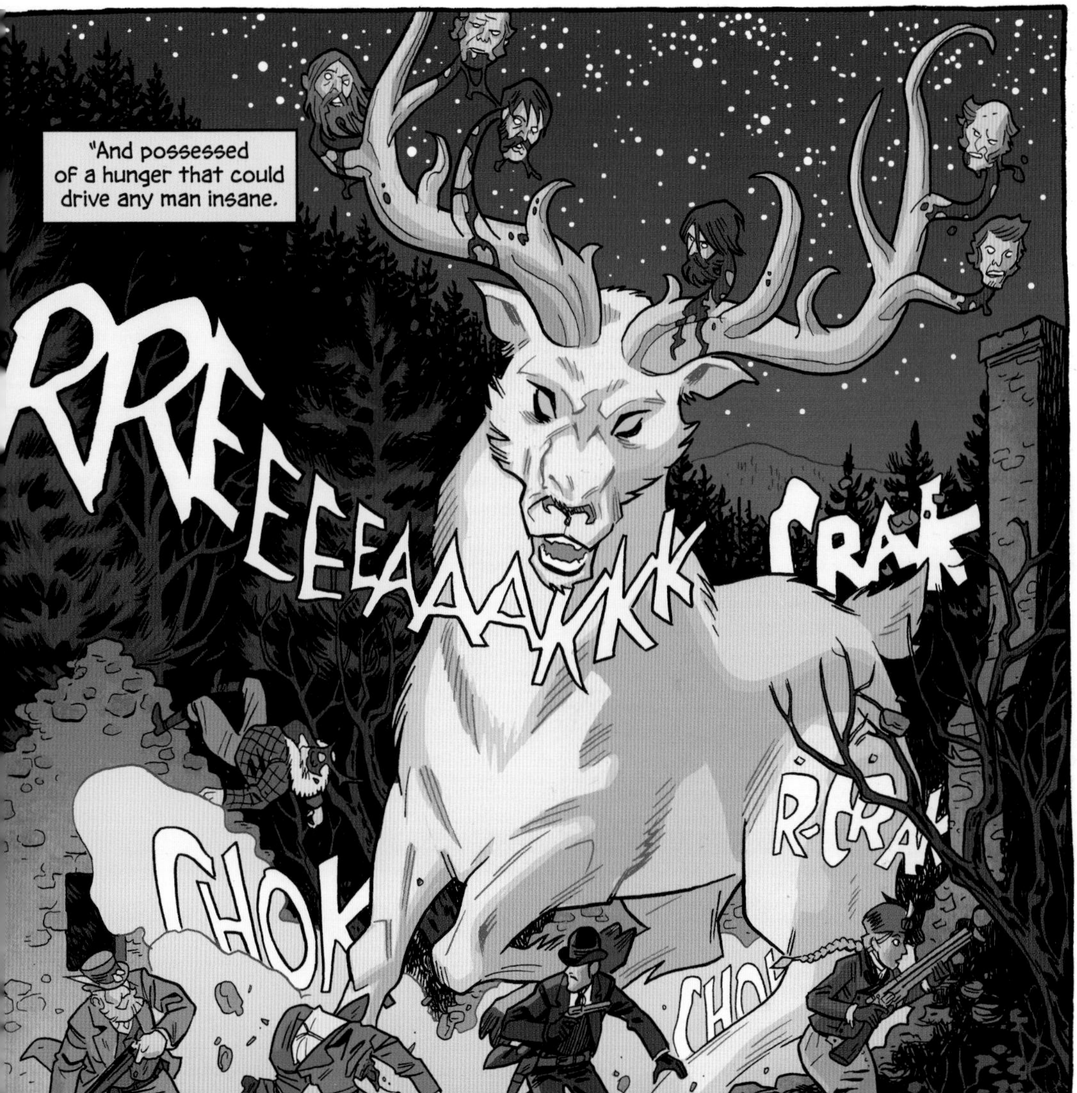
"And possessed of a hunger that could drive any man insane.
RRREEEAAAKKK
CRAK
R-CRAK
CHOK
CHOK

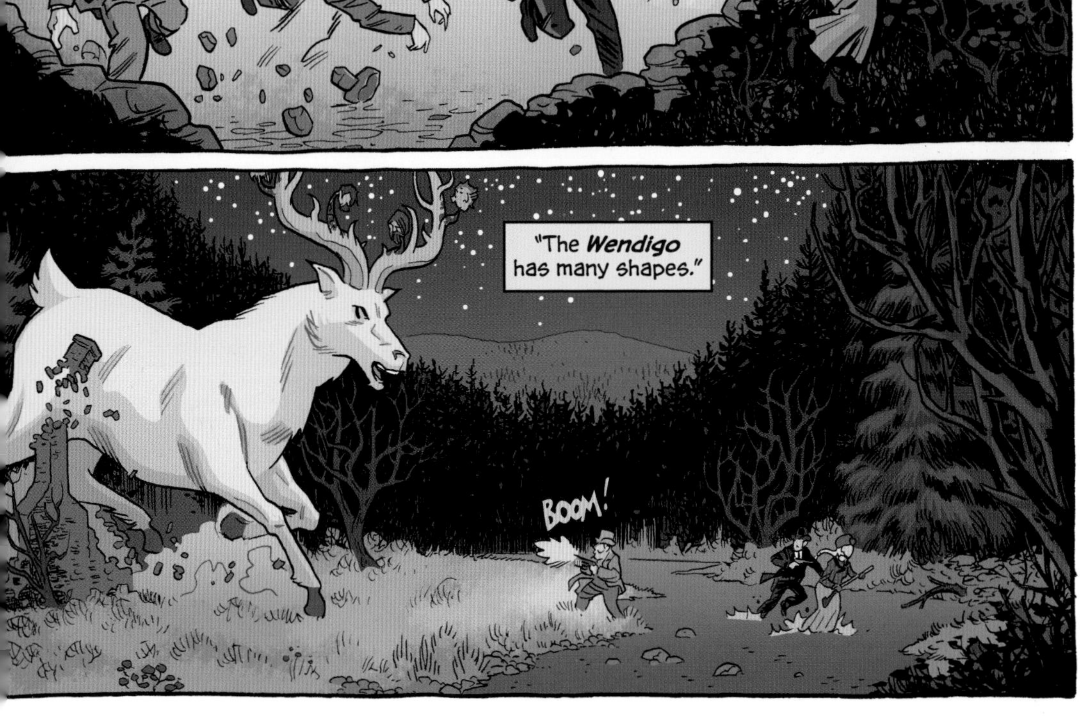
"The *Wendigo* has many shapes."
BOOM!

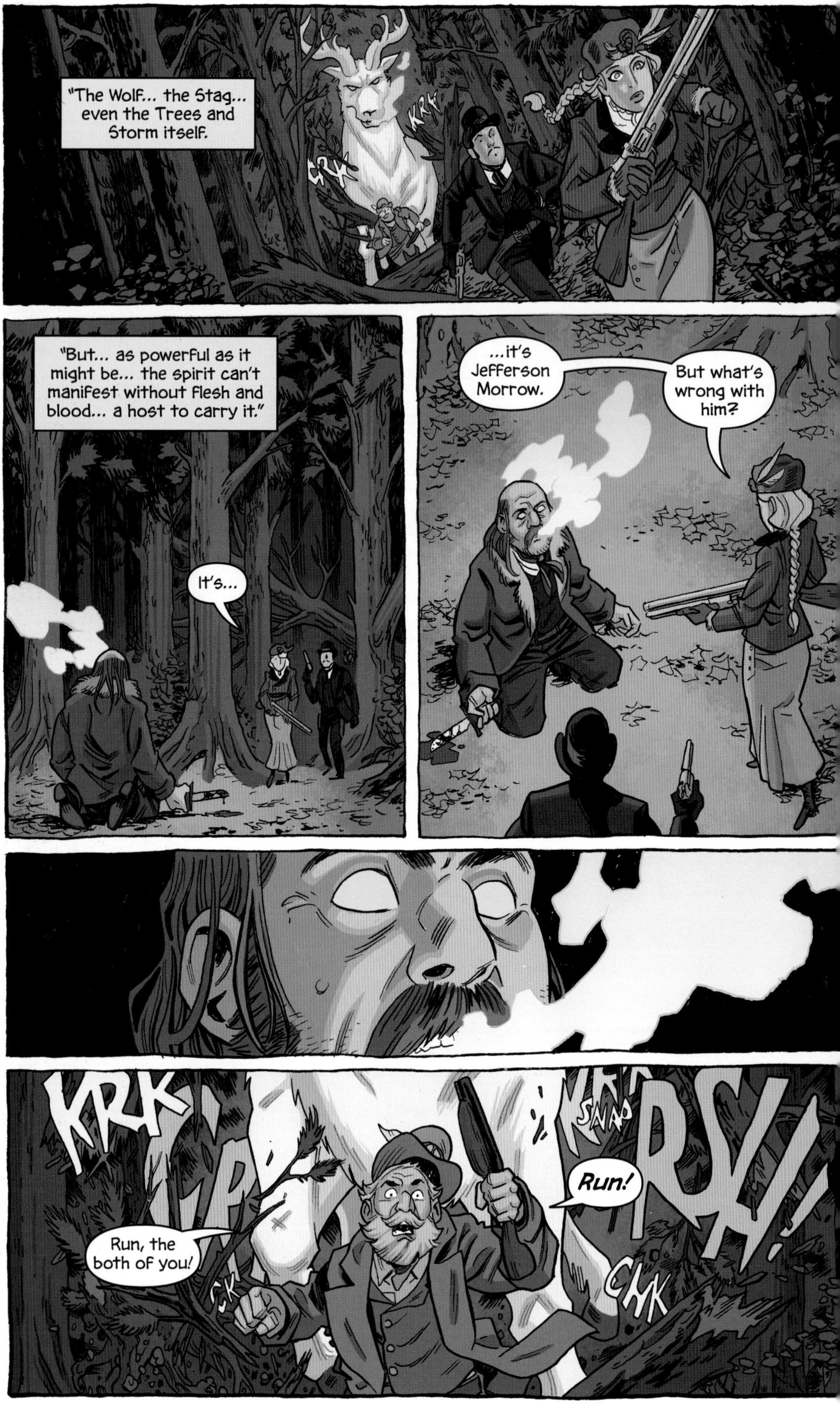
"The Wolf... the Stag... even the Trees and Storm itself.
KRK
"But... as powerful as it might be... the spirit can't manifest without flesh and blood... a host to carry it."
It's...
...it's Jefferson Morrow.
But what's wrong with him?
KRK
Run!
Run, the both of you!
CHK

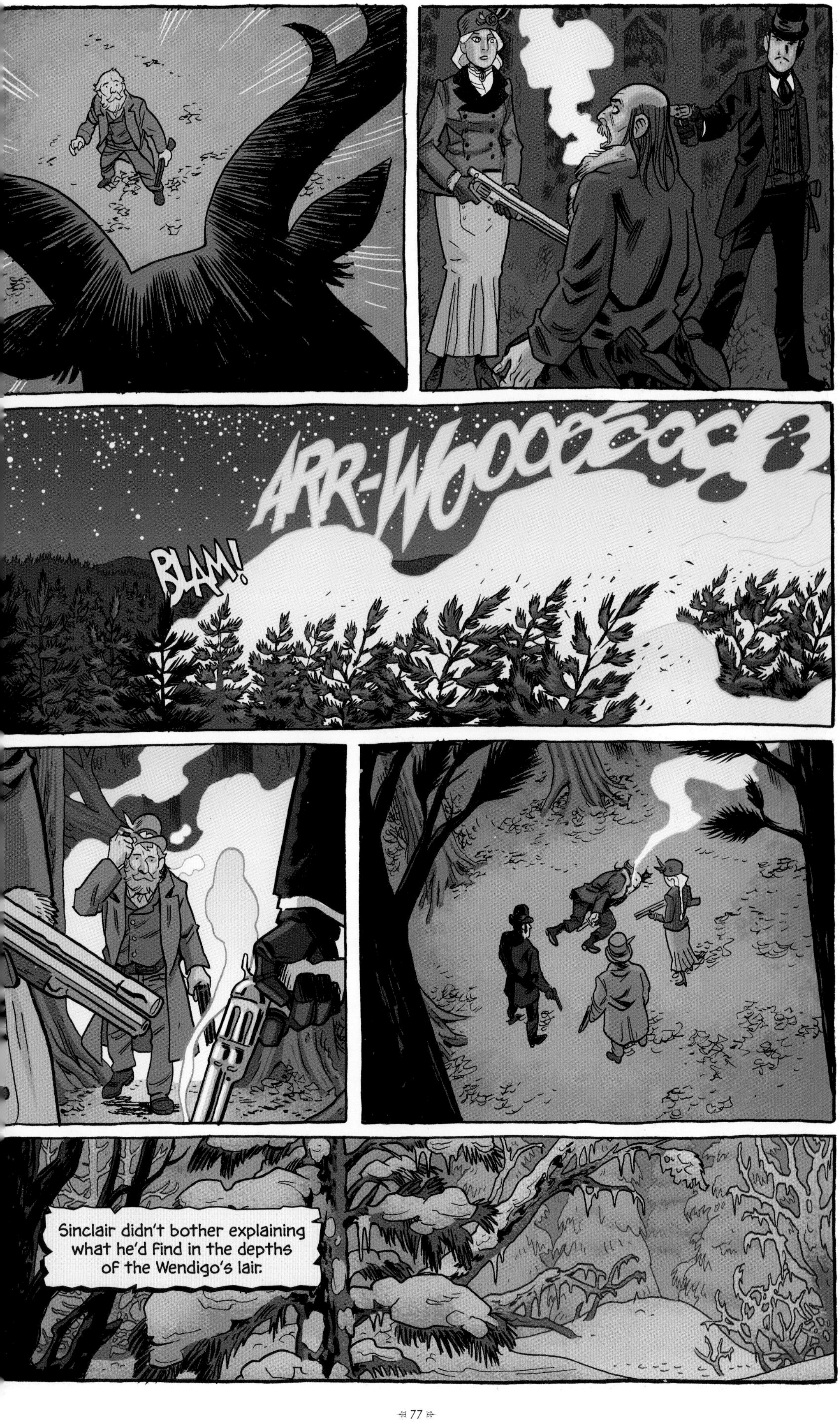
ARR-WOOOOOOO
BLAM!
Sinclair didn't bother explaining what he'd find in the depths of the Wendigo's lair.

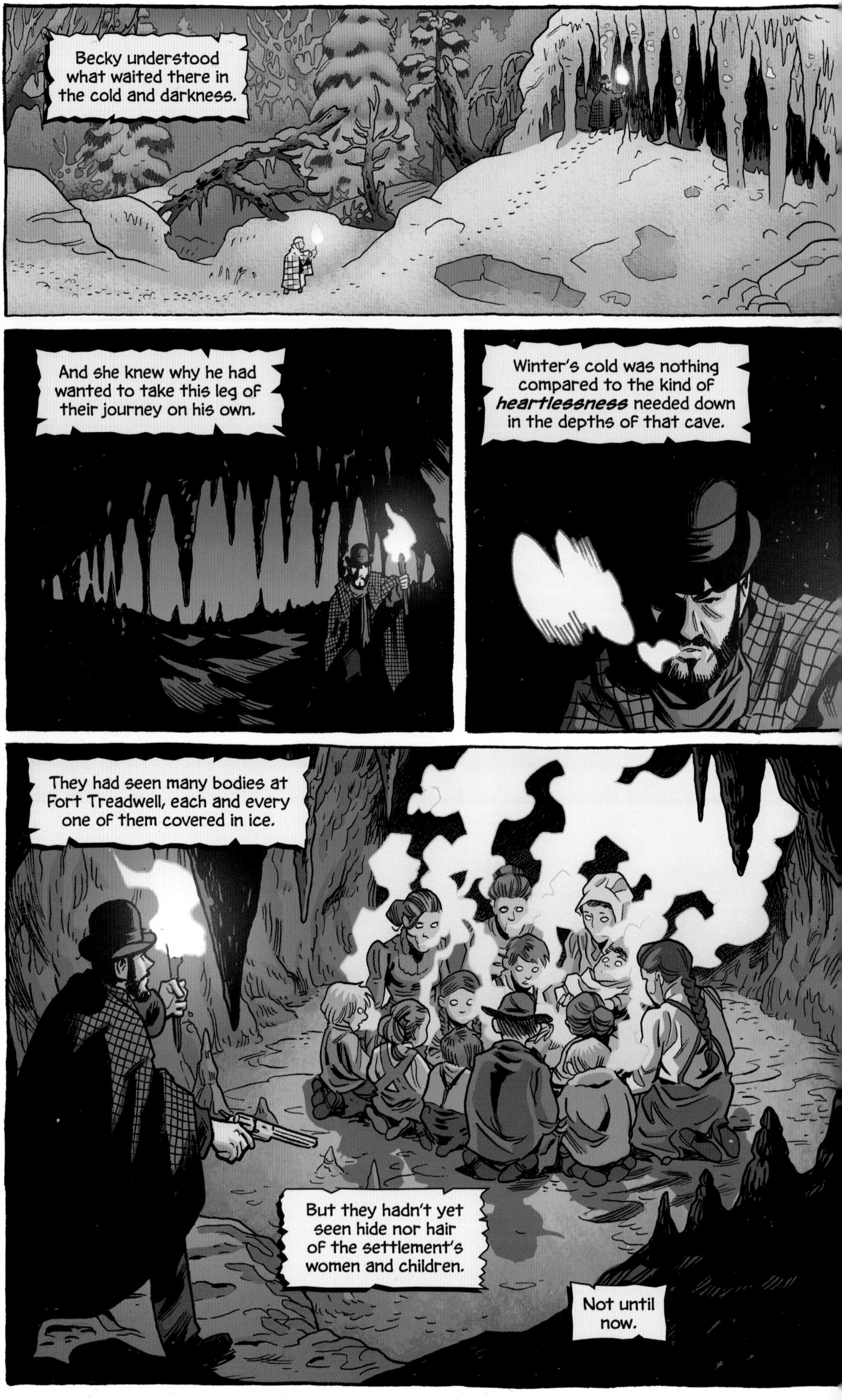
Becky understood what waited there in the cold and darkness.
And she knew why he had wanted to take this leg of their journey on his own.
Winter's cold was nothing compared to the kind of ***heartlessness*** needed down in the depths of that cave.
They had seen many bodies at Fort Treadwell, each and every one of them covered in ice.
But they hadn't yet seen hide nor hair of the settlement's women and children.
Not until now.

CHAPTER
FOUR

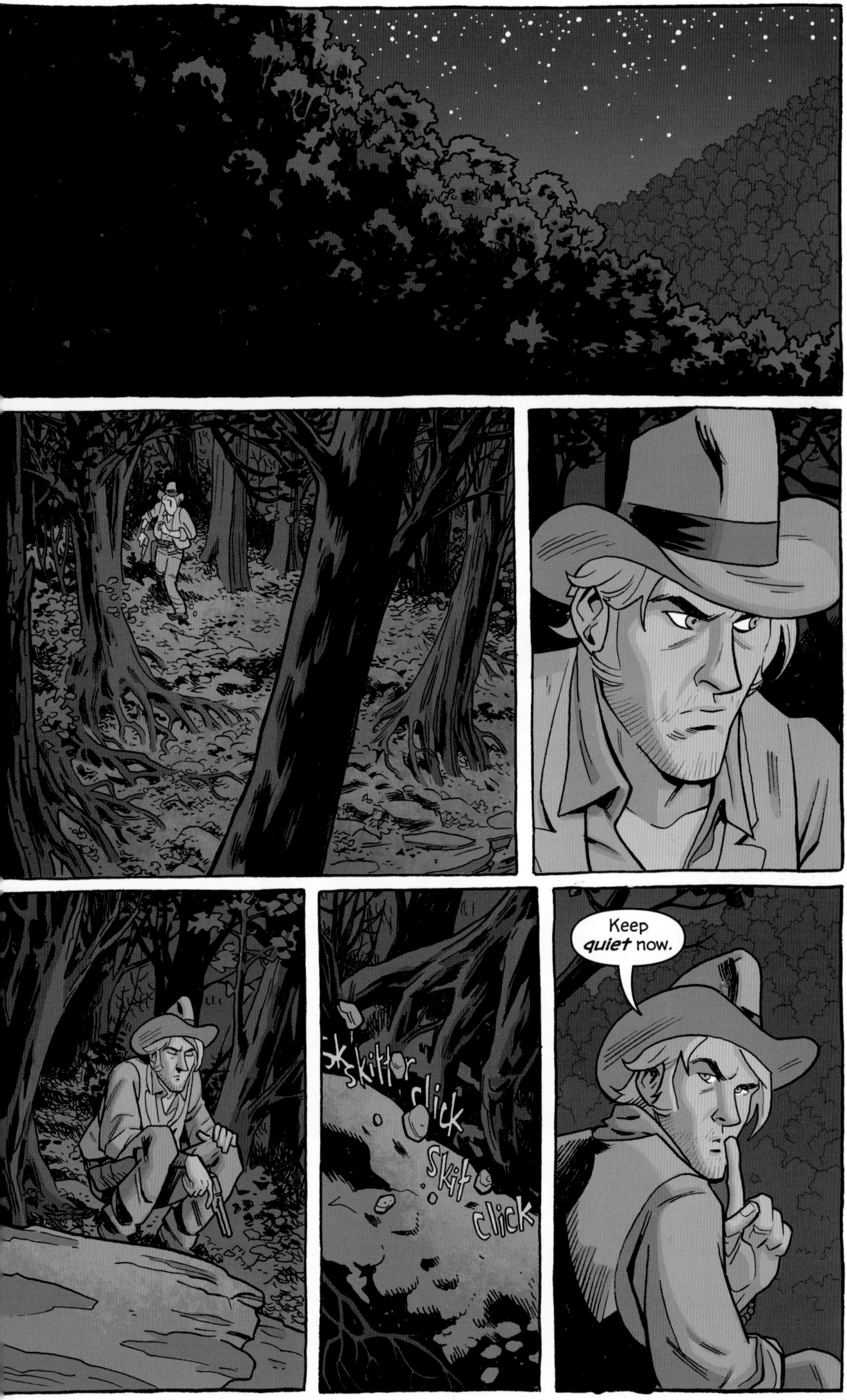
sk skitter
click
skit
click
Keep *quiet* now.

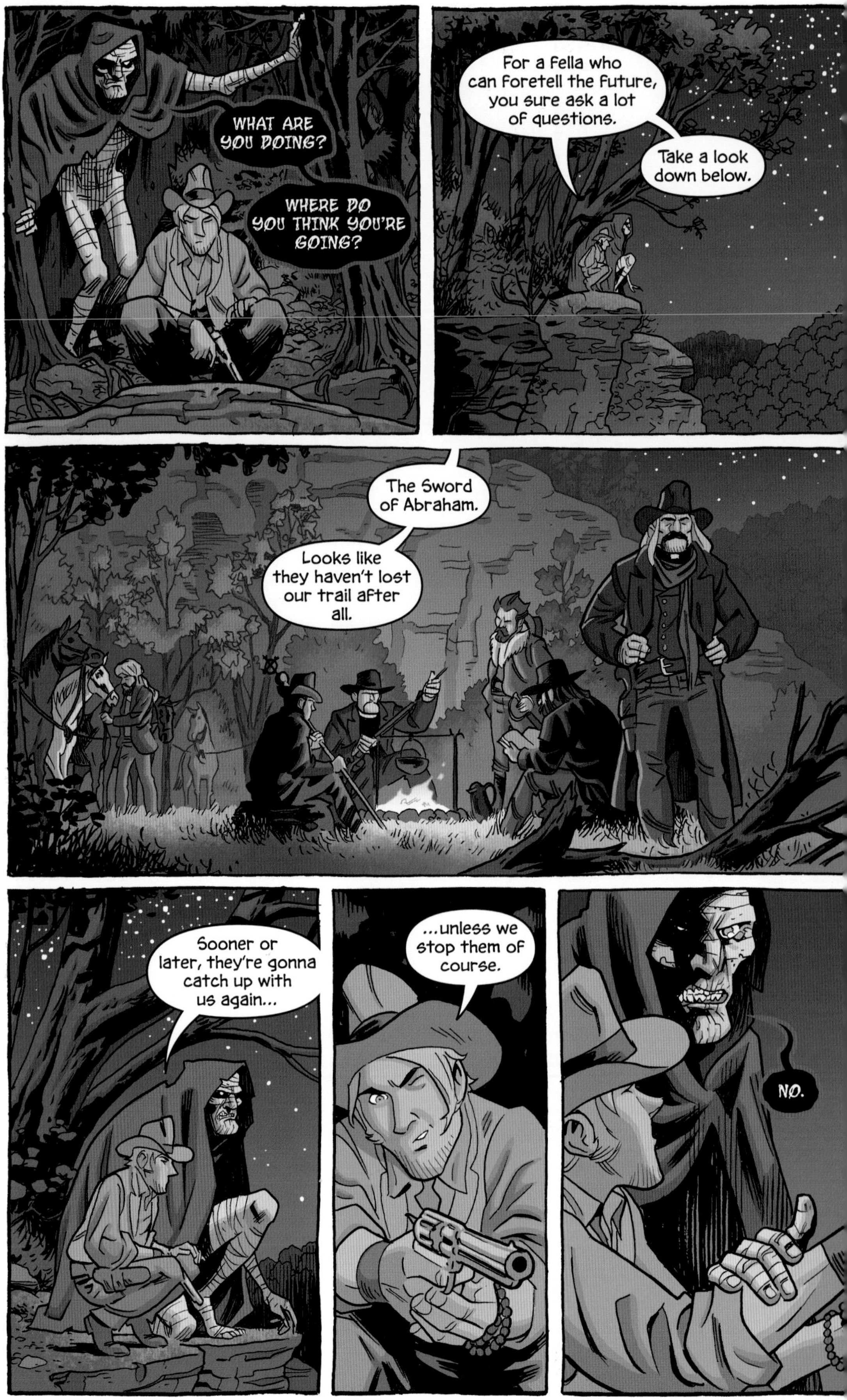
WHAT ARE YOU DOING?
WHERE DO YOU THINK YOU'RE GOING?
For a fella who can foretell the future, you sure ask a lot of questions.
Take a look down below.
The Sword of Abraham.
Looks like they haven't lost our trail after all.
Sooner or later, they're gonna catch up with us again...
...unless we stop them of course.
NO.

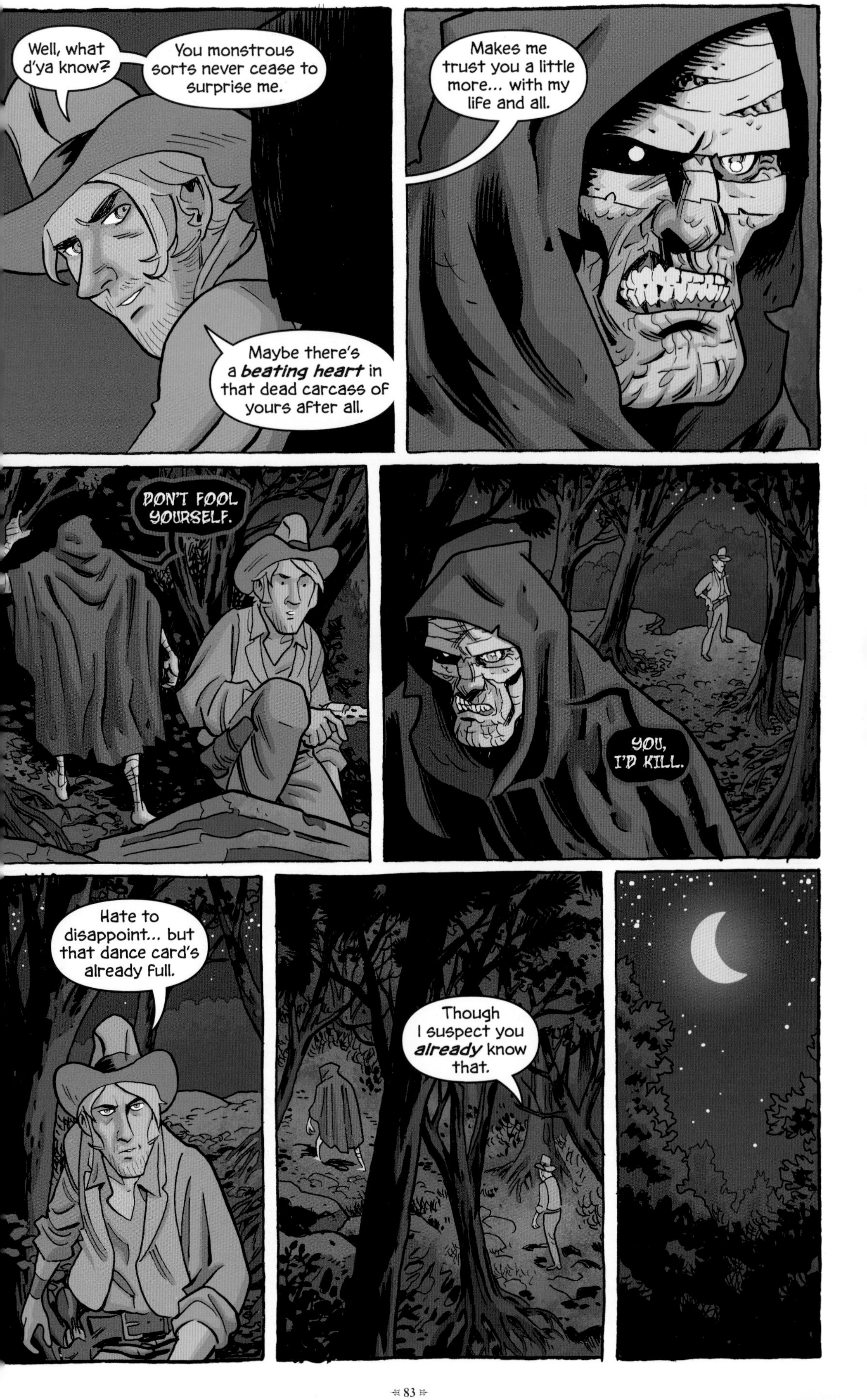
Well, what d'ya know?
You monstrous sorts never cease to surprise me.
Maybe there's a *beating heart* in that dead carcass of yours after all.
Makes me trust you a little more... with my life and all.
DON'T FOOL YOURSELF.
YOU, I'D KILL.
Hate to disappoint... but that dance card's already full.
Though I suspect you *already* know that.

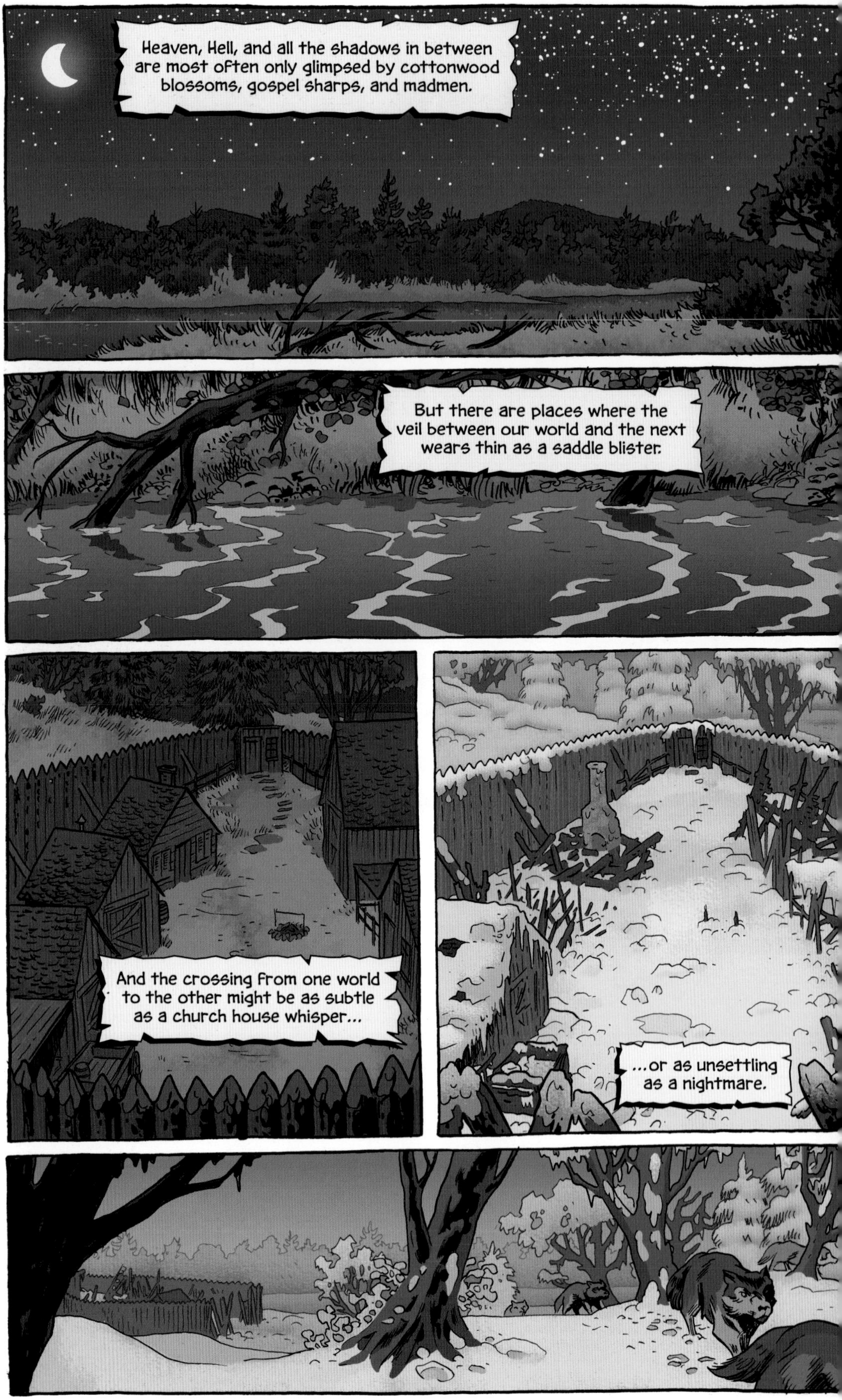
Heaven, Hell, and all the shadows in between are most often only glimpsed by cottonwood blossoms, gospel sharps, and madmen.
But there are places where the veil between our world and the next wears thin as a saddle blister.
And the crossing from one world to the other might be as subtle as a church house whisper...
...or as unsettling as a nightmare.

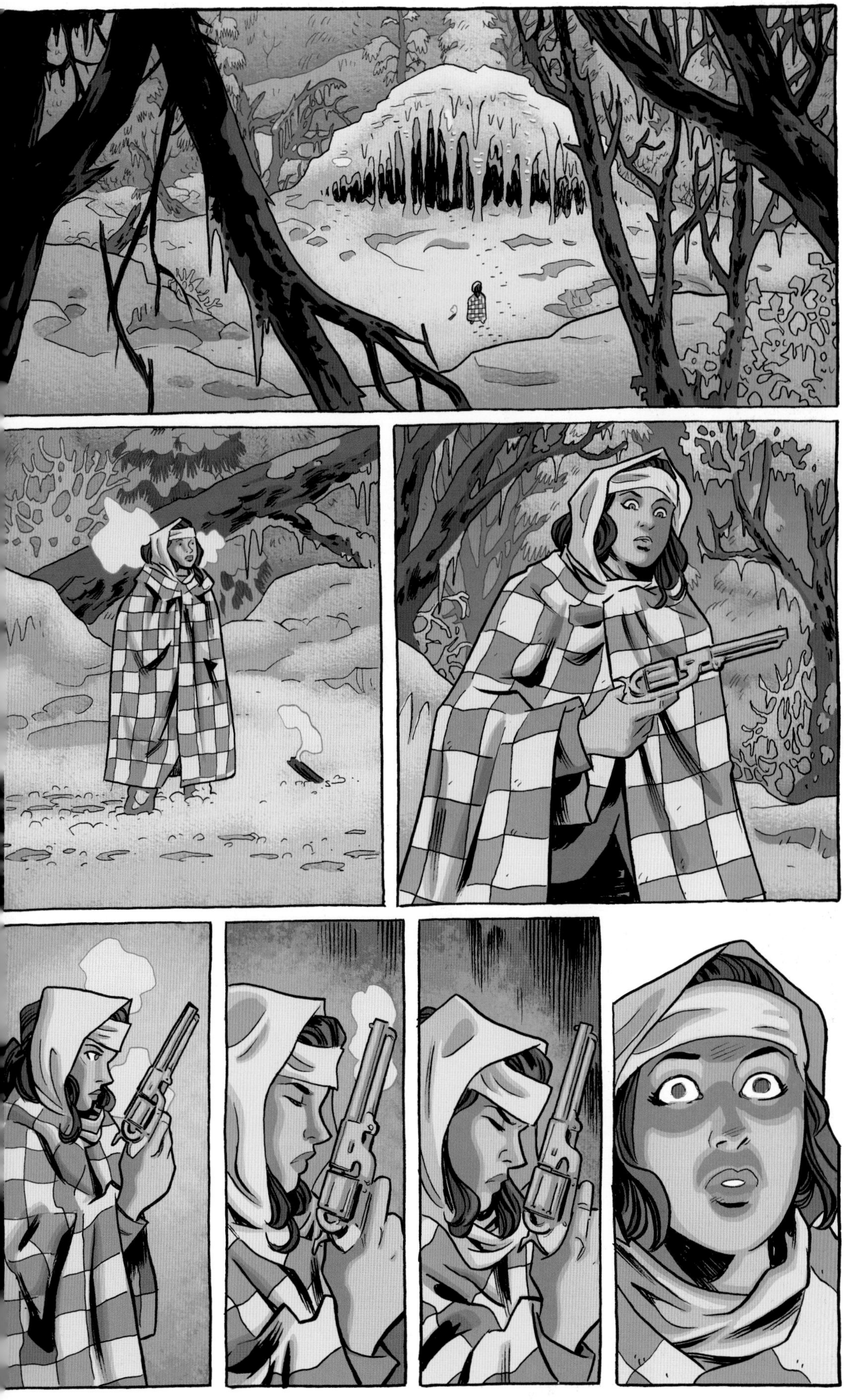

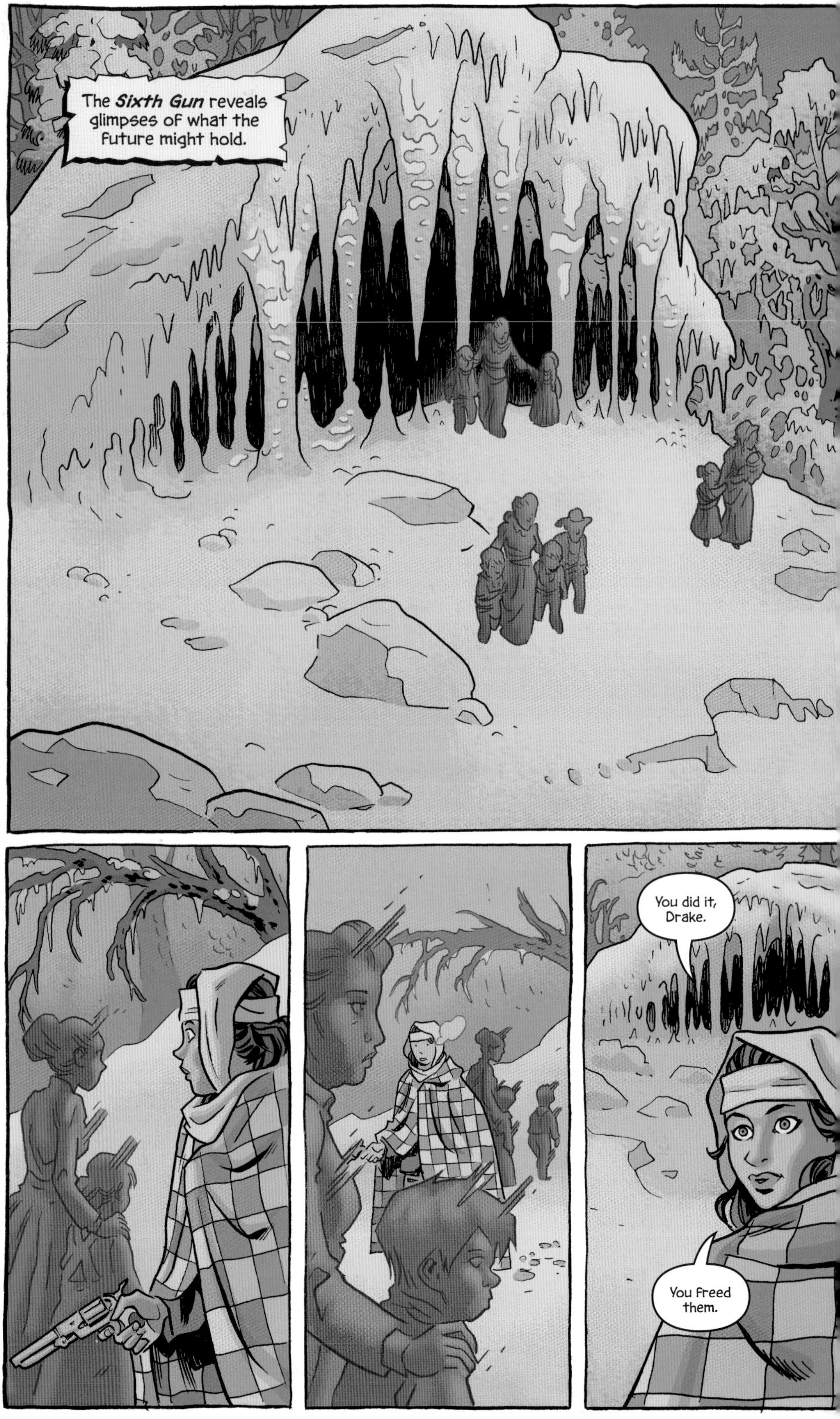
The *Sixth Gun* reveals glimpses of what the future might hold.
You did it, Drake.
You freed them.

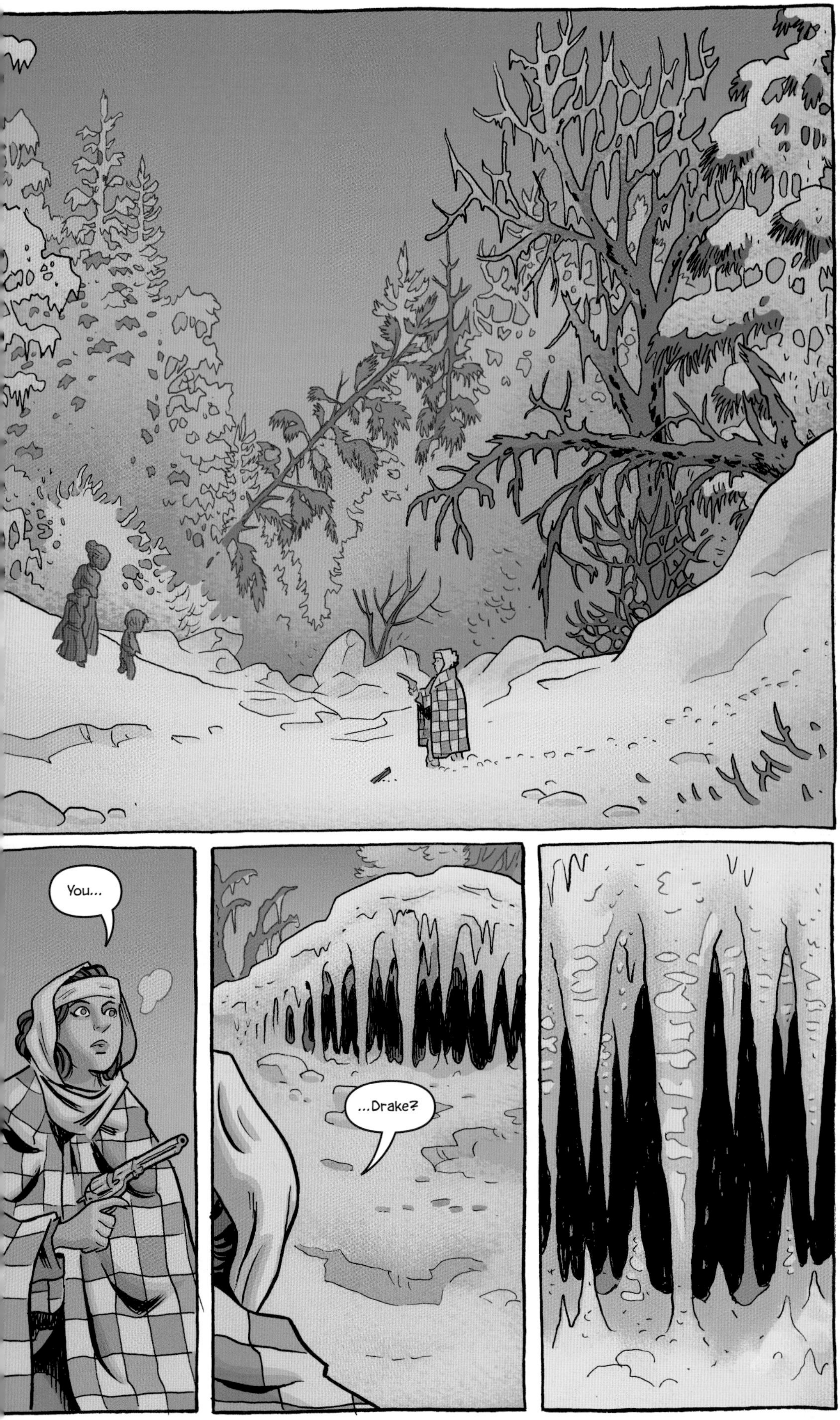
You...
...Drake?

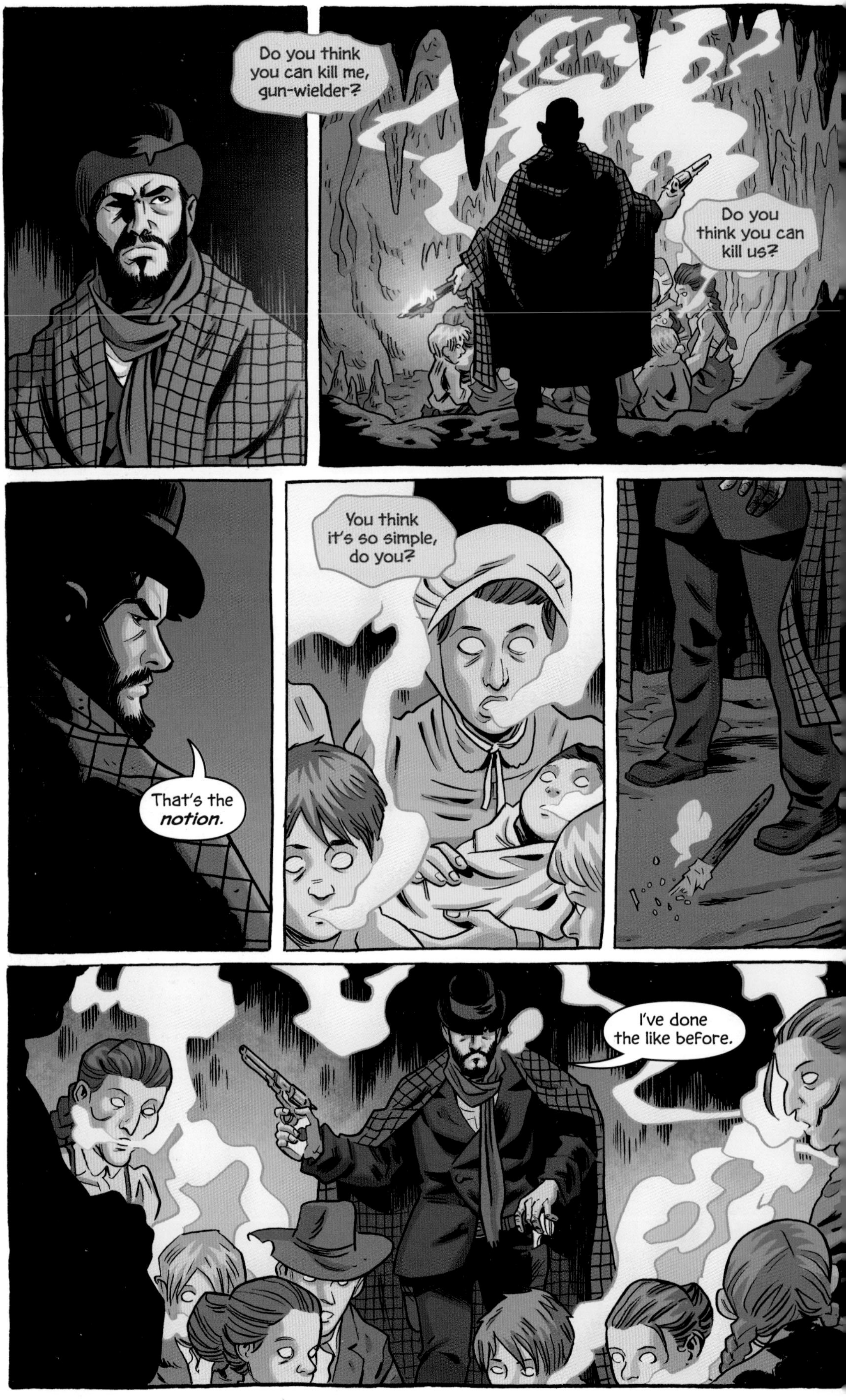
Do you think you can kill me, gun-wielder?
Do you think you can kill us?
That's the *notion.*
You think it's so simple, do you?
I've done the like before.

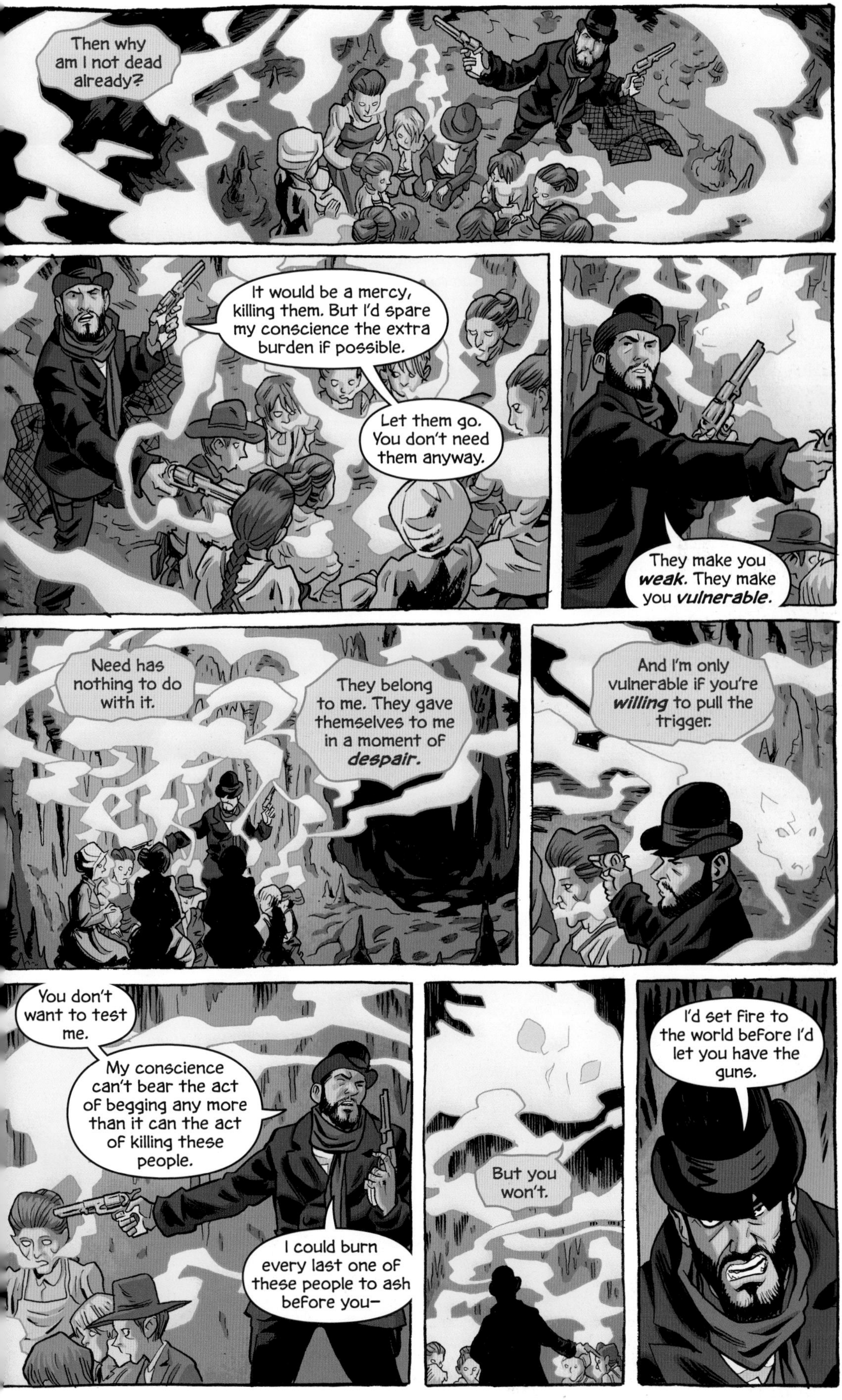
Then why am I not dead already?
It would be a mercy, killing them. But I'd spare my conscience the extra burden if possible.
Let them go. You don't need them anyway.
They make you *weak*. They make you *vulnerable*.
Need has nothing to do with it.
They belong to me. They gave themselves to me in a moment of *despair*.
And I'm only vulnerable if you're *willing* to pull the trigger.
You don't want to test me.
My conscience can't bear the act of begging any more than it can the act of killing these people.
I could burn every last one of these people to ash before you—
But you won't.
I'd set fire to the world before I'd let you have the guns.

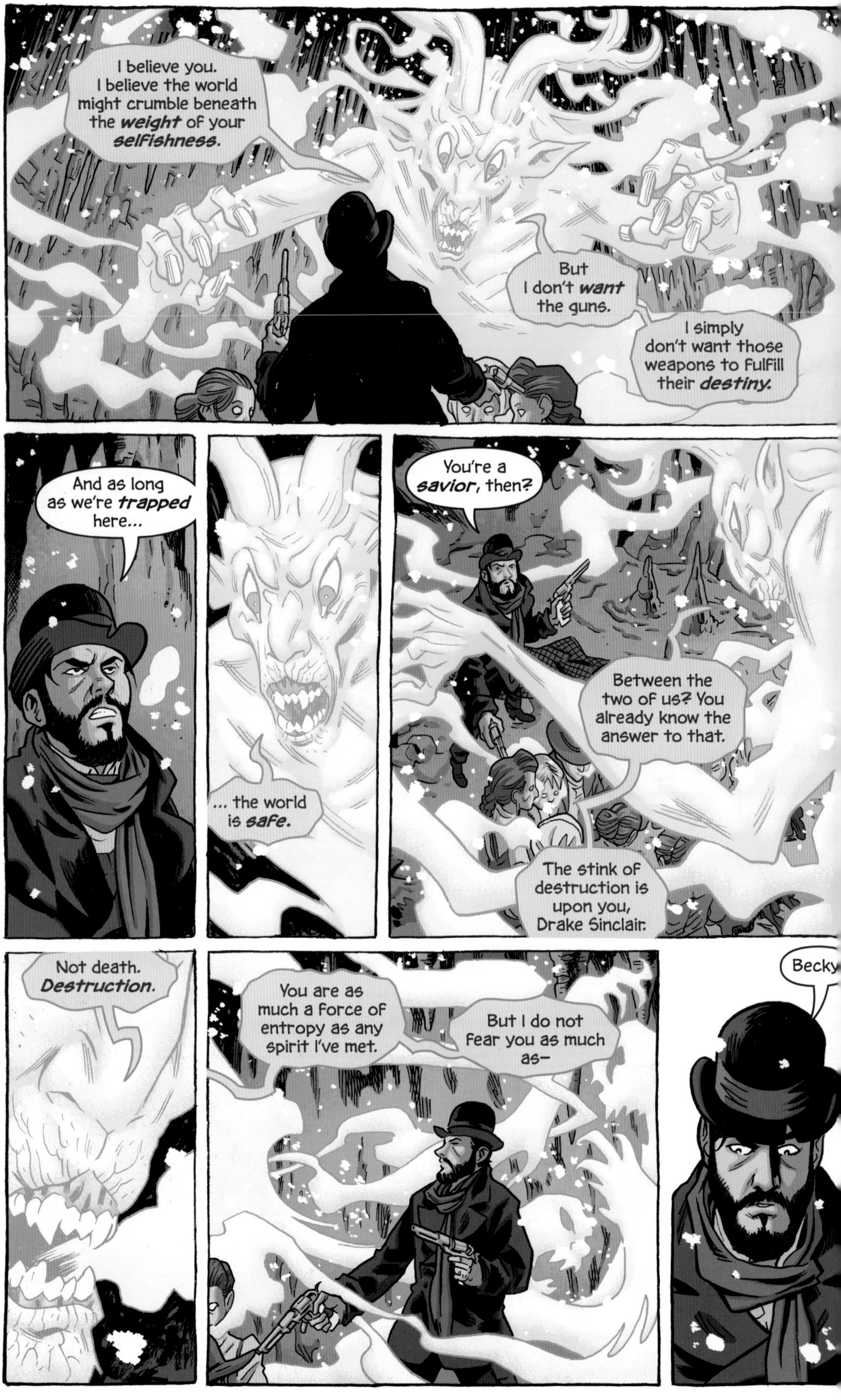
I believe you. I believe the world might crumble beneath the *weight* of your *selfishness.*
But I don't *want* the guns.
I simply don't want those weapons to fulfill their *destiny.*
And as long as we're *trapped* here...
... the world is *safe.*
You're a *savior,* then?
Between the two of us? You already know the answer to that.
The stink of destruction is upon you, Drake Sinclair.
Not death. *Destruction.*
You are as much a force of entropy as any spirit I've met.
But I do not fear you as much as–
Becky

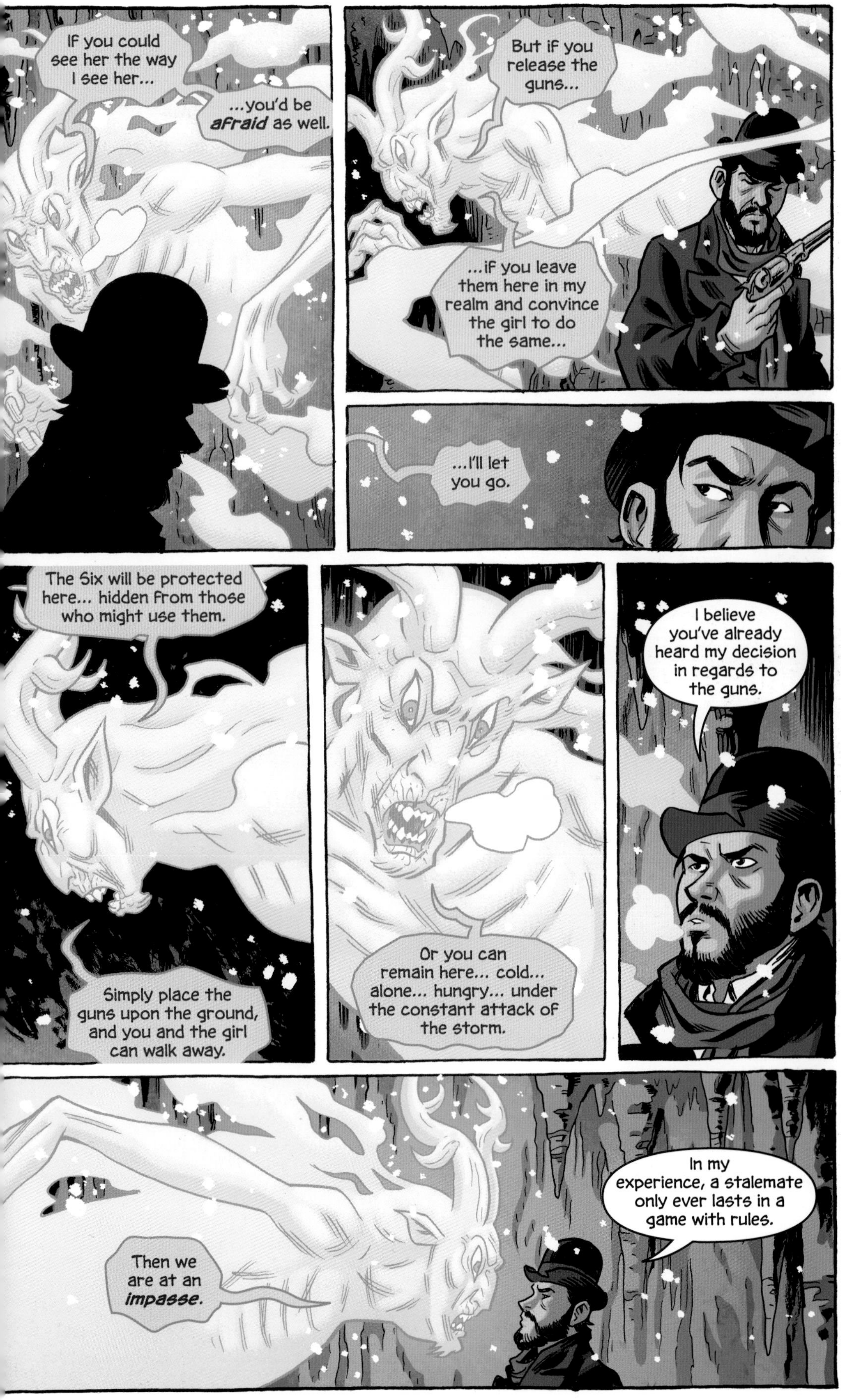
If you could see her the way I see her...
...you'd be *afraid* as well.
But if you release the guns...
...if you leave them here in my realm and convince the girl to do the same...
...I'll let you go.
The Six will be protected here... hidden from those who might use them.
Simply place the guns upon the ground, and you and the girl can walk away.
Or you can remain here... cold... alone... hungry... under the constant attack of the storm.
I believe you've already heard my decision in regards to the guns.
Then we are at an *impasse.*
In my experience, a stalemate only ever lasts in a game with rules.

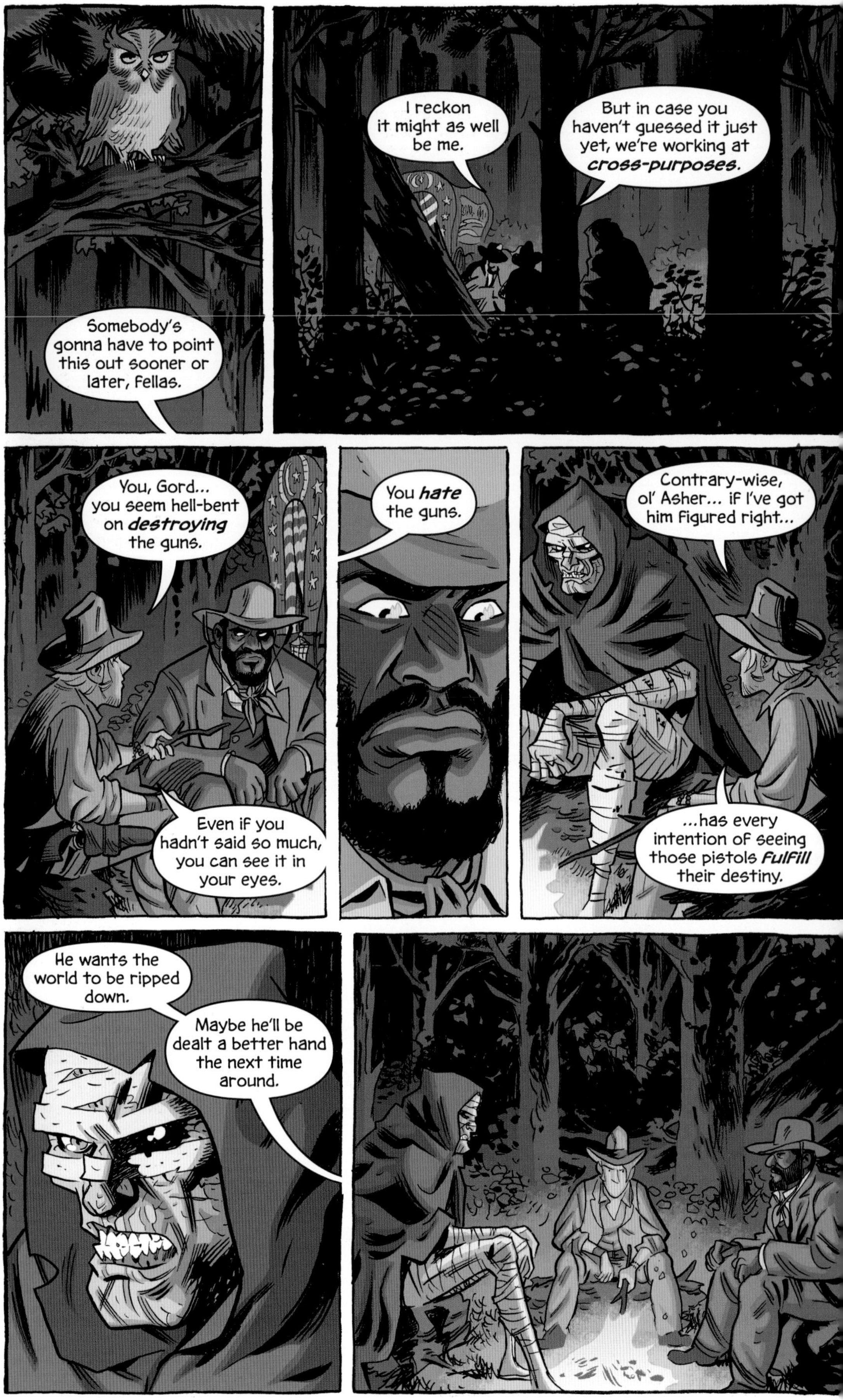
Somebody's gonna have to point this out sooner or later, fellas.
I reckon it might as well be me.
But in case you haven't guessed it just yet, we're working at *cross-purposes.*
You, Gord... you seem hell-bent on *destroying* the guns.
Even if you hadn't said so much, you can see it in your eyes.
You *hate* the guns.
Contrary-wise, ol' Asher... if I've got him figured right...
...has every intention of seeing those pistols *fulfill* their destiny.
He wants the world to be ripped down.
Maybe he'll be dealt a better hand the next time around.

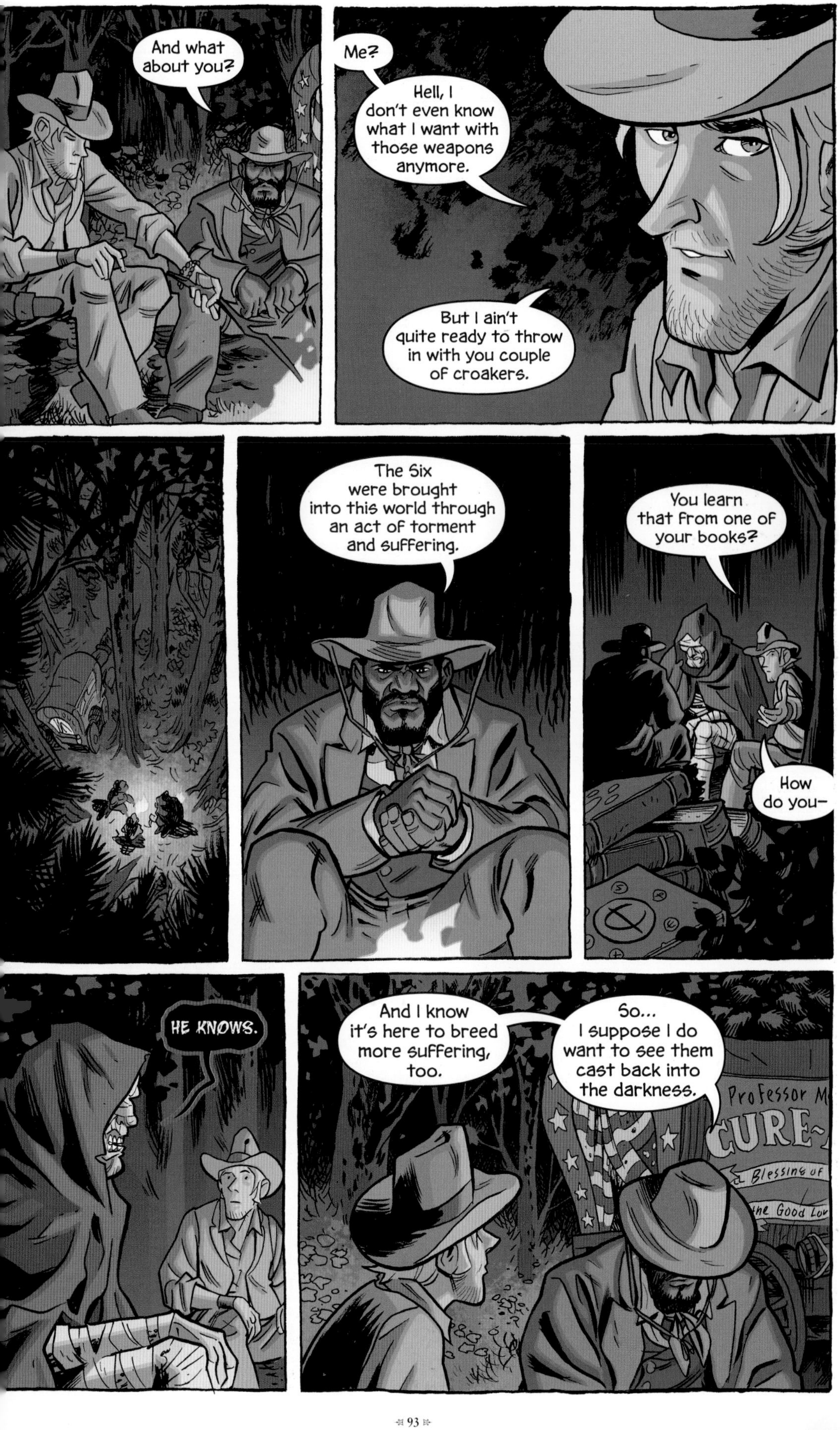

And what about you?
Me?
Hell, I don't even know what I want with those weapons anymore.
But I ain't quite ready to throw in with you couple of croakers.
The Six were brought into this world through an act of torment and suffering.
You learn that from one of your books?
How do you–
HE KNOWS.
And I know it's here to breed more suffering, too.
So... I suppose I do want to see them cast back into the darkness.
Professor M
CURE-
a Blessing of
the Good Lo

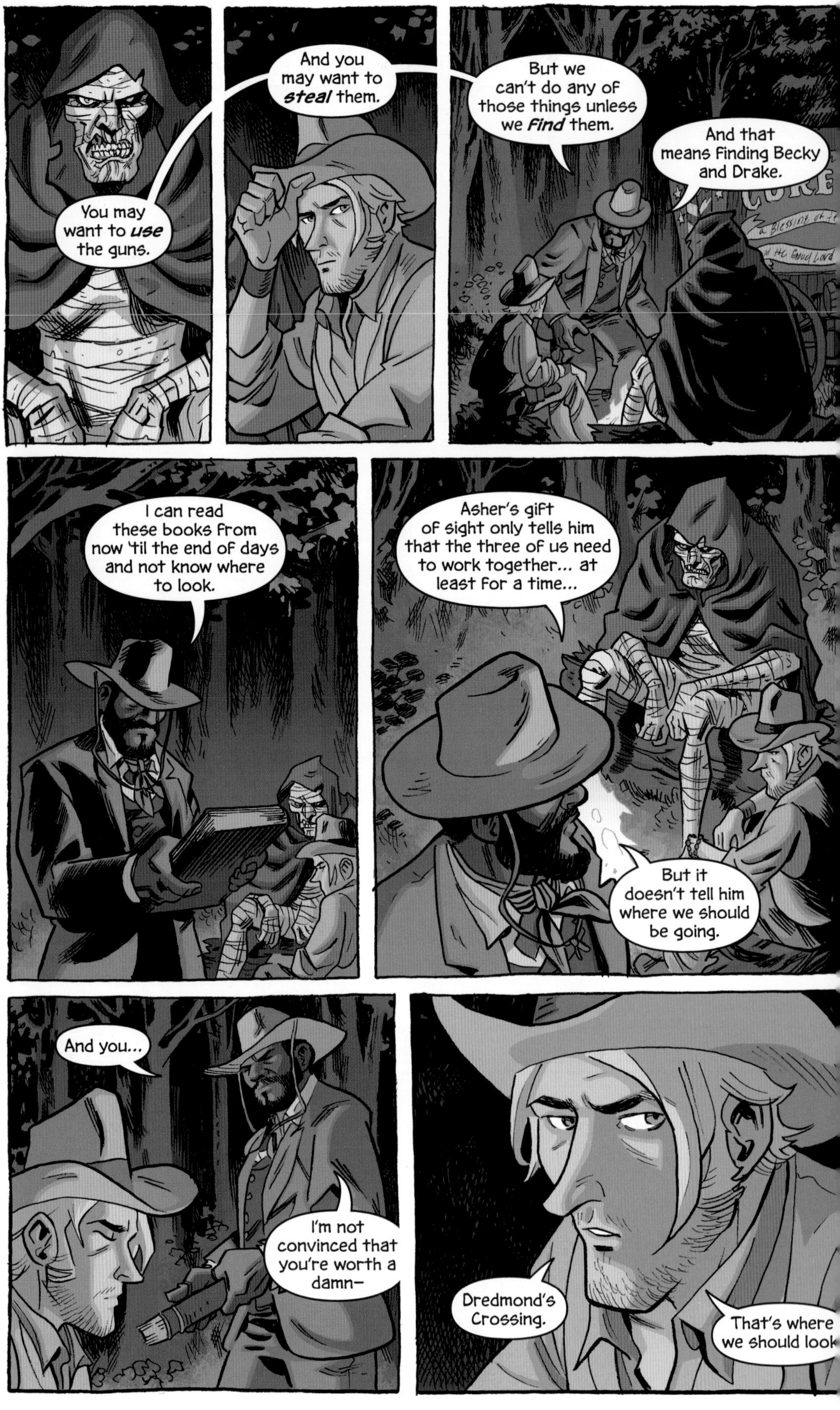
You may want to use the guns.
And you may want to steal them.
But we can't do any of those things unless we find them.
And that means finding Becky and Drake.
CURE
a Blessing of the
the Good Lord
I can read these books from now 'til the end of days and not know where to look.
Asher's gift of sight only tells him that the three of us need to work together... at least for a time...
But it doesn't tell him where we should be going.
And you...
I'm not convinced that you're worth a damn—
Dredmond's Crossing.
That's where we should look

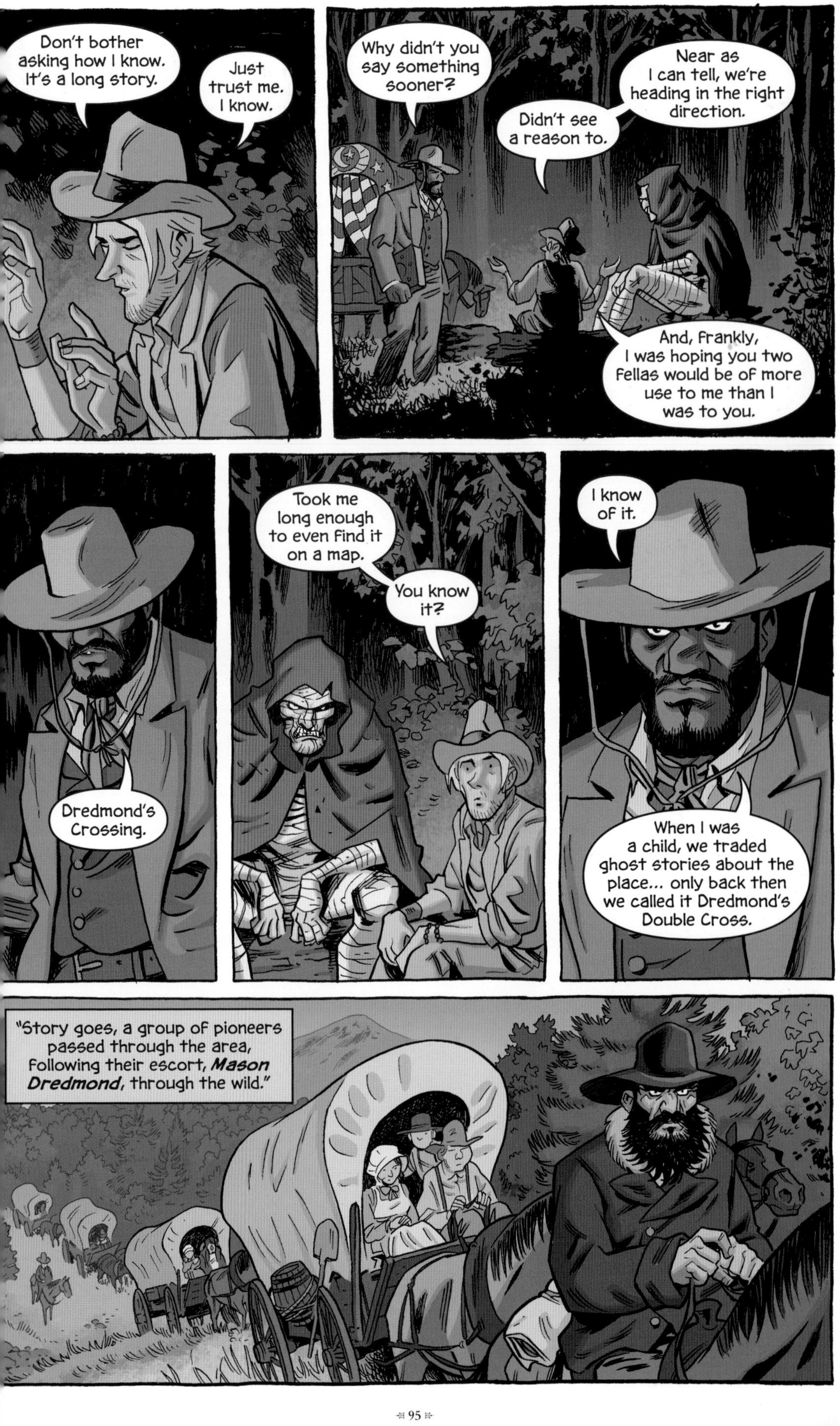
Don't bother asking how I know. It's a long story.
Just trust me. I know.
Why didn't you say something sooner?
Didn't see a reason to.
Near as I can tell, we're heading in the right direction.
And, frankly, I was hoping you two fellas would be of more use to me than I was to you.
Dredmond's Crossing.
Took me long enough to even find it on a map.
You know it?
I know of it.
When I was a child, we traded ghost stories about the place... only back then we called it Dredmond's Double Cross.
"Story goes, a group of pioneers passed through the area, following their escort, ***Mason Dredmond***, through the wild."

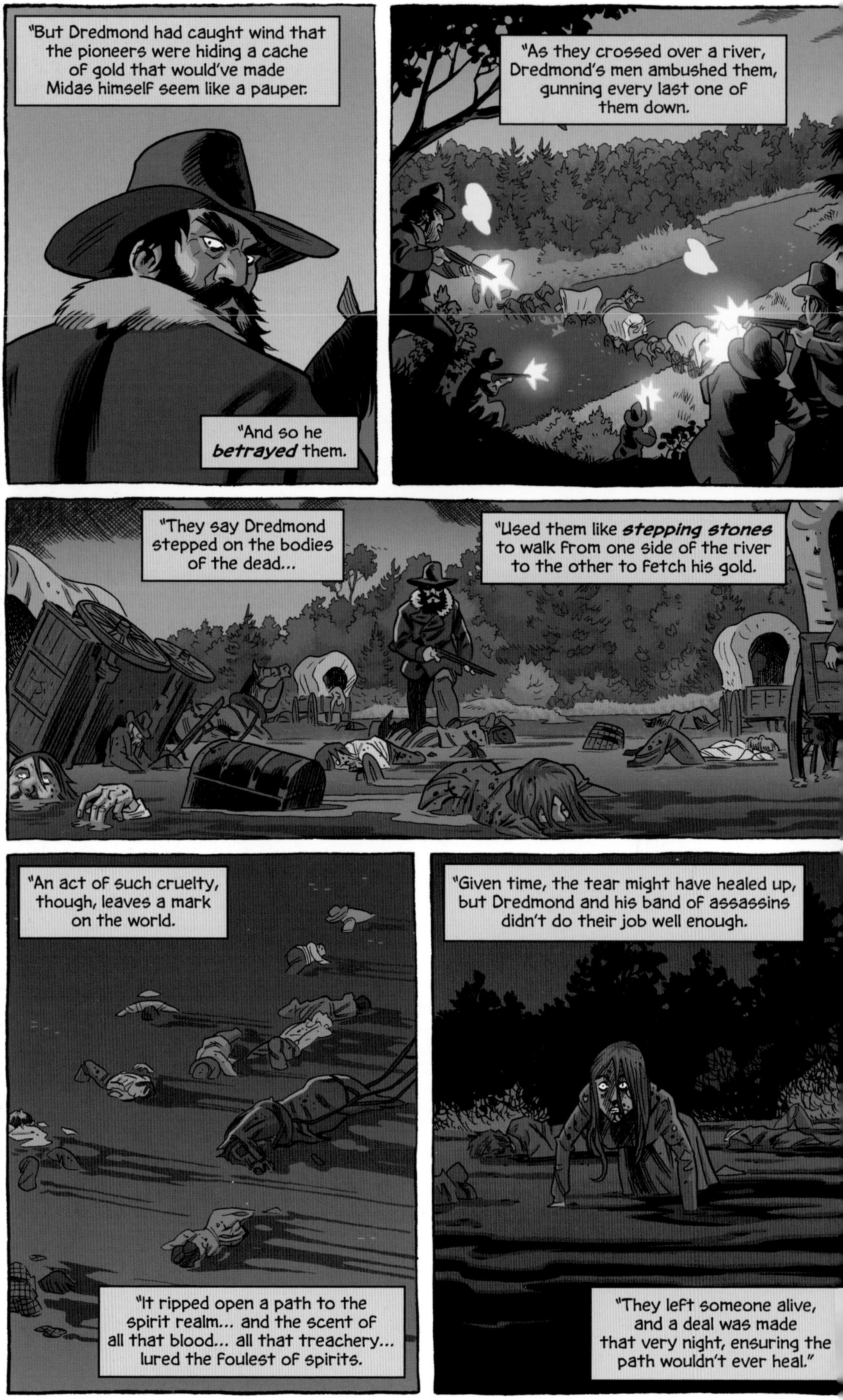
"But Dredmond had caught wind that the pioneers were hiding a cache of gold that would've made Midas himself seem like a pauper.
"And so he *betrayed* them.
"As they crossed over a river, Dredmond's men ambushed them, gunning every last one of them down.
"They say Dredmond stepped on the bodies of the dead...
"Used them like *stepping stones* to walk from one side of the river to the other to fetch his gold.
"An act of such cruelty, though, leaves a mark on the world.
"It ripped open a path to the spirit realm... and the scent of all that blood... all that treachery... lured the foulest of spirits.
"Given time, the tear might have healed up, but Dredmond and his band of assassins didn't do their job well enough.
"They left someone alive, and a deal was made that very night, ensuring the path wouldn't ever heal."

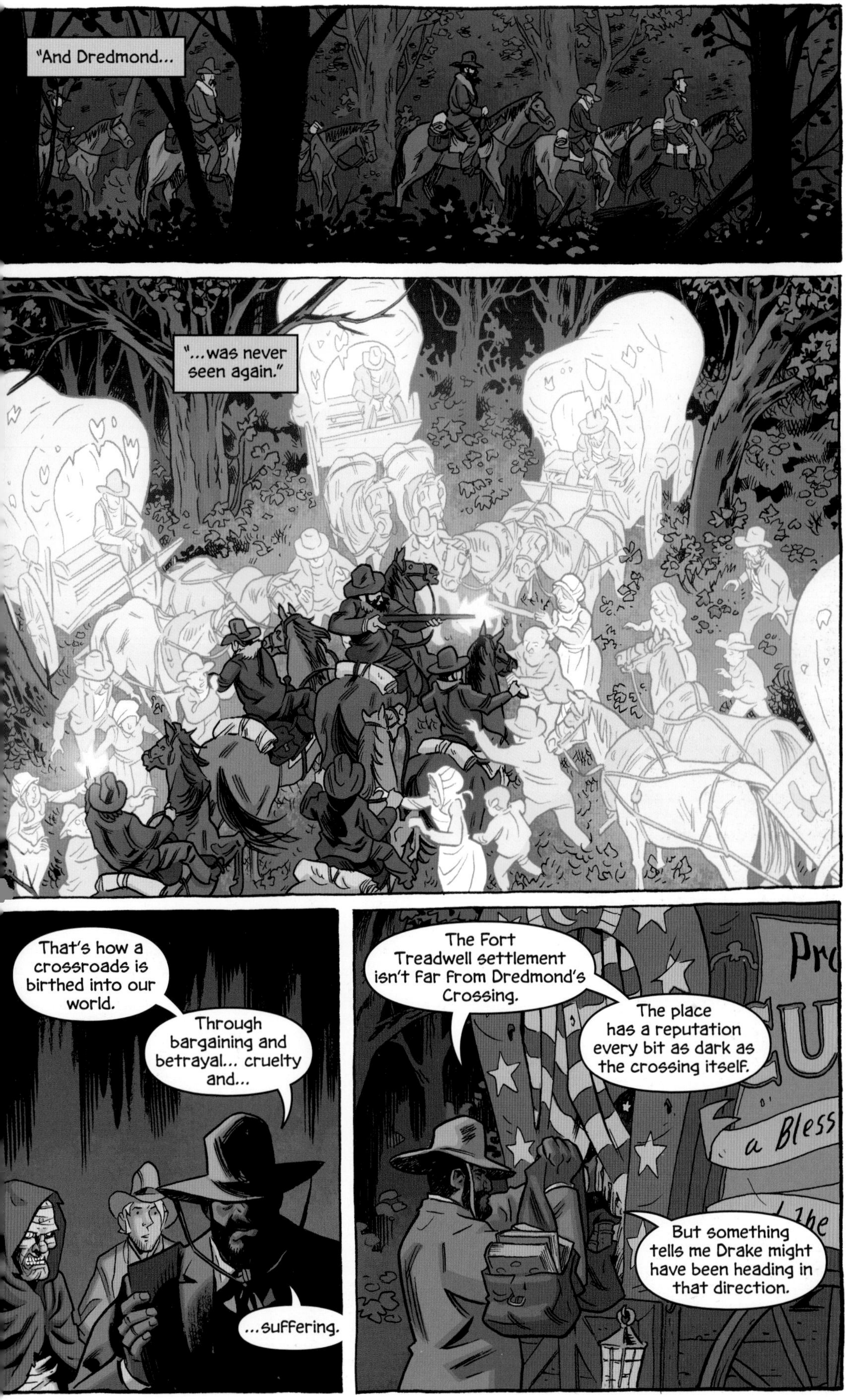
"And Dredmond...
"...was never seen again."
That's how a crossroads is birthed into our world.
Through bargaining and betrayal... cruelty and...
...suffering.
The Fort Treadwell settlement isn't far from Dredmond's Crossing.
The place has a reputation every bit as dark as the crossing itself.
But something tells me Drake might have been heading in that direction.

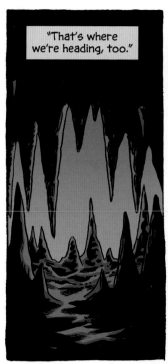

"That's where we're heading, too."

She thinks you'll betray her.

The girl.

She thinks you'll betray everyone and everything.

She doesn't trust you.

She's just as *clever* as I suspected then.

If you're trying to rattle me, you'll have to do better than—

...

CLATTER

NnnNnnn

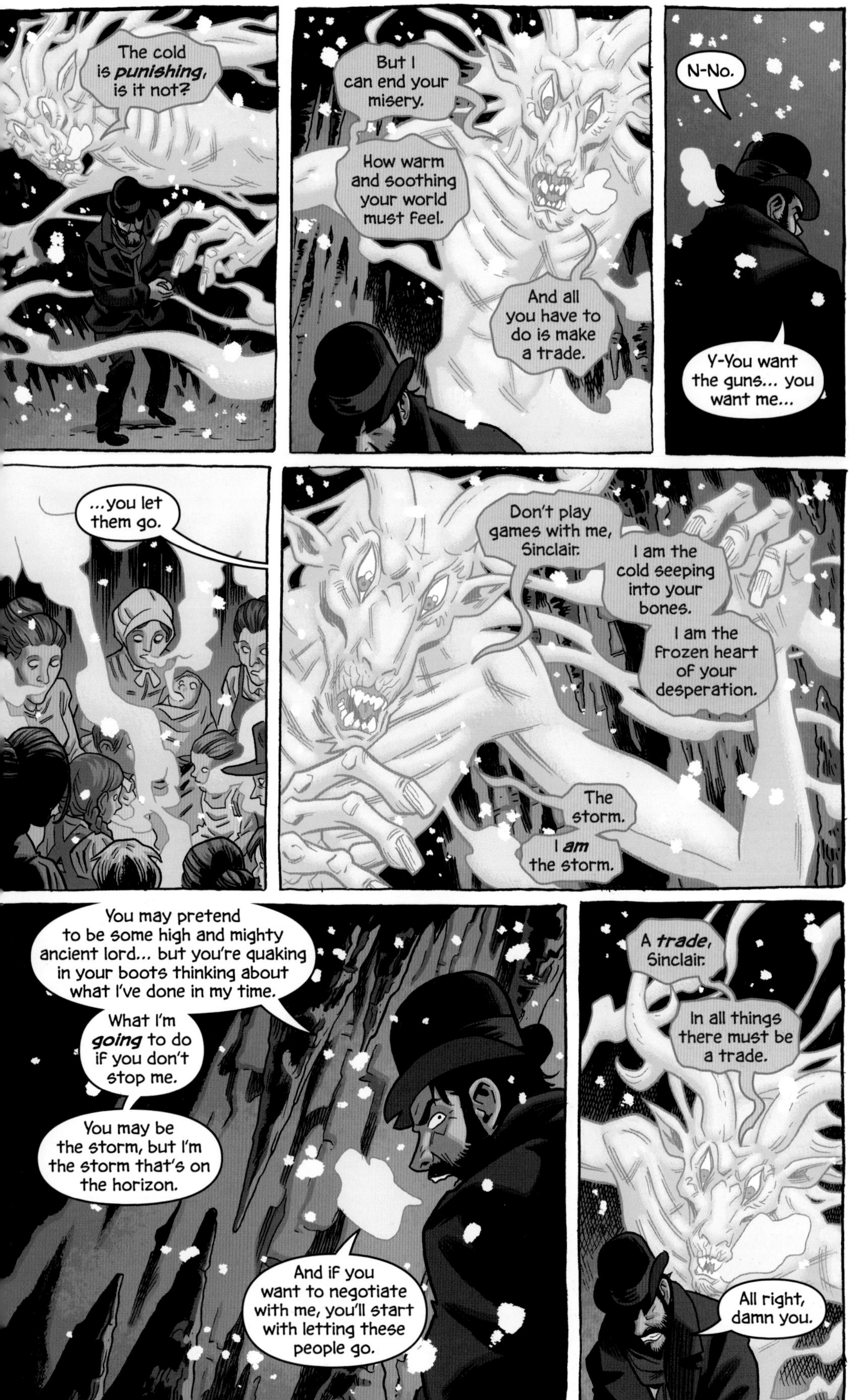

The cold is *punishing*, is it not?
But I can end your misery.
How warm and soothing your world must feel.
And all you have to do is make a trade.
N-No.
Y-You want the guns... you want me...
...you let them go.
Don't play games with me, Sinclair.
I am the cold seeping into your bones.
I am the frozen heart of your desperation.
The storm.
I *am* the storm.
You may pretend to be some high and mighty ancient lord... but you're quaking in your boots thinking about what I've done in my time.
What I'm *going* to do if you don't stop me.
You may be the storm, but I'm the storm that's on the horizon.
And if you want to negotiate with me, you'll start with letting these people go.
A *trade*, Sinclair.
In all things there must be a trade.
All right, damn you.

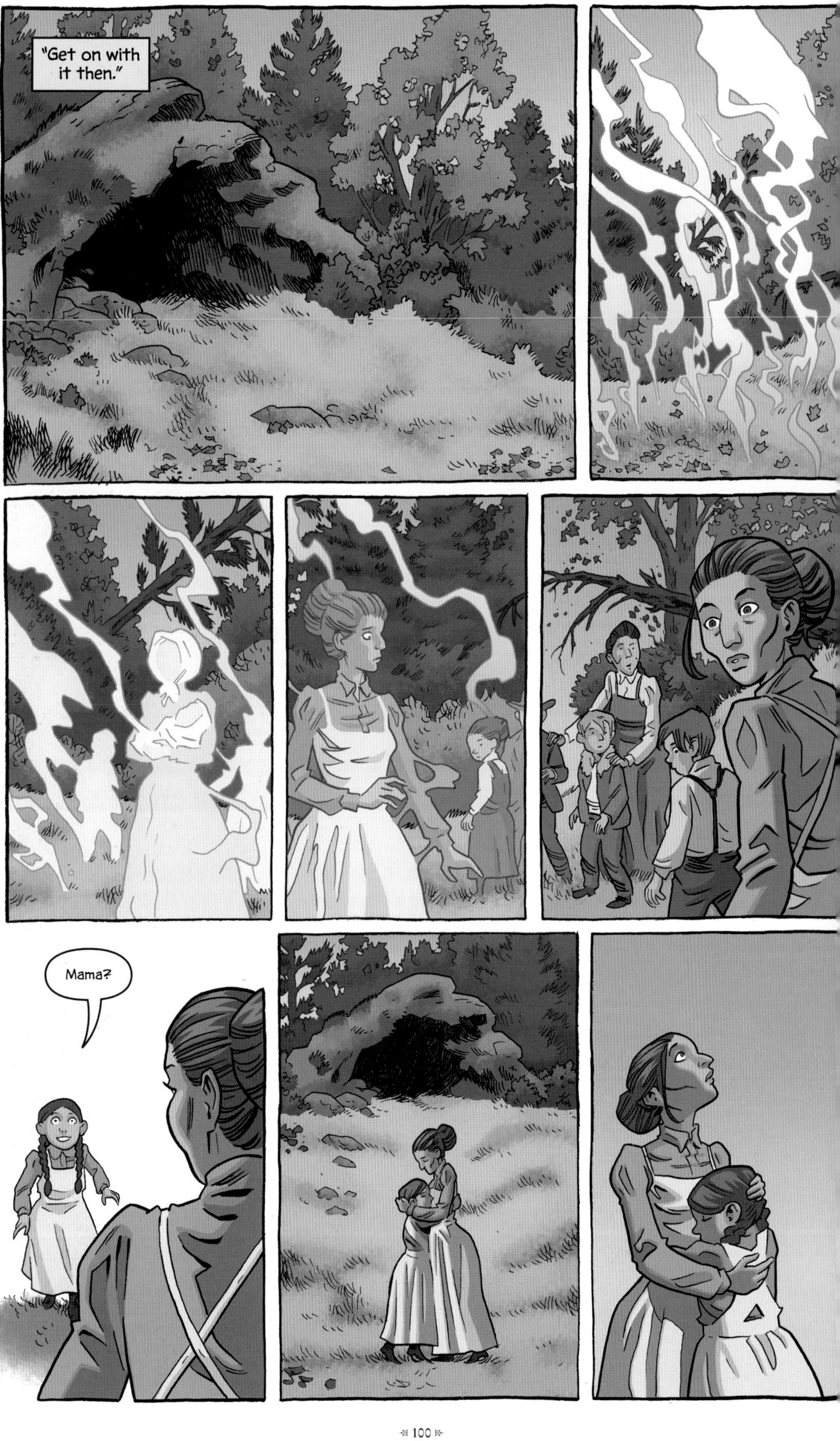
"Get on with it then."
Mama?

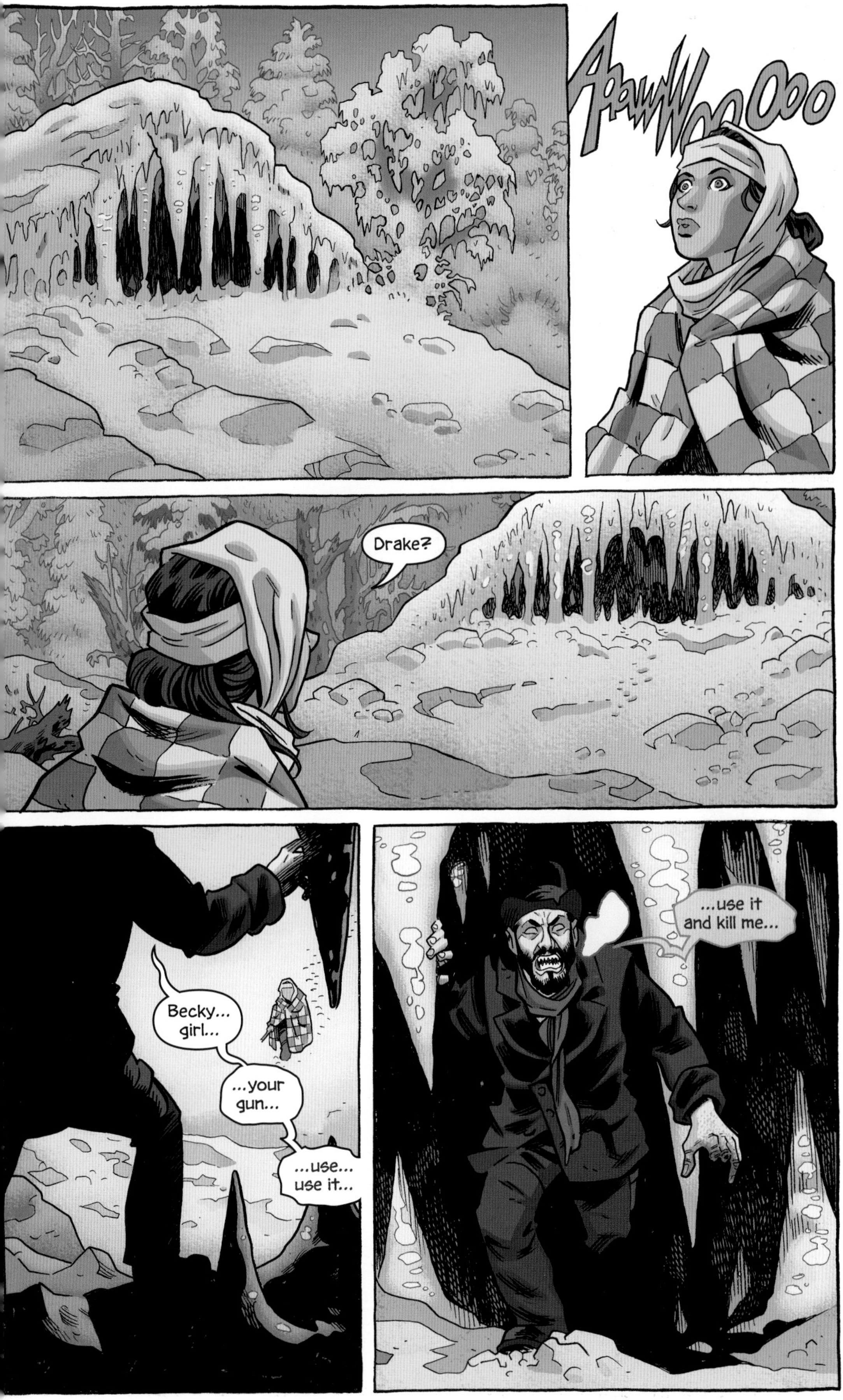
AooowWooOOoo
Drake?
Becky... girl...
...your gun...
...use... use it...
...use it and kill me...

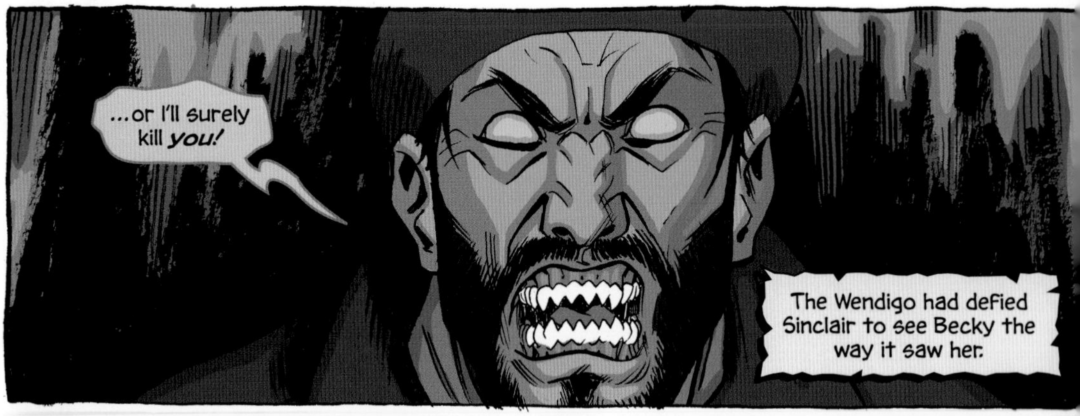
...or I'll surely kill *you!*
The Wendigo had defied Sinclair to see Becky the way it saw her.

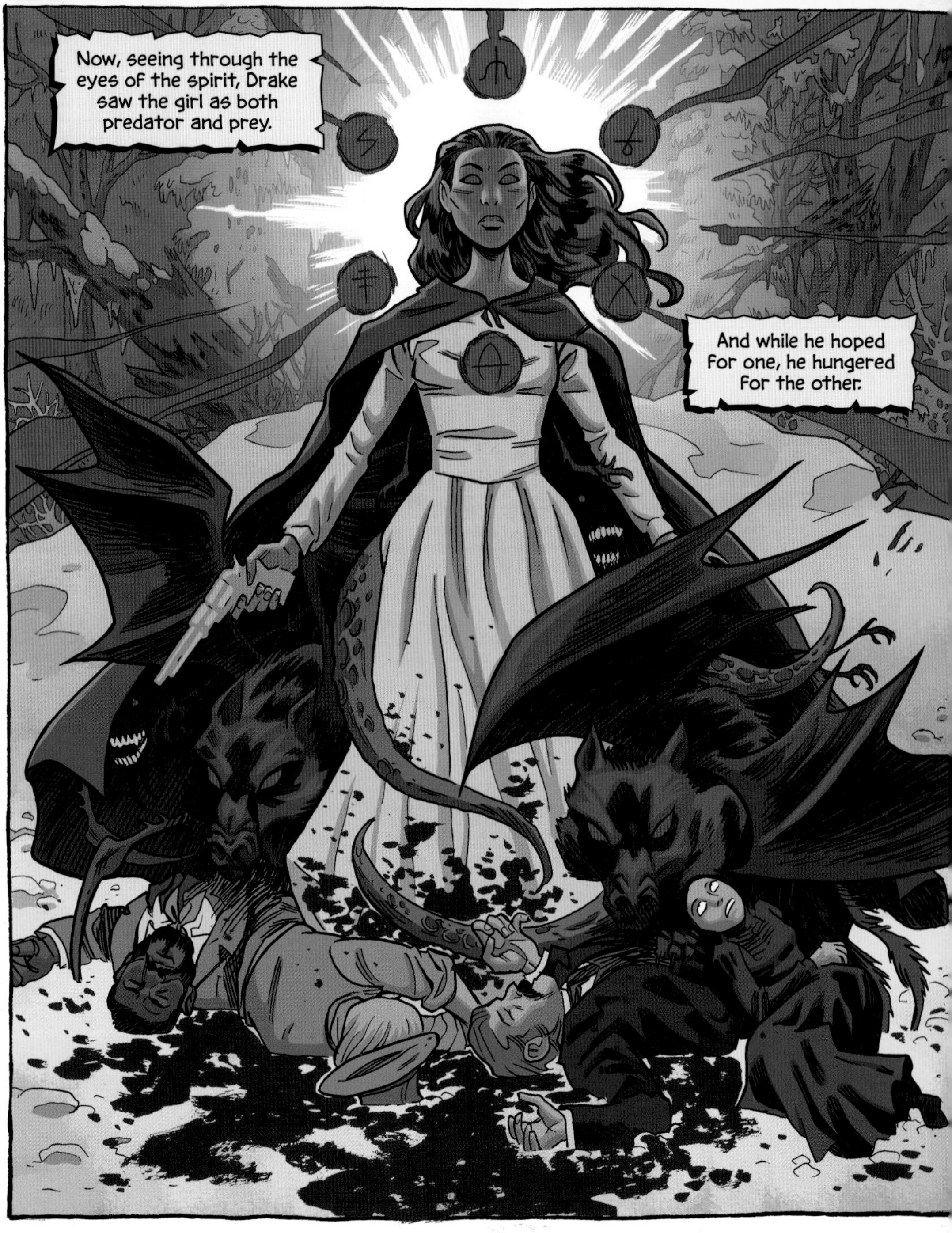
Now, seeing through the eyes of the spirit, Drake saw the girl as both predator and prey.
And while he hoped for one, he hungered for the other.

CHAPTER FIVE

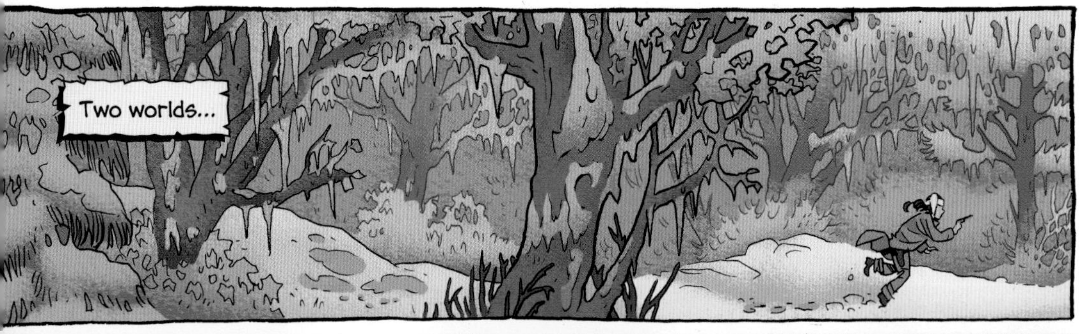
Two worlds...

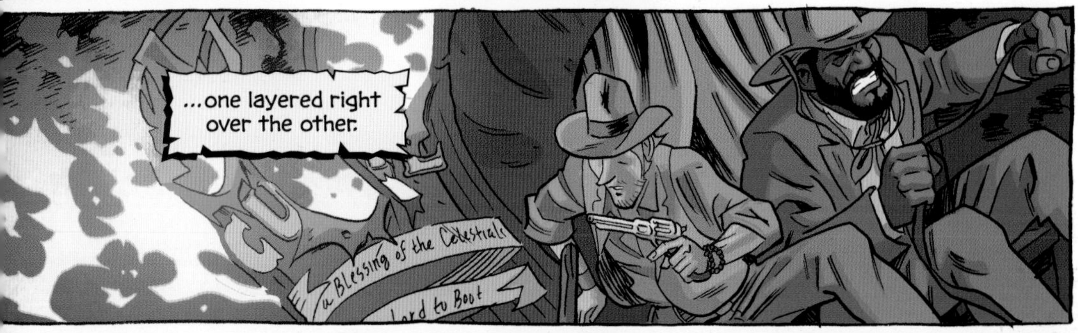
...one layered right over the other.
a Blessing of the Celestials
Lord to Boot

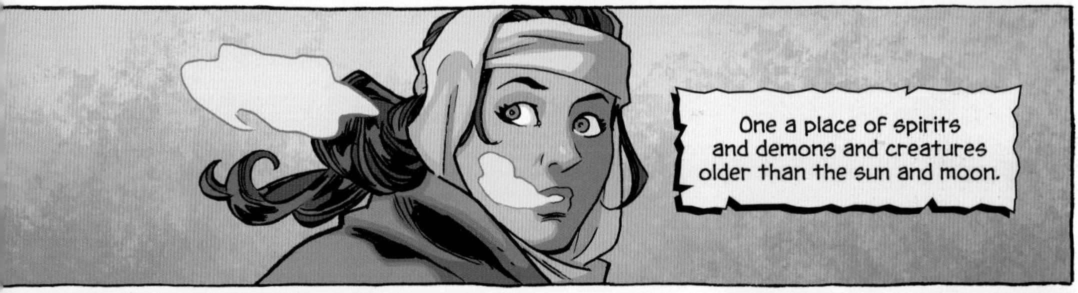
One a place of spirits and demons and creatures older than the sun and moon.

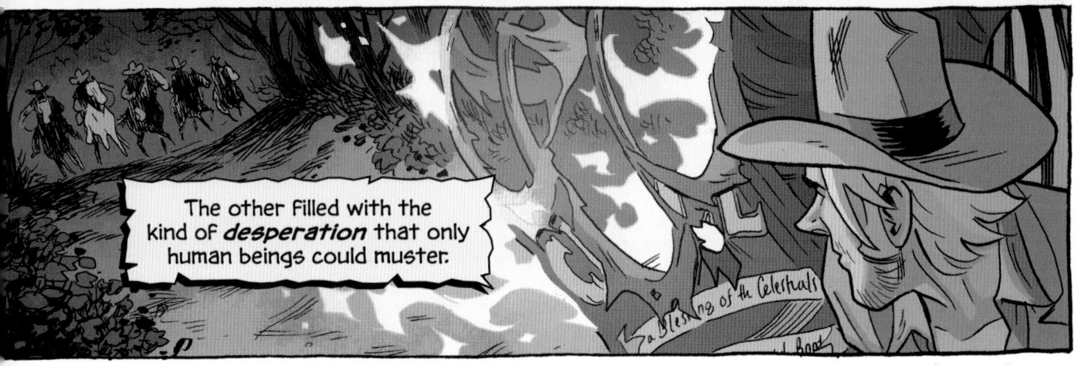
The other filled with the kind of ***desperation*** that only human beings could muster.
a Blessing of the Celestials

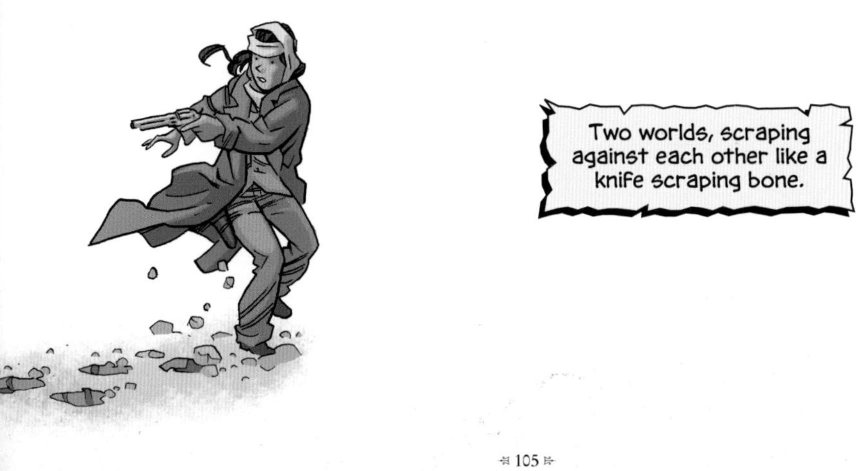
Two worlds, scraping against each other like a knife scraping bone.

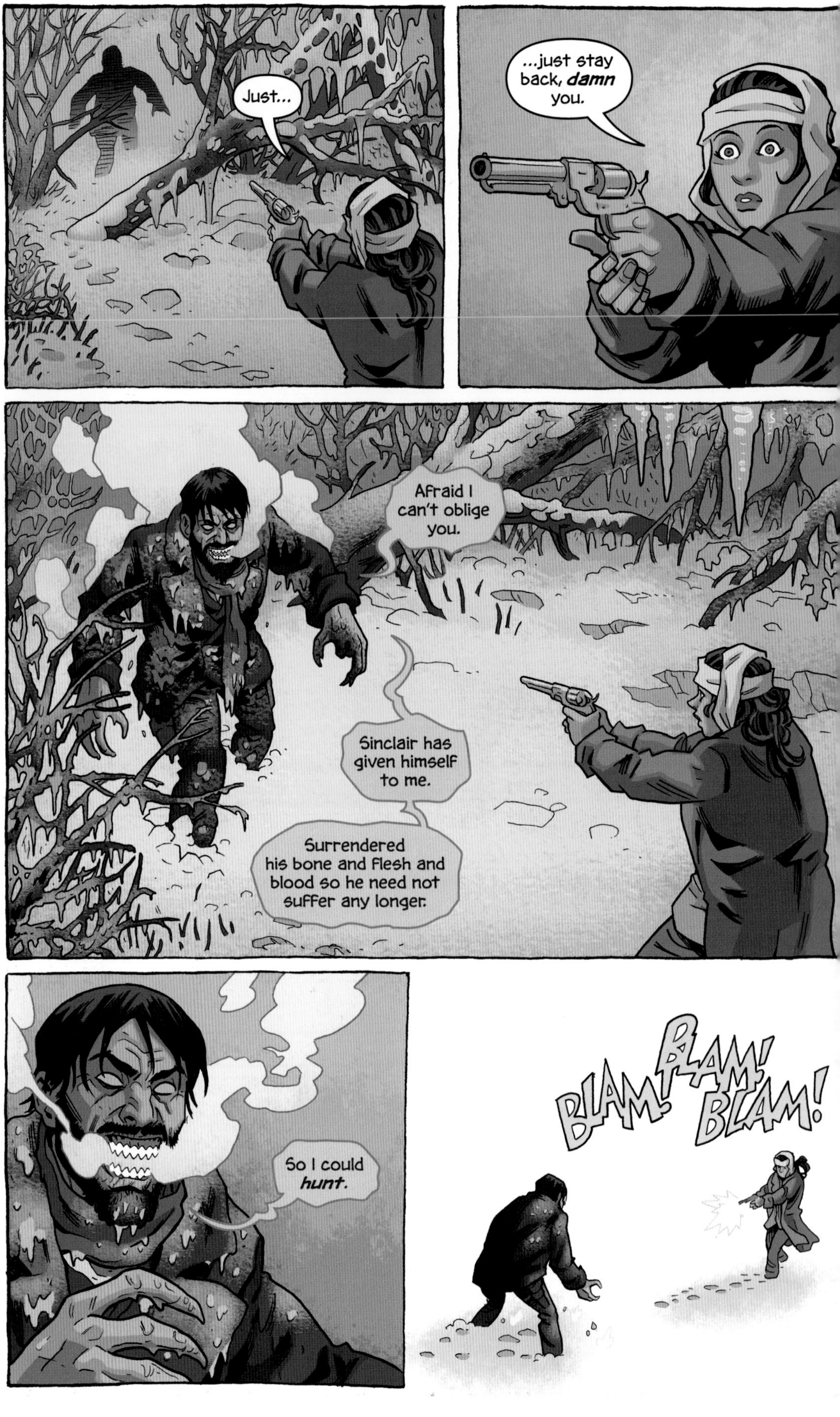
Just...
...just stay back, *damn* you.
Afraid I can't oblige you.
Sinclair has given himself to me.
Surrendered his bone and flesh and blood so he need not suffer any longer.
So I could *hunt*.
BLAM! BLAM! BLAM!

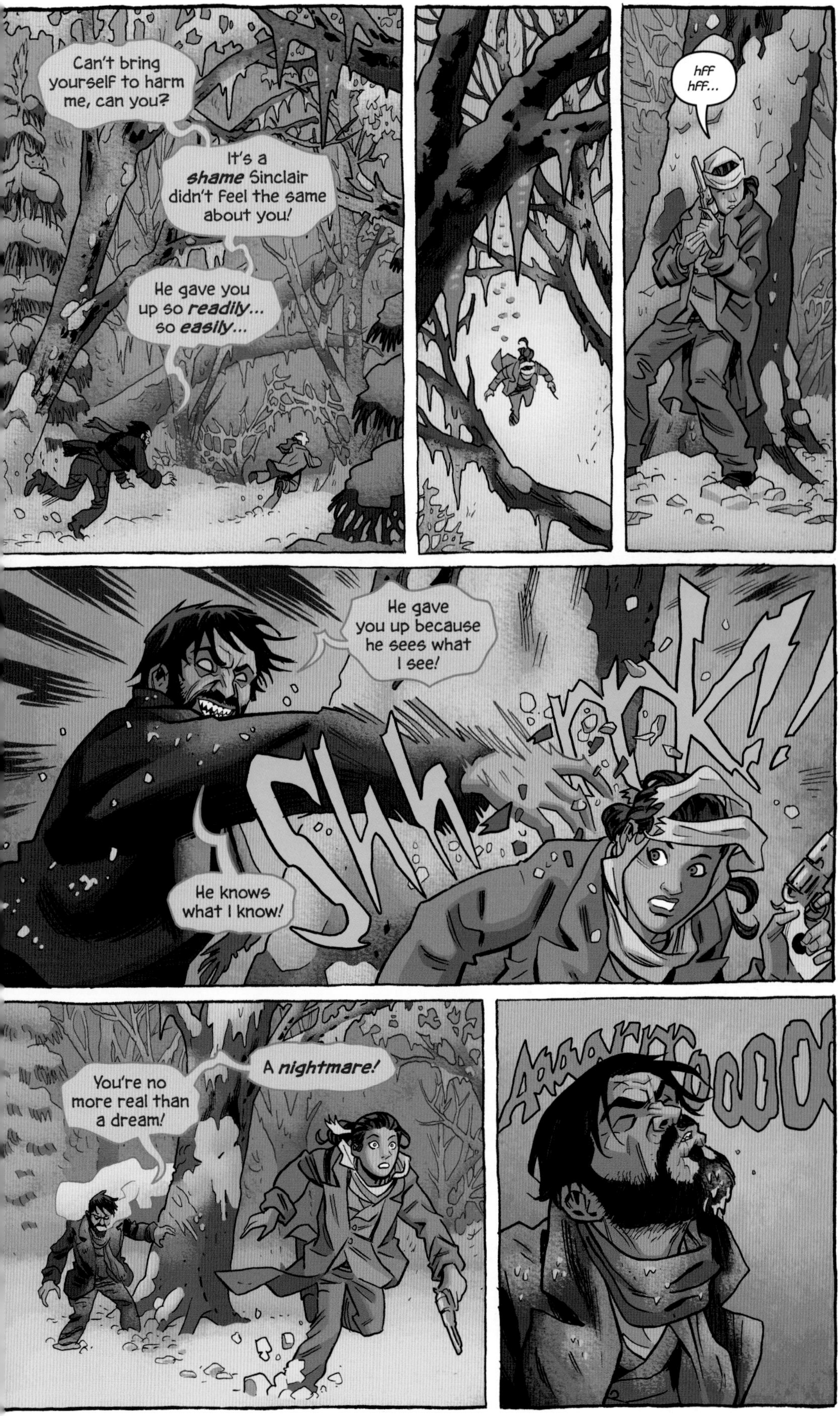
Can't bring yourself to harm me, can you?
It's a *shame* Sinclair didn't feel the same about you!
He gave you up so *readily*... so *easily*...
hff hff...
He gave you up because he sees what I see!
Shh
He knows what I know!
You're no more real than a dream!
A *nightmare!*

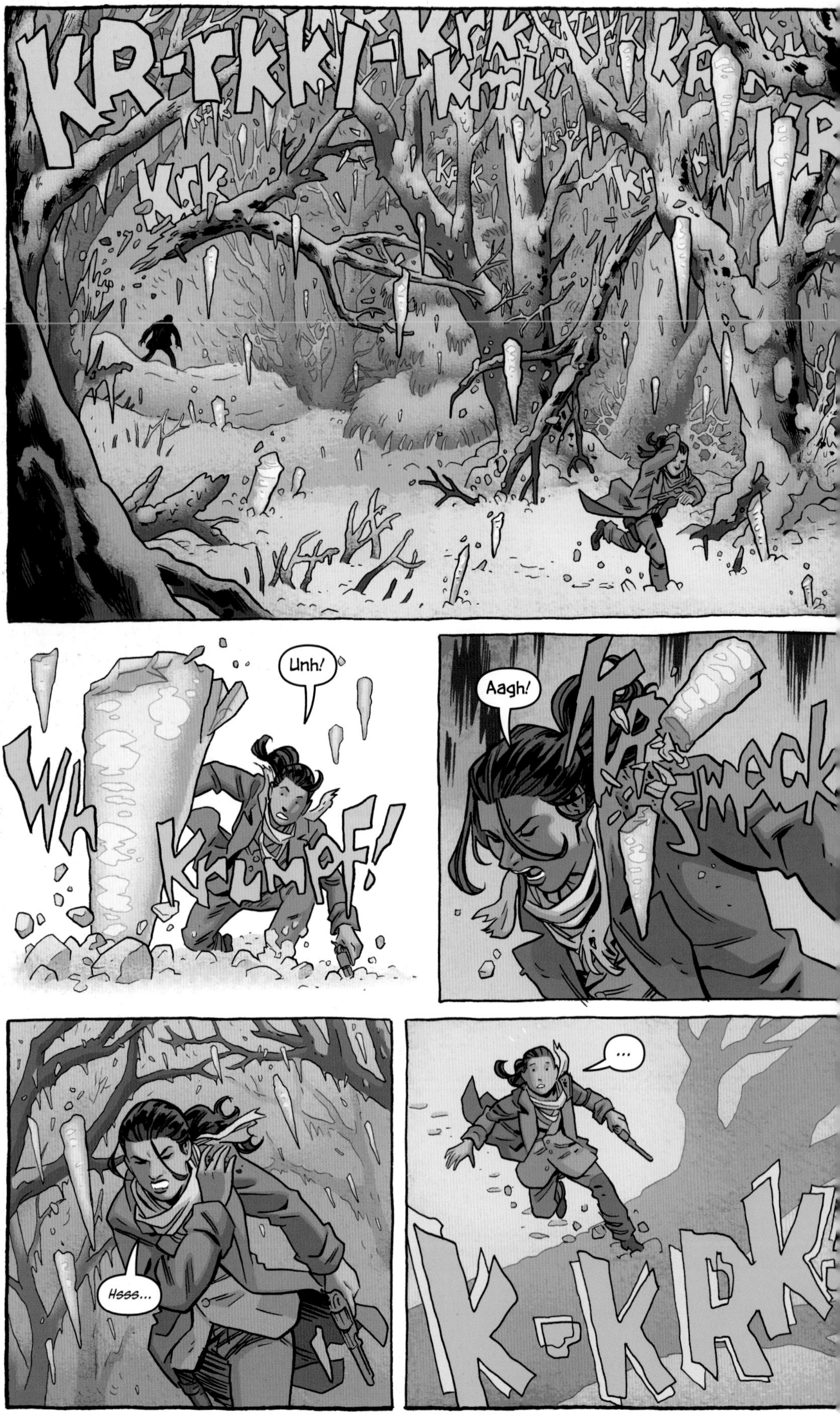
KR-RKKI-KRK
Unh!
WH KRUMPF!
Aagh!
SMECK
Hsss...
...
K-KRK

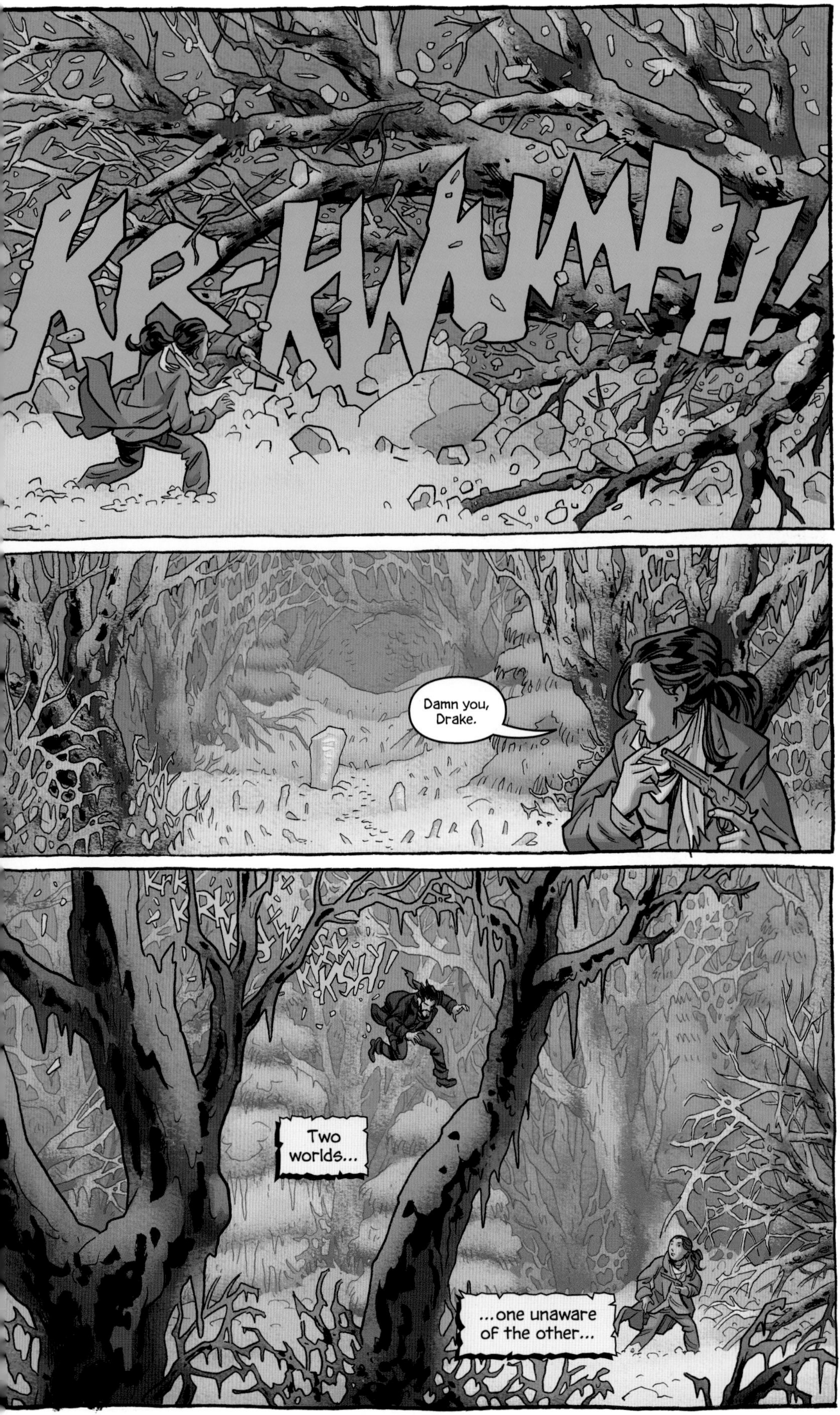
KR-KWUMPH!!
Damn you, Drake.
Two worlds...
...one unaware of the other...

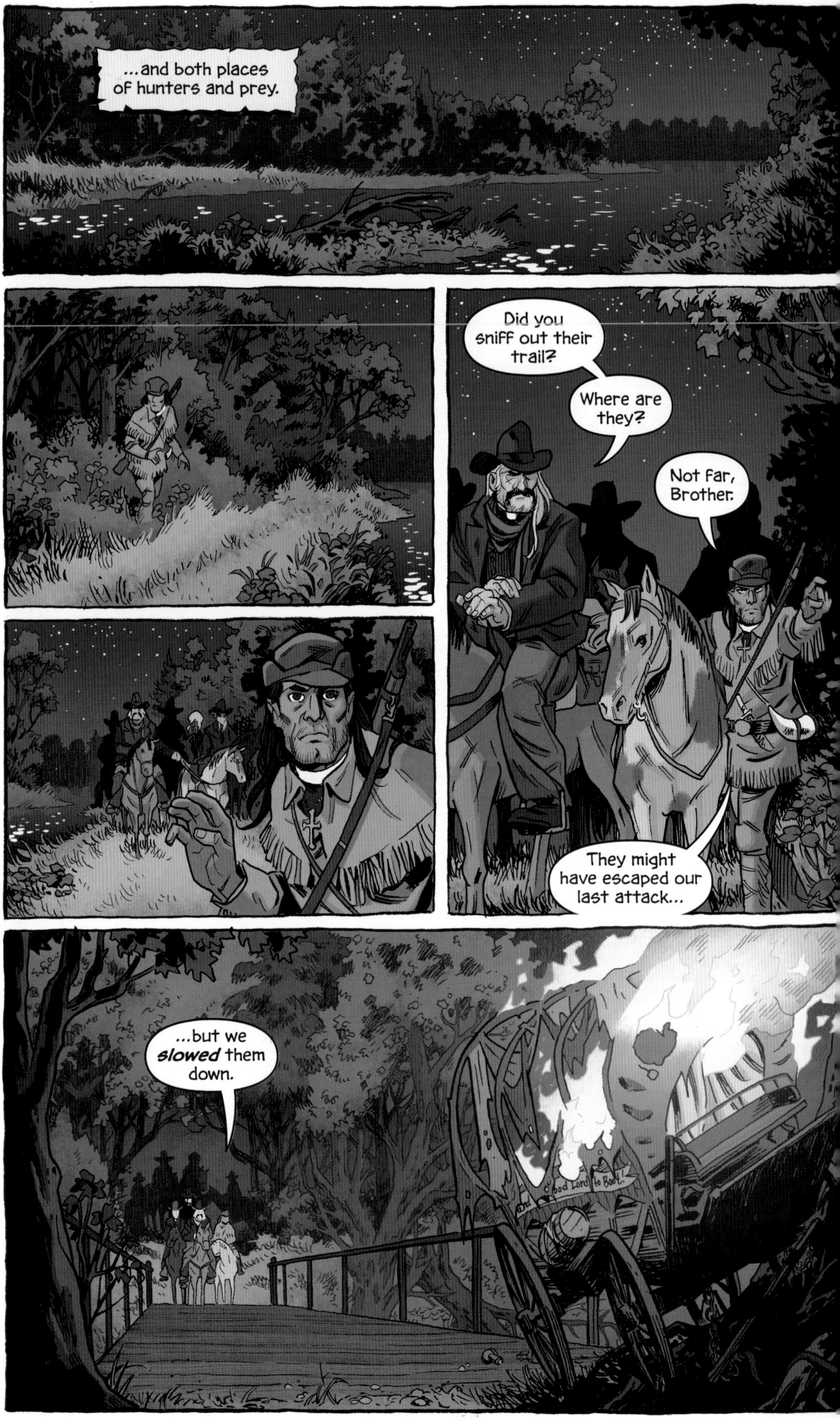
...and both places of hunters and prey.
Did you sniff out their trail?
Where are they?
Not far, Brother.
They might have escaped our last attack...
...but we *slowed* them down.

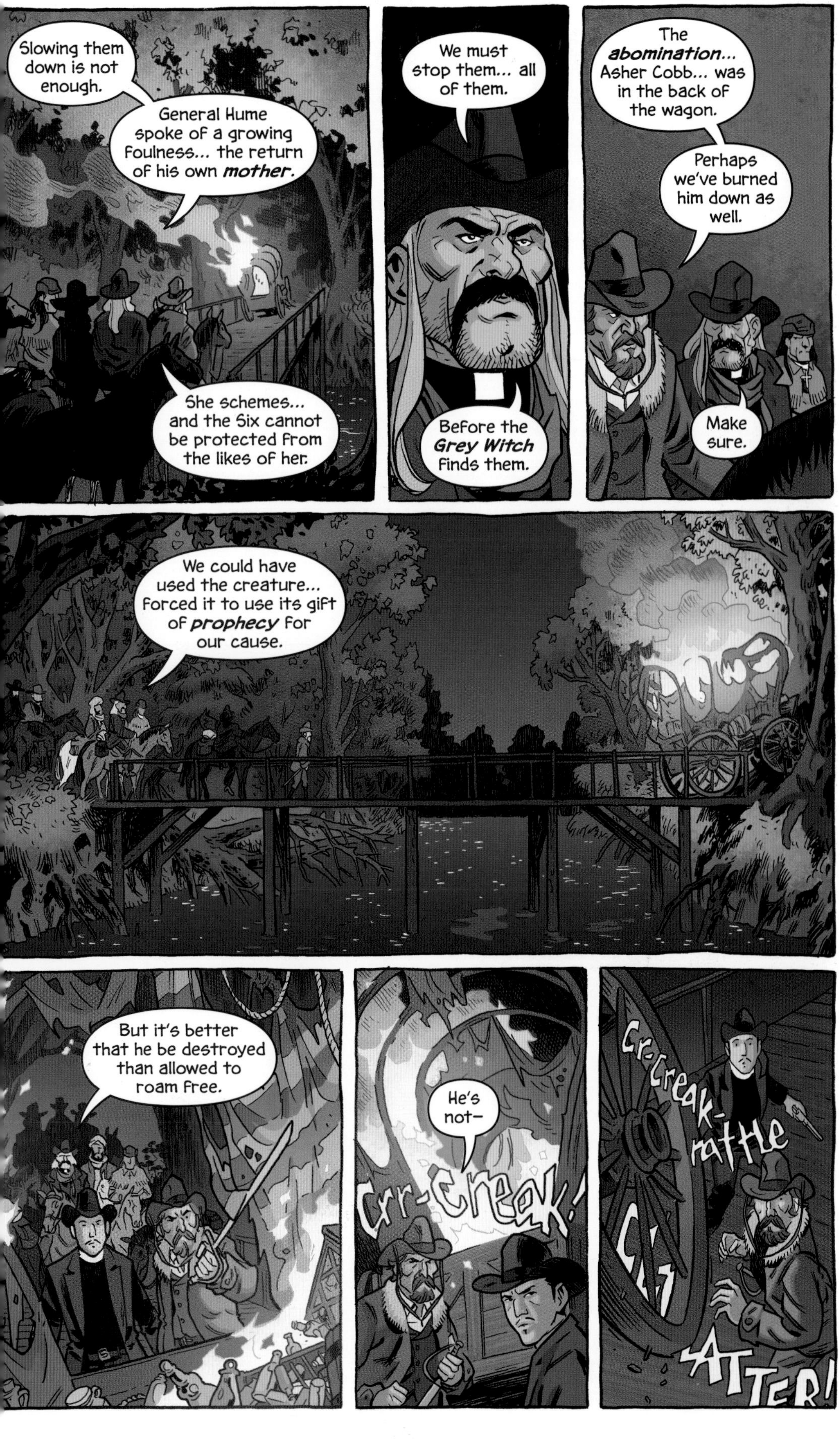
Slowing them down is not enough.
General Hume spoke of a growing foulness... the return of his own *mother*.
She schemes... and the Six cannot be protected from the likes of her.
We must stop them... all of them.
Before the *Grey Witch* finds them.
The *abomination*... Asher Cobb... was in the back of the wagon.
Perhaps we've burned him down as well.
Make sure.
We could have used the creature... forced it to use its gift of *prophecy* for our cause.
But it's better that he be destroyed than allowed to roam free.
He's not—
Cr-creak!
Cr-creak-rattle
ATTER!

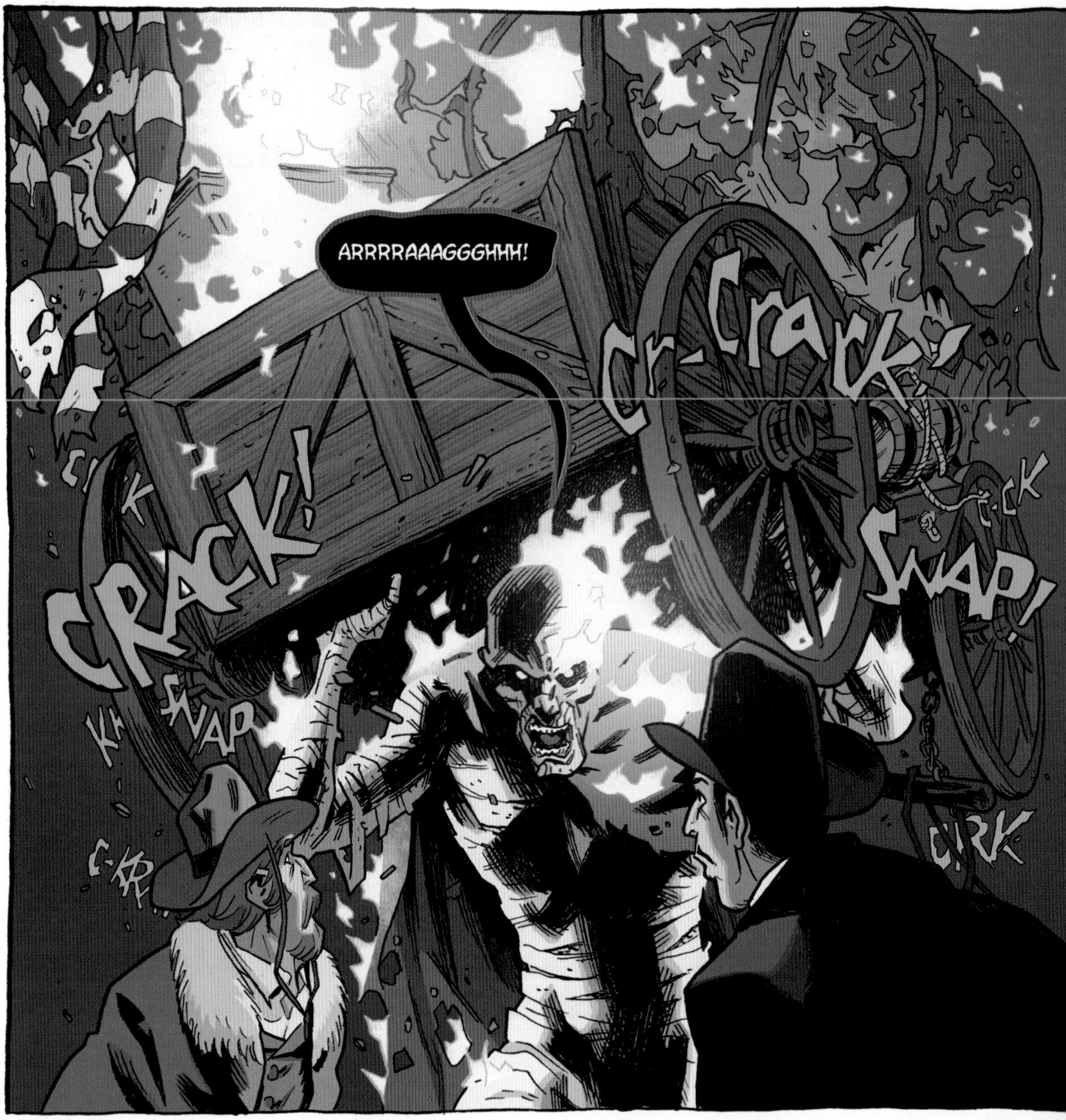
ARRRRAAAGGGHHH!
CR-CRACK!
CRACK!
SWAP!
SWAP
CIRK

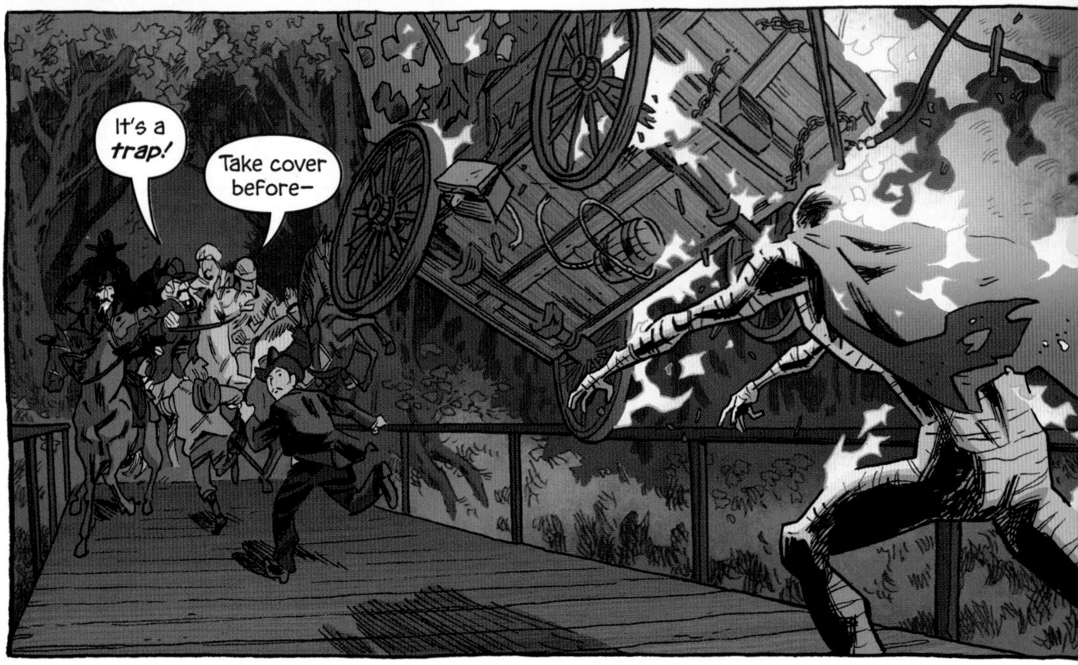
It's a *trap!*
Take cover before–

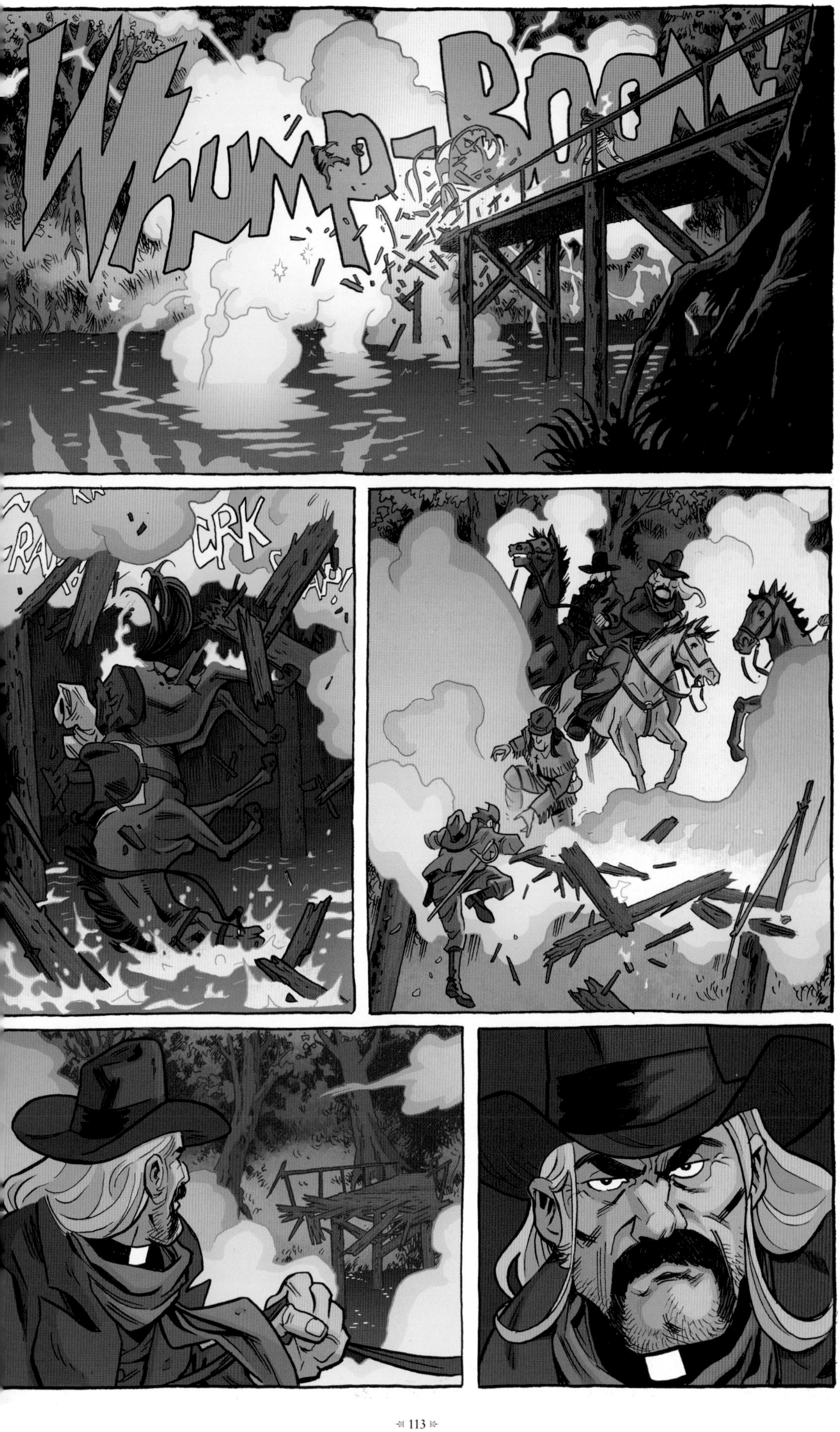

WHUMP-BOOM
CRK

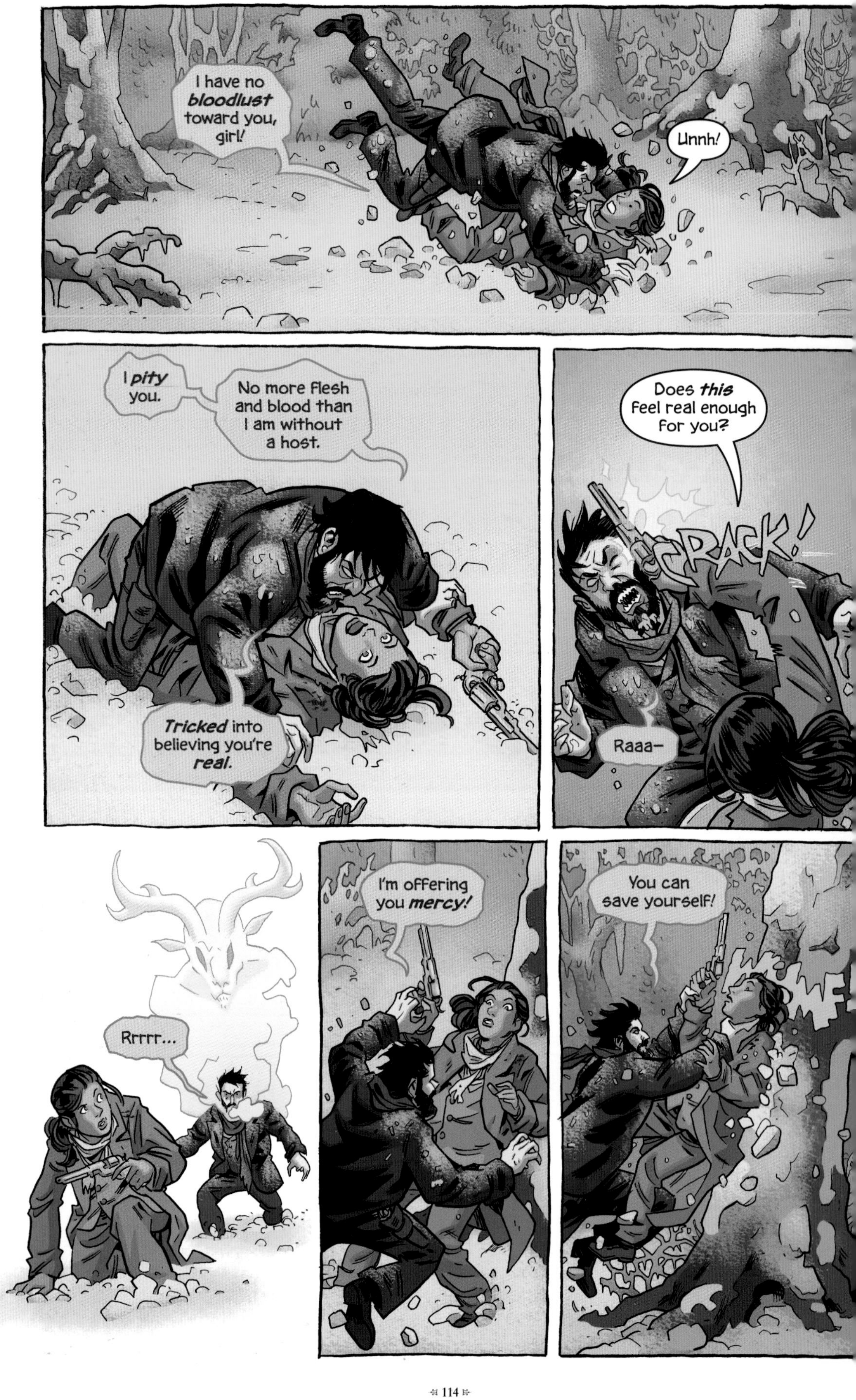
I have no *bloodlust* toward you, girl!
Unnh!
I *pity* you.
No more flesh and blood than I am without a host.
Tricked into believing you're *real*.
Does *this* feel real enough for you?
CRACK!
Raaa–
Rrrrr...
I'm offering you *mercy!*
You can save yourself!

If the world is *recast*, what do you think would happen to something so *fleeting* as yourself?

Give me the gun and I'll let you live.

I can guard the weapons. I can keep them hidden and useless here in my realm.

Give it to me! It's what your friend *wanted*.

Nnnnn—

It's why he let me nest within his flesh.

No.

He let you take his body so I'd have something to *kill*.

I'm *not* giving you this pistol.

I've *seen* what will happen.

"You'll hide the guns for a time... but sooner or later, *others* will come searching for them.

"And you *might* be powerful enough to kill them... but I know what you'll do if you ever have all six of the weapons."

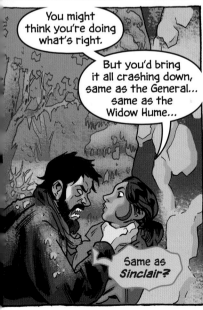

You might think you're doing what's right.

But you'd bring it all crashing down, same as the General... same as the Widow Hume...

Same as *Sinclair?*

You follow him like a mewling pup... and you know what he'll do when he has the chance!

Your only choices are to die... give me the gun...

Or...

Or...

Kill me, Becky.

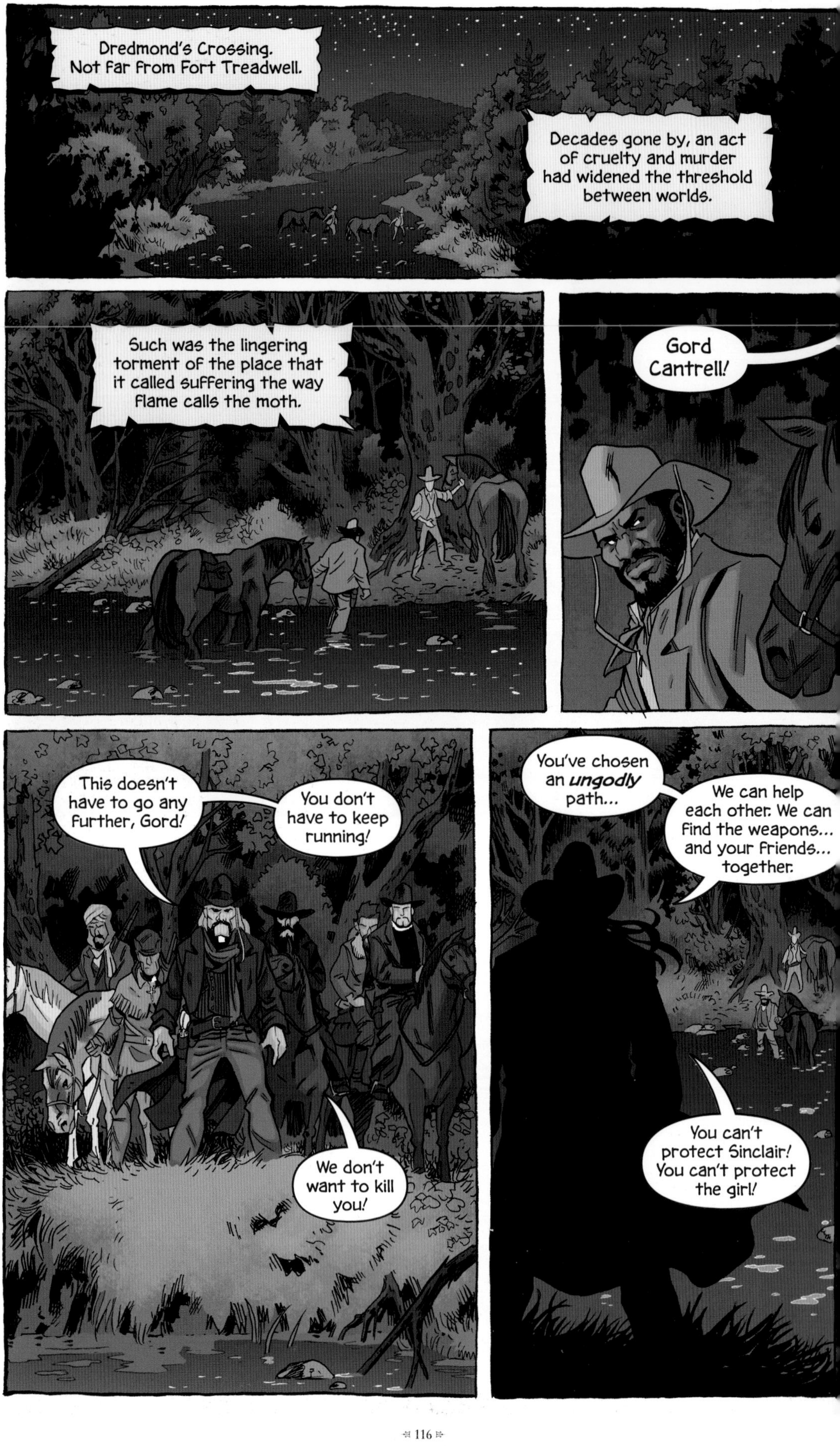
Dredmond's Crossing.
Not far from Fort Treadwell.
Decades gone by, an act of cruelty and murder had widened the threshold between worlds.
Such was the lingering torment of the place that it called suffering the way flame calls the moth.
Gord Cantrell!
This doesn't have to go any further, Gord!
You don't have to keep running!
We don't want to kill you!
You've chosen an *ungodly* path...
We can help each other. We can find the weapons... and your friends... together.
You can't protect Sinclair! You can't protect the girl!

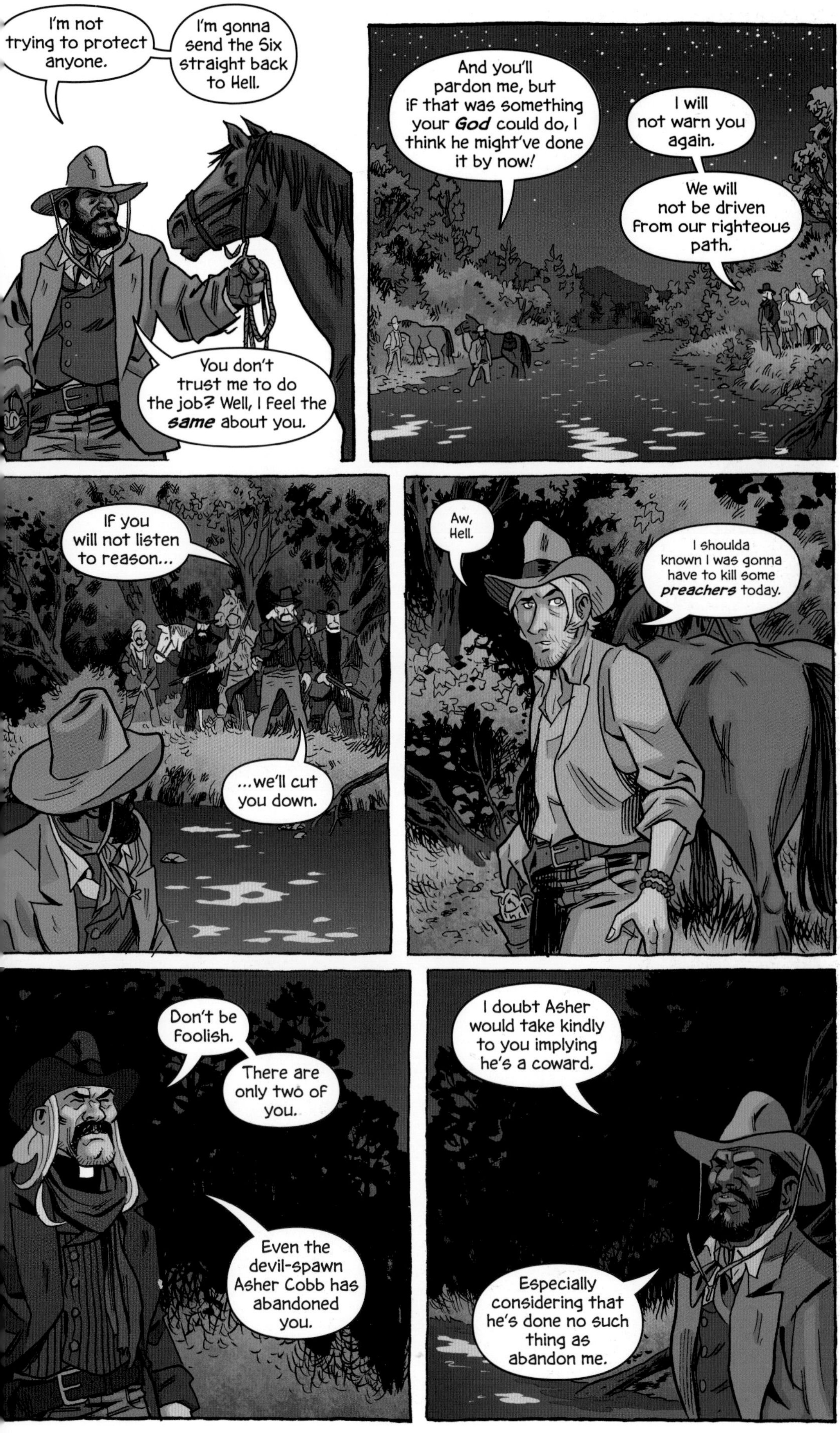
I'm not trying to protect anyone.
I'm gonna send the Six straight back to Hell.
You don't trust me to do the job? Well, I feel the *same* about you.
And you'll pardon me, but if that was something your *God* could do, I think he might've done it by now!
I will not warn you again.
We will not be driven from our righteous path.
If you will not listen to reason...
...we'll cut you down.
Aw, Hell.
I shoulda known I was gonna have to kill some *preachers* today.
Don't be foolish.
There are only two of you.
Even the devil-spawn Asher Cobb has abandoned you.
I doubt Asher would take kindly to you implying he's a coward.
Especially considering that he's done no such thing as abandon me.

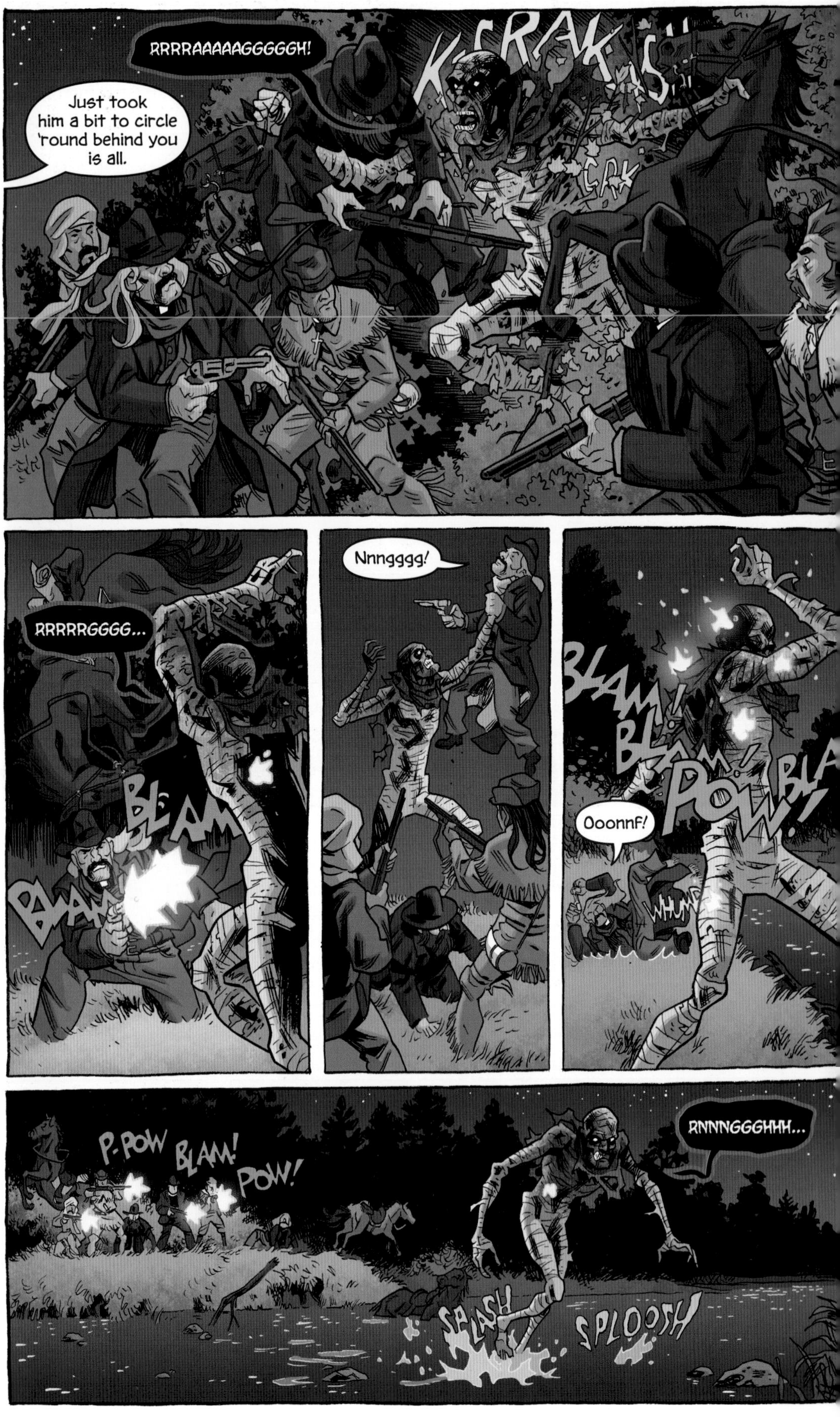
RRRRAAAAAAGGGGGH!
Just took him a bit to circle 'round behind you is all.
KRAK
CRK
RRRRRGGGG...
BLAM
BLAM
Nnngggg!
BLAM!
BLAM!
POW!
Ooonnf!
WHUMP
P-POW
BLAM!
POW!
RNNNGGGHHH...
SPLASH
SPLOOSH

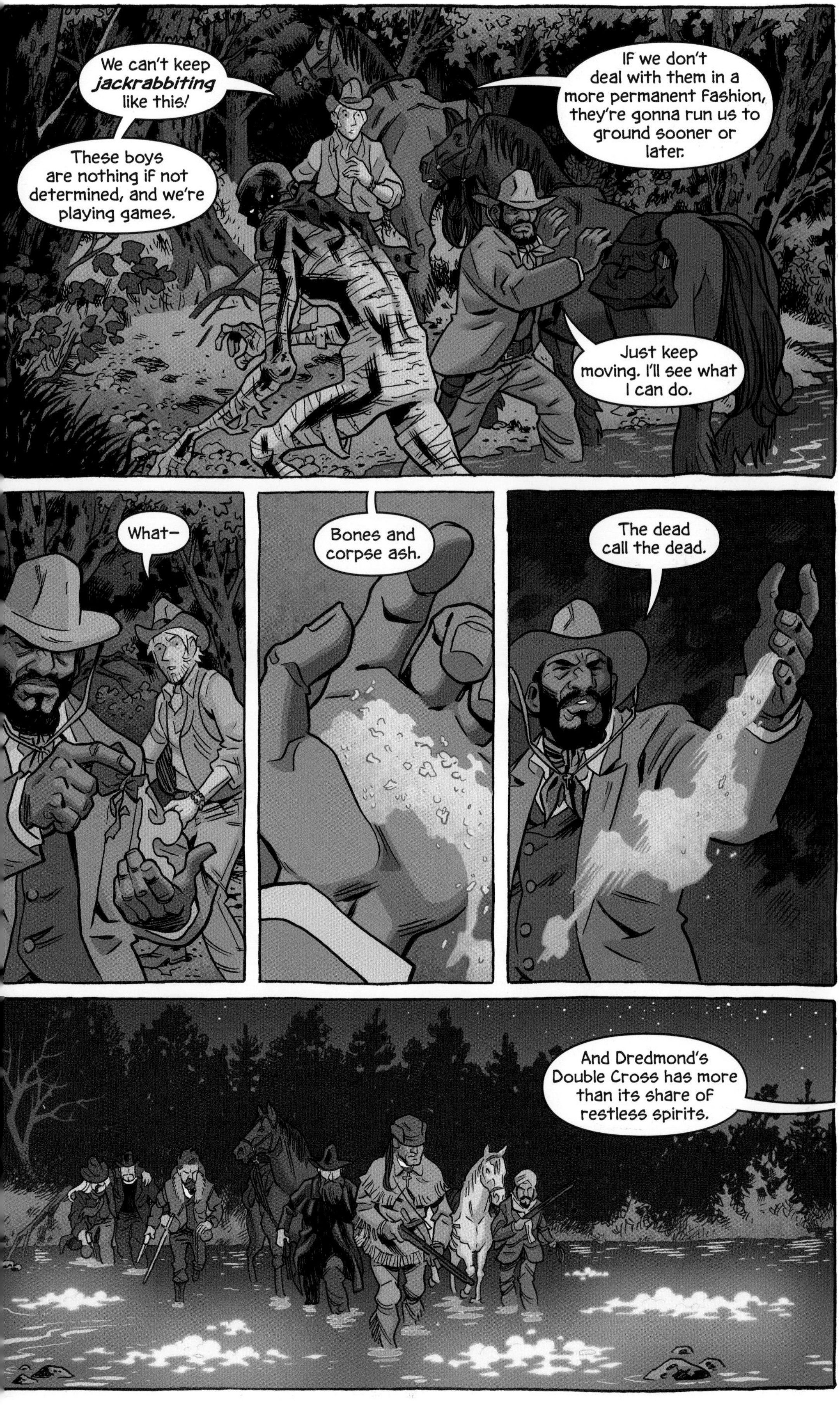
We can't keep *jackrabbiting* like this!
These boys are nothing if not determined, and we're playing games.
If we don't deal with them in a more permanent fashion, they're gonna run us to ground sooner or later.
Just keep moving. I'll see what I can do.
What–
Bones and corpse ash.
The dead call the dead.
And Dredmond's Double Cross has more than its share of restless spirits.

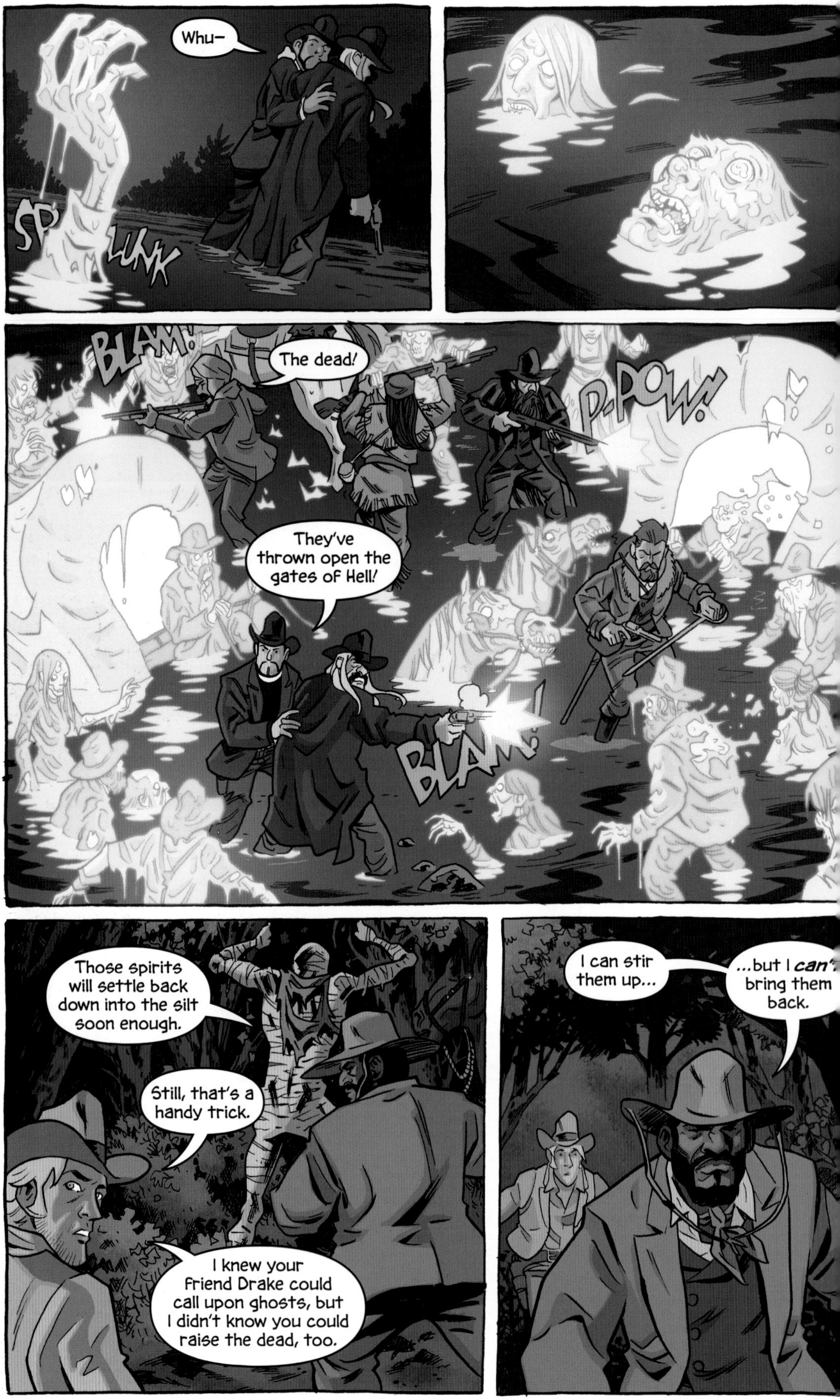

Whu–
SPLUNK
BLAM!
The dead!
P-POW!
They've thrown open the gates of Hell!
BLAM!
Those spirits will settle back down into the silt soon enough.
Still, that's a handy trick.
I knew your friend Drake could call upon ghosts, but I didn't know you could raise the dead, too.
I can stir them up...
...but I *can't* bring them back.

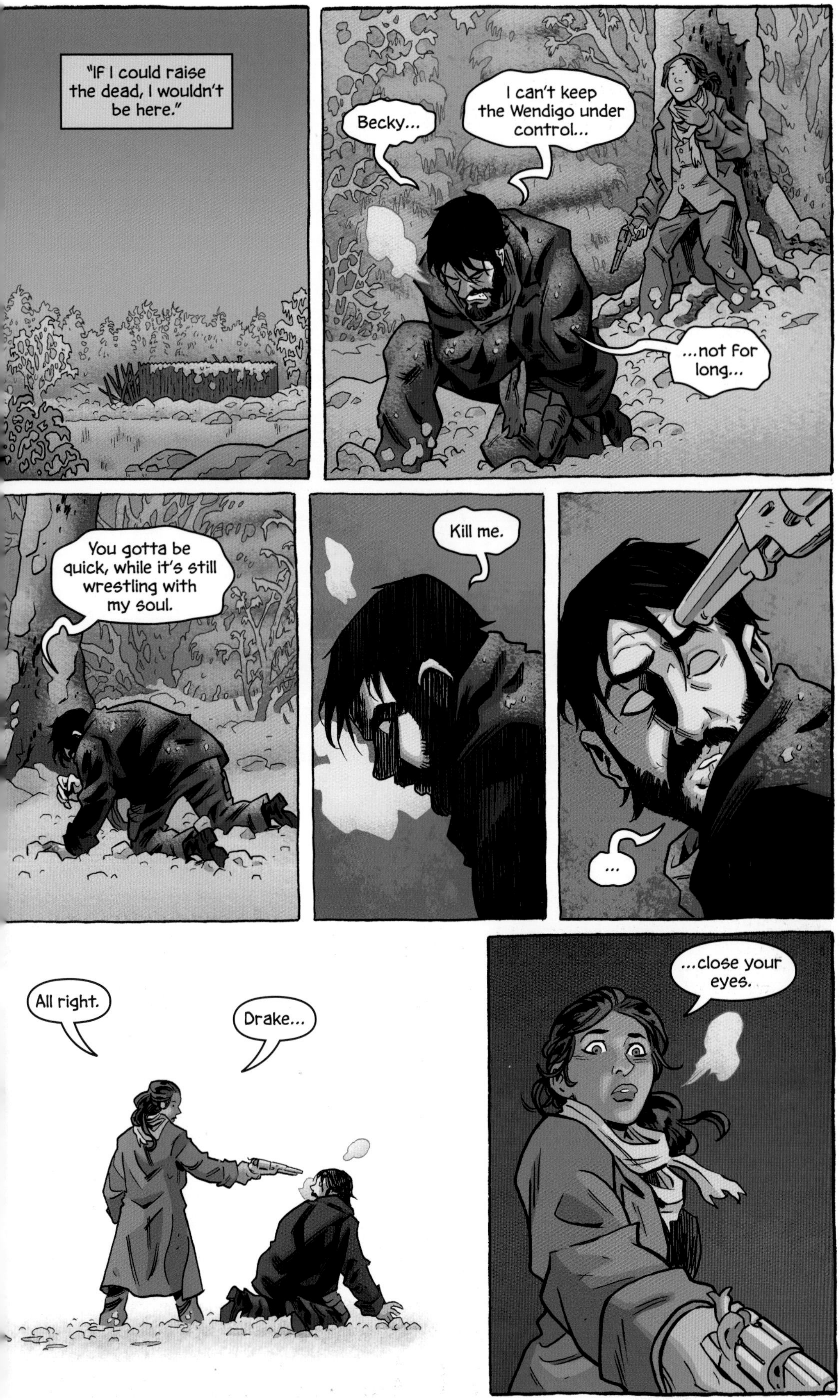
"If I could raise the dead, I wouldn't be here."
Becky...
I can't keep the Wendigo under control...
...not for long...
You gotta be quick, while it's still wrestling with my soul.
Kill me.
...
All right.
Drake...
...close your eyes.

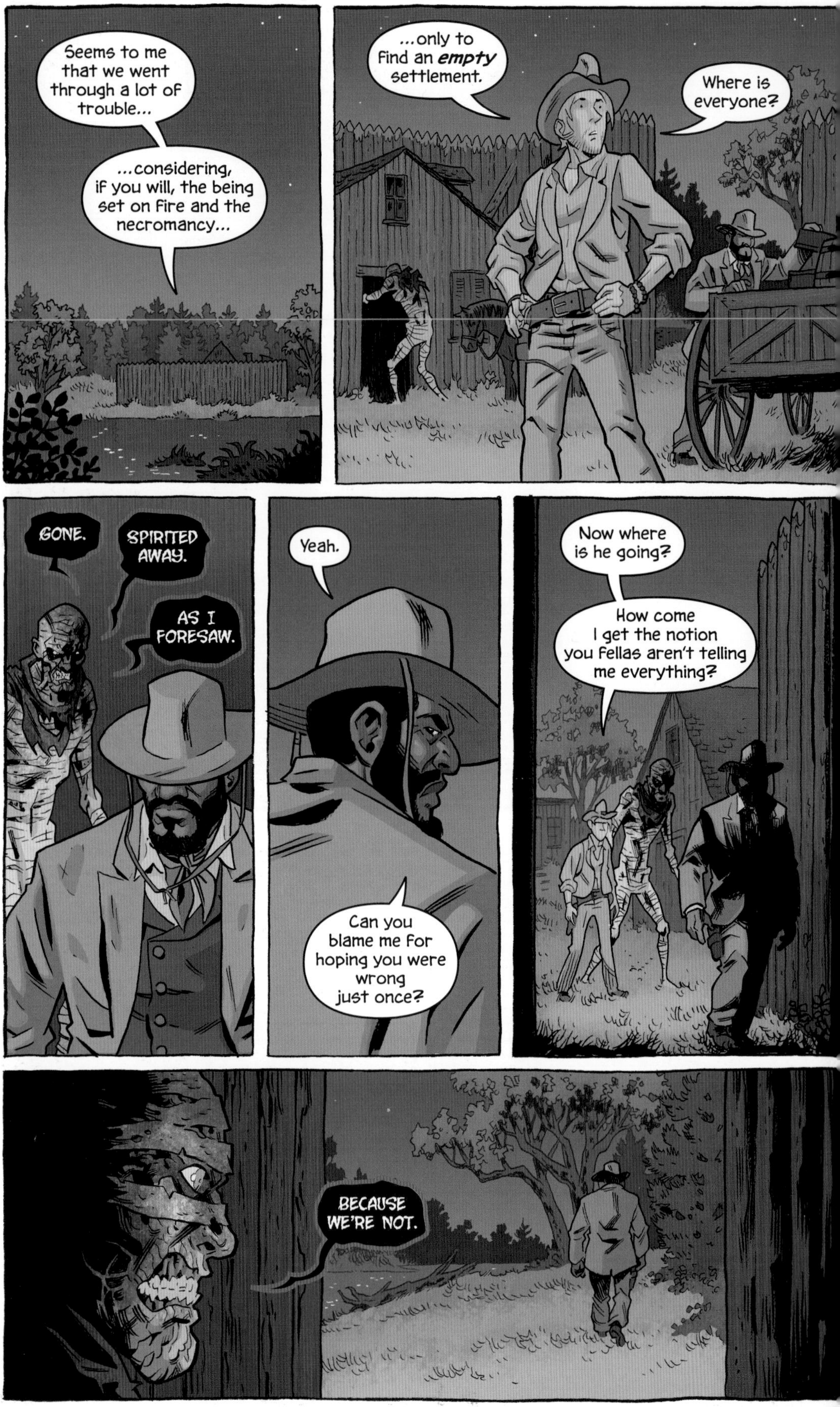

Seems to me that we went through a lot of trouble...
...considering, if you will, the being set on fire and the necromancy...
...only to find an *empty* settlement.
Where is everyone?
GONE.
SPIRITED AWAY.
AS I FORESAW.
Yeah.
Can you blame me for hoping you were wrong just once?
Now where is he going?
How come I get the notion you fellas aren't telling me everything?
BECAUSE WE'RE NOT.

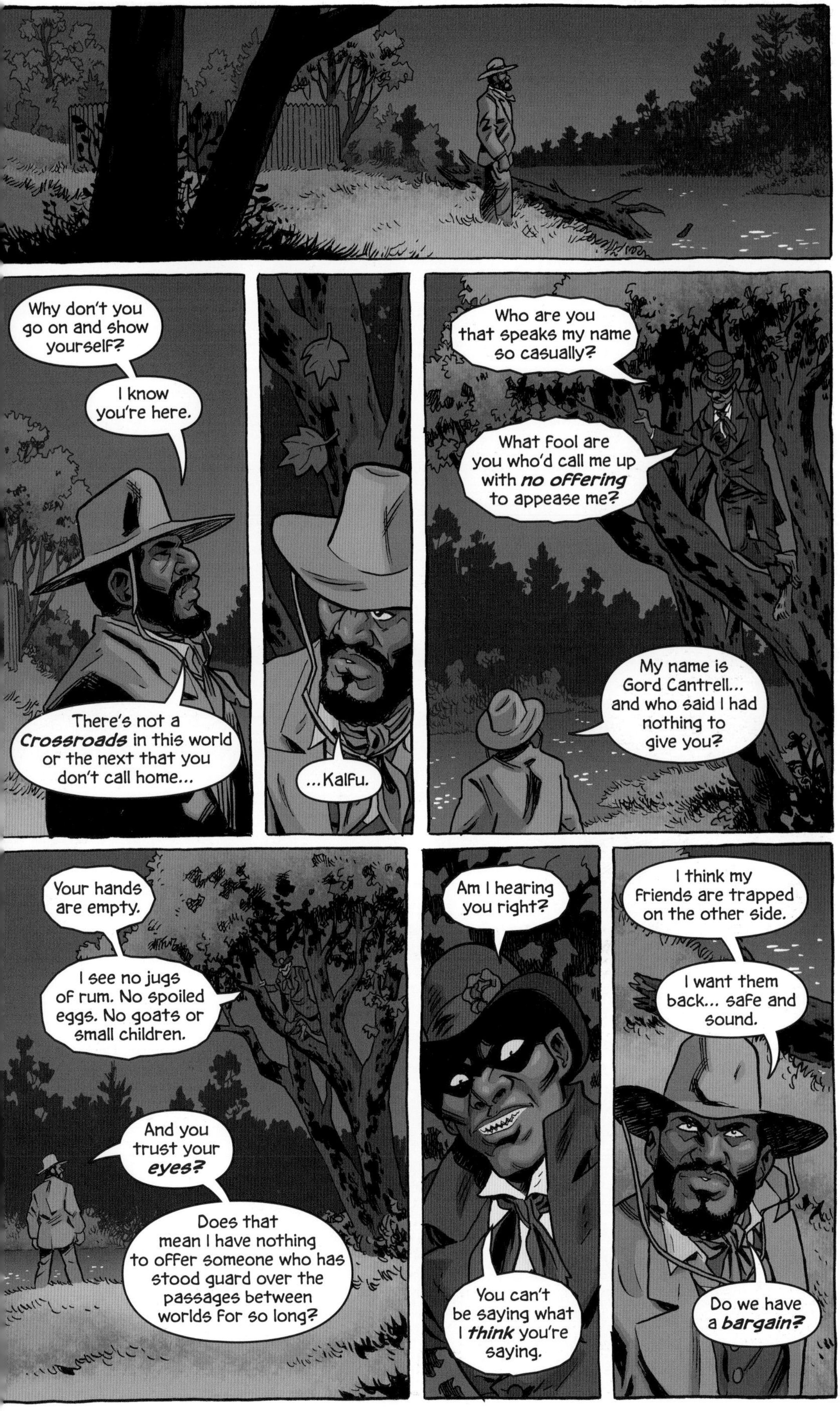
Why don't you go on and show yourself?
I know you're here.
There's not a Crossroads in this world or the next that you don't call home...
...Kalfu.
Who are you that speaks my name so casually?
What fool are you who'd call me up with no offering to appease me?
My name is Gord Cantrell... and who said I had nothing to give you?
Your hands are empty.
I see no jugs of rum. No spoiled eggs. No goats or small children.
And you trust your eyes?
Does that mean I have nothing to offer someone who has stood guard over the passages between worlds for so long?
Am I hearing you right?
You can't be saying what I think you're saying.
I think my friends are trapped on the other side.
I want them back... safe and sound.
Do we have a bargain?

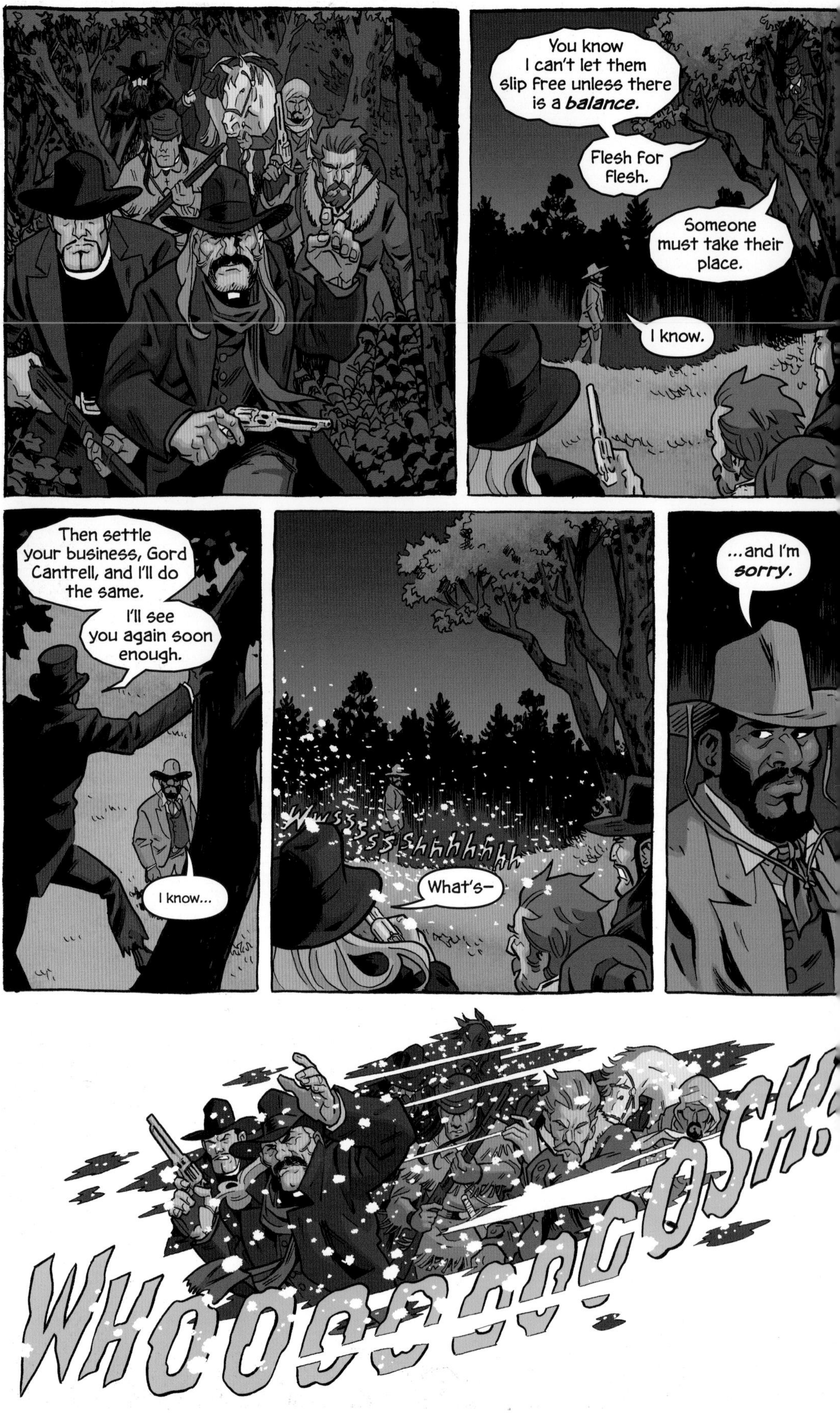

You know I can't let them slip free unless there is a ***balance.***
Flesh for flesh.
Someone must take their place.
I know.
Then settle your business, Gord Cantrell, and I'll do the same.
I'll see you again soon enough.
I know...
Wwsssssshhhhhhhhh
What's–
...and I'm ***sorry.***
WHOOOOOOOOSH!

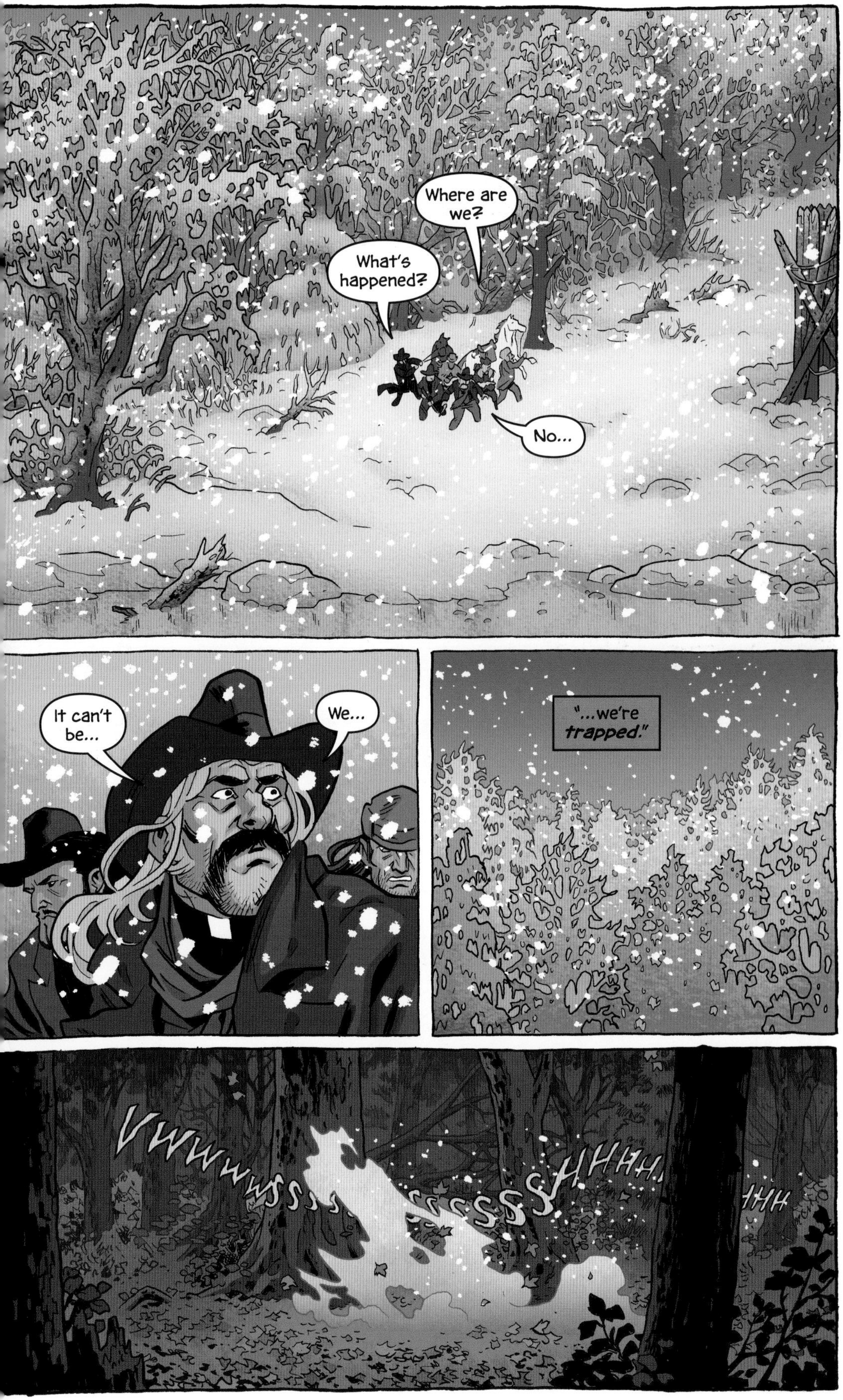

What's happened?
Where are we?
No...
It can't be...
We...
"...we're *trapped*."
VWWWWSSSSSSSSSSSSHHHHHHHHH

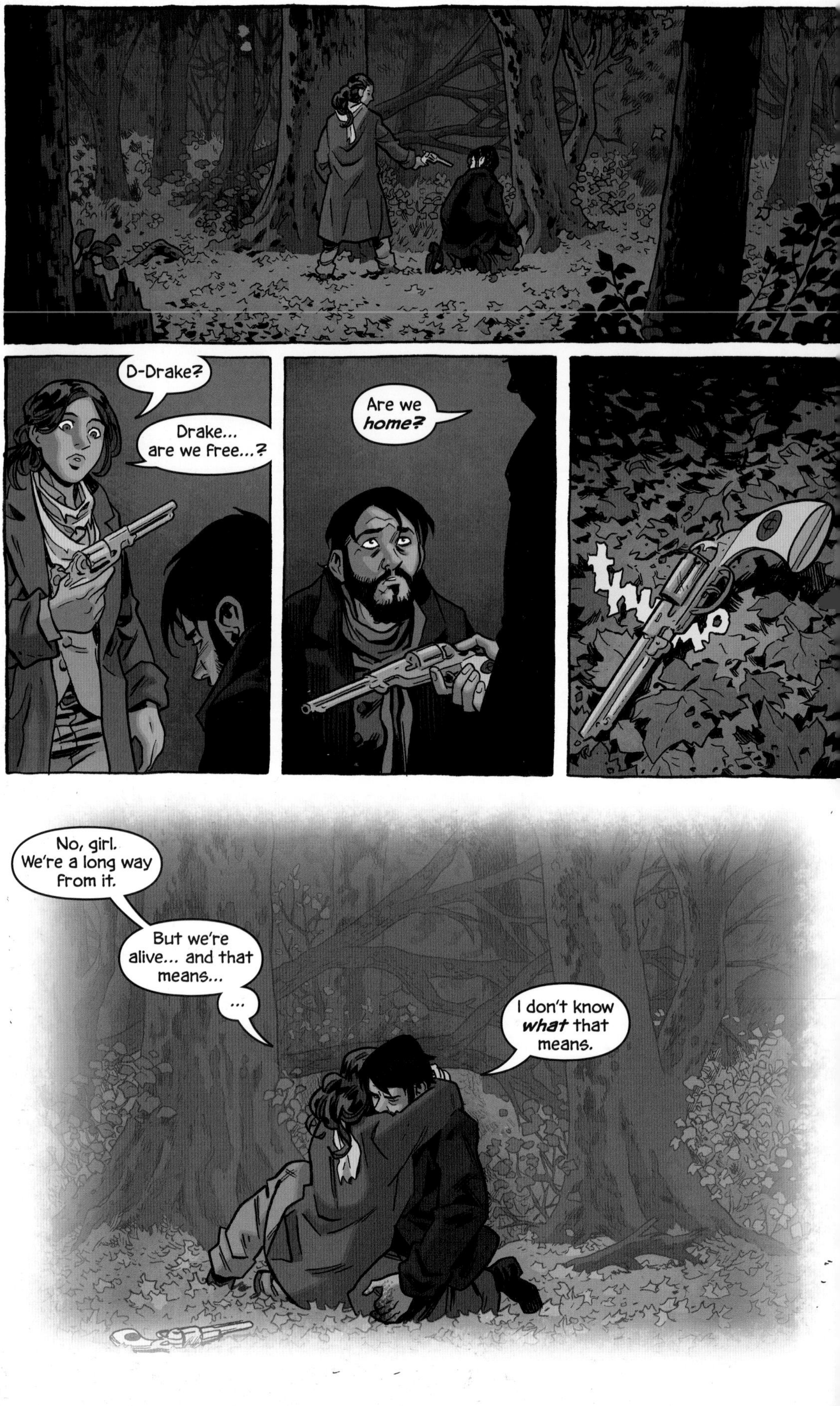
D-Drake?
Drake... are we free...?
Are we *home?*
thump
No, girl. We're a long way from it.
But we're alive... and that means...
...
I don't know *what* that means.

CHAPTER SIX

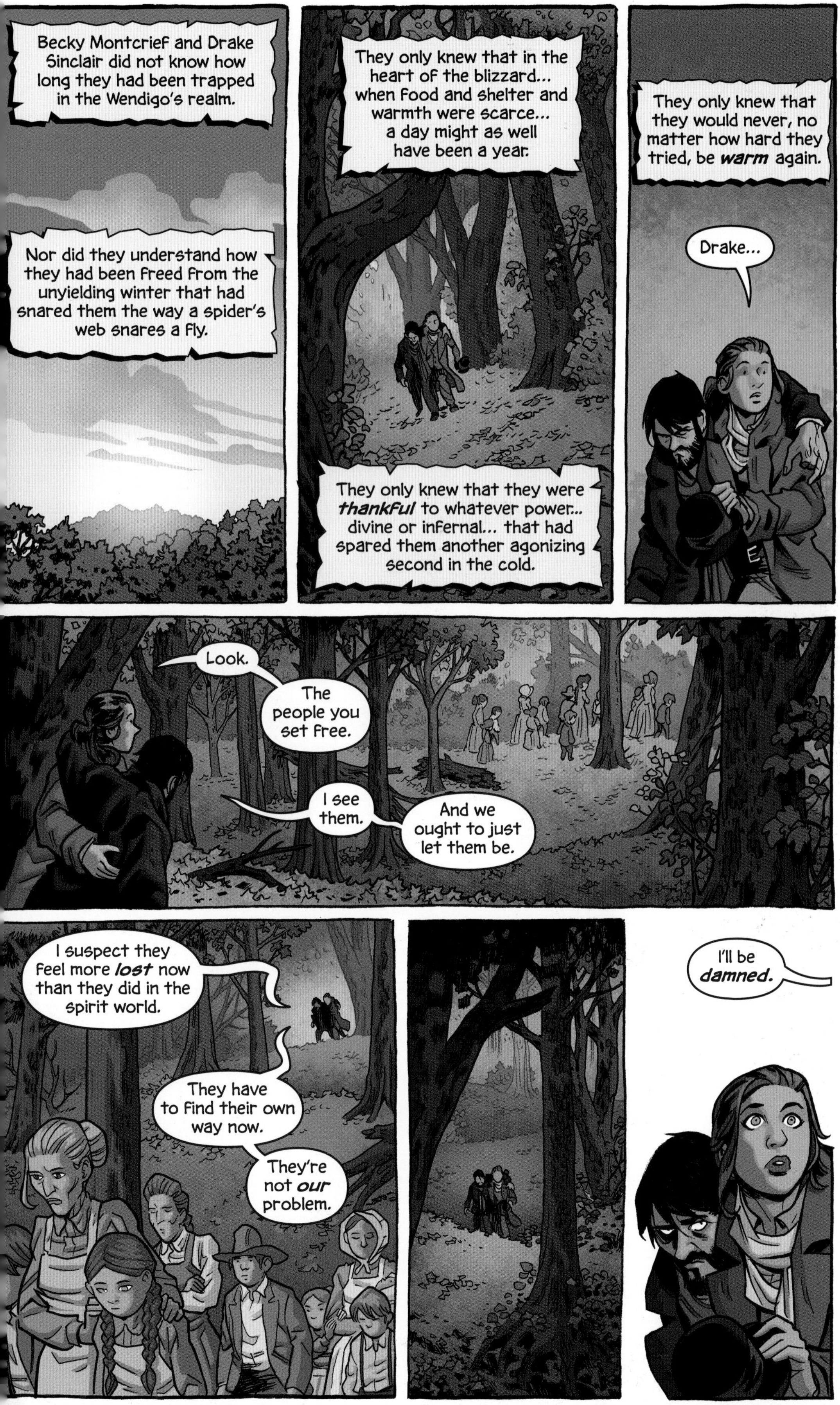
Becky Montcrief and Drake Sinclair did not know how long they had been trapped in the Wendigo's realm.
Nor did they understand how they had been freed from the unyielding winter that had snared them the way a spider's web snares a fly.
They only knew that in the heart of the blizzard... when food and shelter and warmth were scarce... a day might as well have been a year.
They only knew that they were *thankful* to whatever power... divine or infernal... that had spared them another agonizing second in the cold.
They only knew that they would never, no matter how hard they tried, be ***warm*** again.
Drake...
Look.
The people you set free.
I see them.
And we ought to just let them be.
I suspect they feel more *lost* now than they did in the spirit world.
They have to find their own way now.
They're not *our* problem.
I'll be *damned.*

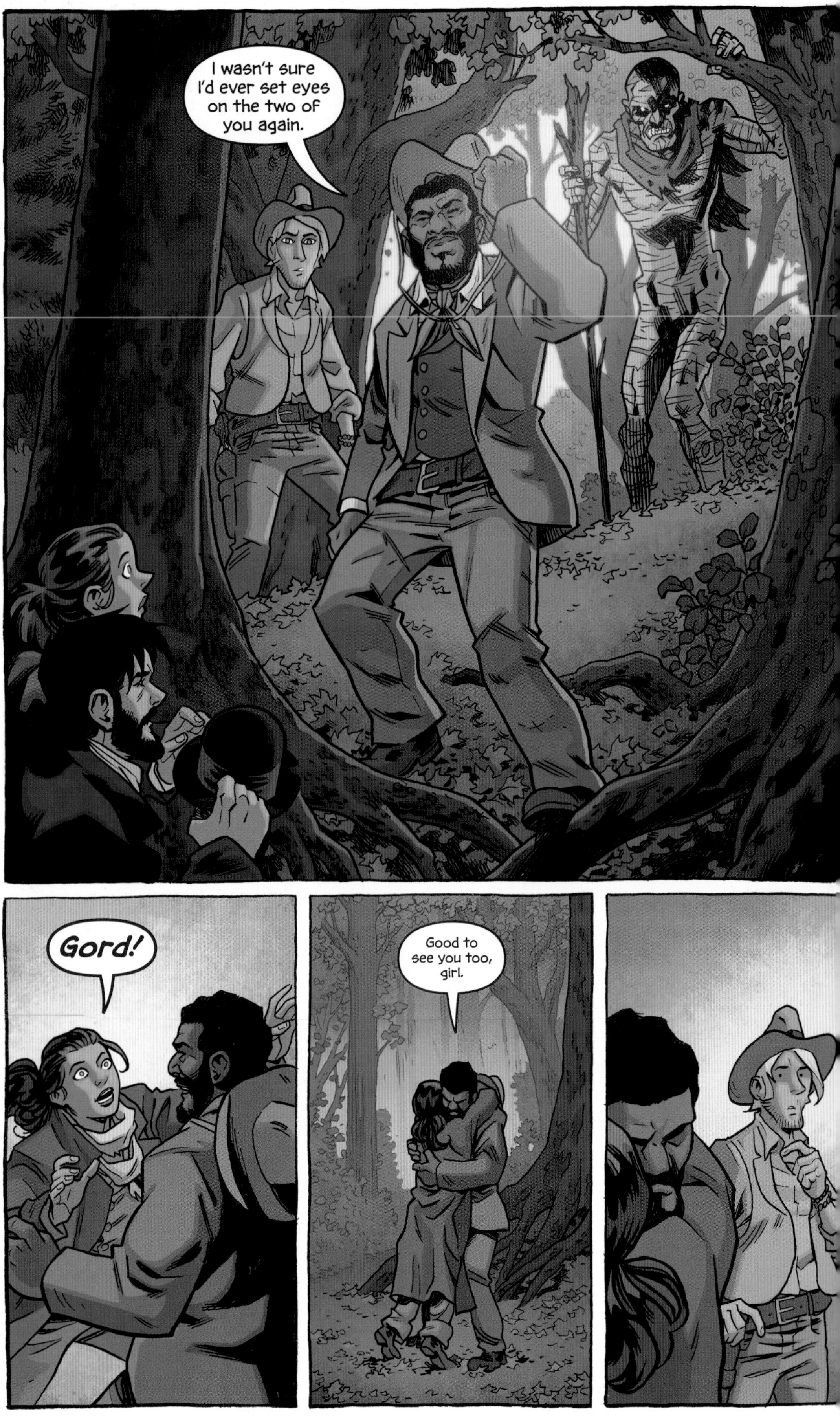
I wasn't sure I'd ever set eyes on the two of you again.
Gord!
Good to see you too, girl.

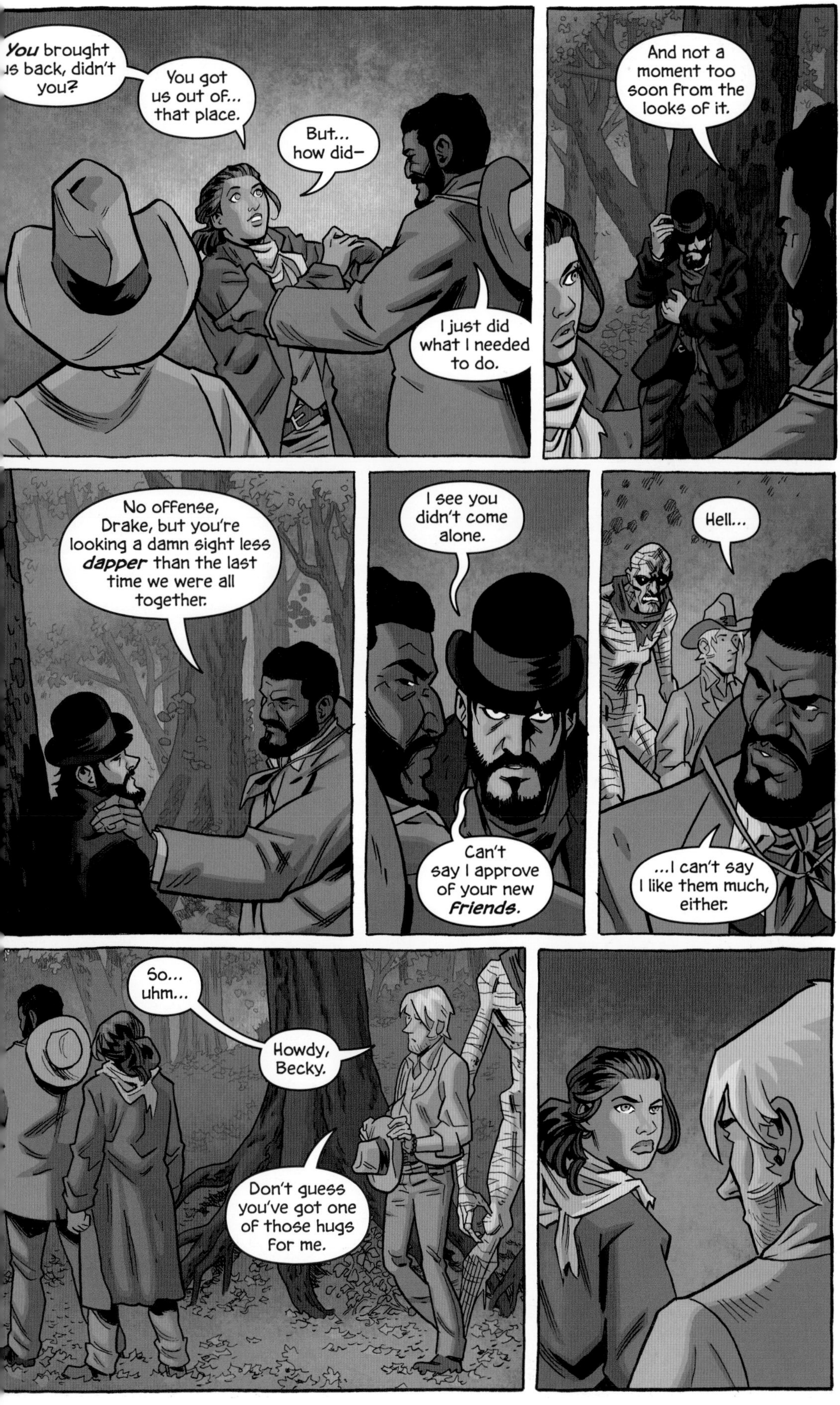

You brought us back, didn't you?
You got us out of... that place.
But... how did–
I just did what I needed to do.
And not a moment too soon from the looks of it.
No offense, Drake, but you're looking a damn sight less *dapper* than the last time we were all together.
I see you didn't come alone.
Can't say I approve of your new *friends*.
Hell...
...I can't say I like them much, either.
So... uhm...
Howdy, Becky.
Don't guess you've got one of those hugs for me.

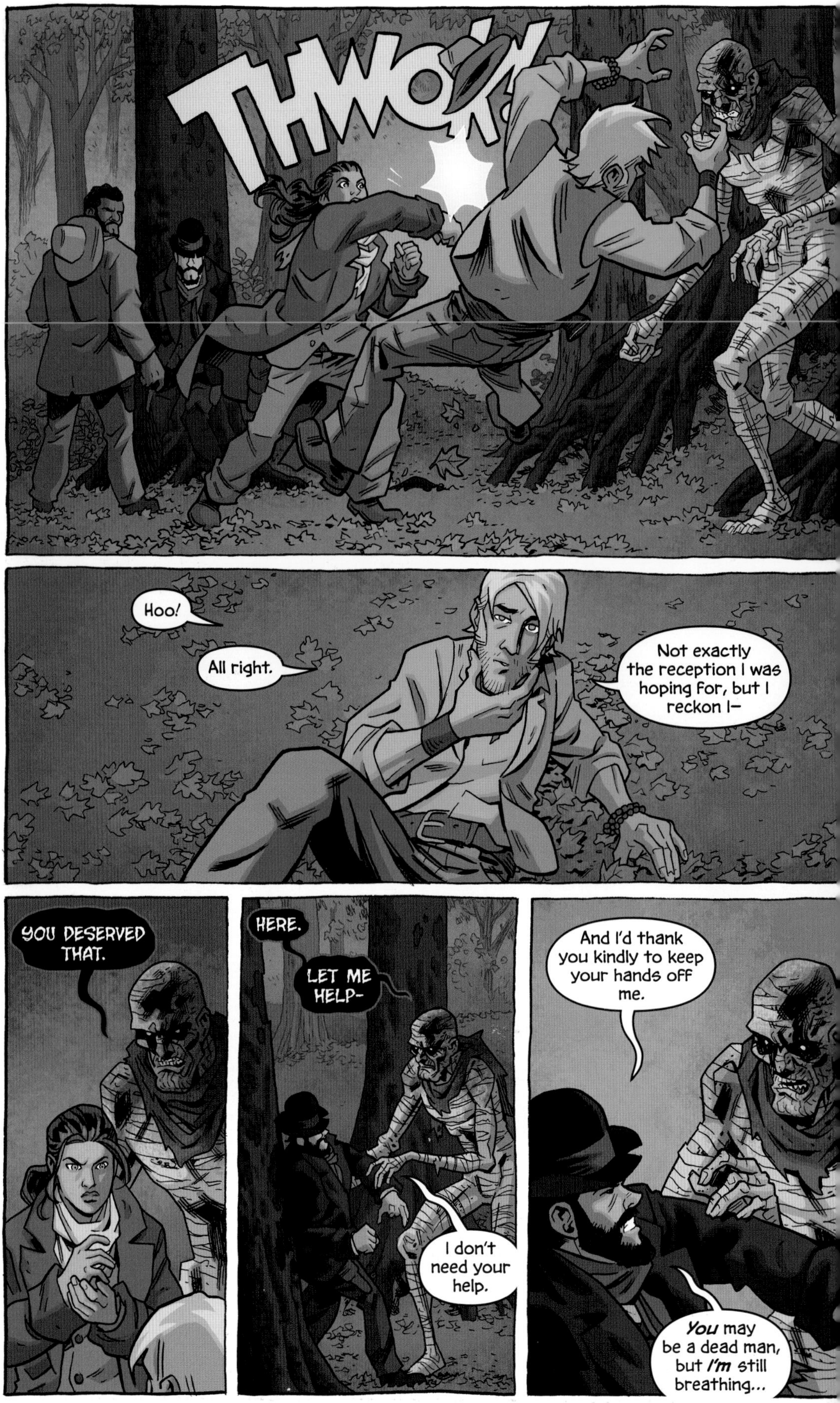
THWOK!
Hoo!
All right.
Not exactly the reception I was hoping for, but I reckon I—
YOU DESERVED THAT.
HERE.
LET ME HELP-
I don't need your help.
And I'd thank you kindly to keep your hands off me.
You may be a dead man, but *I'm* still breathing...

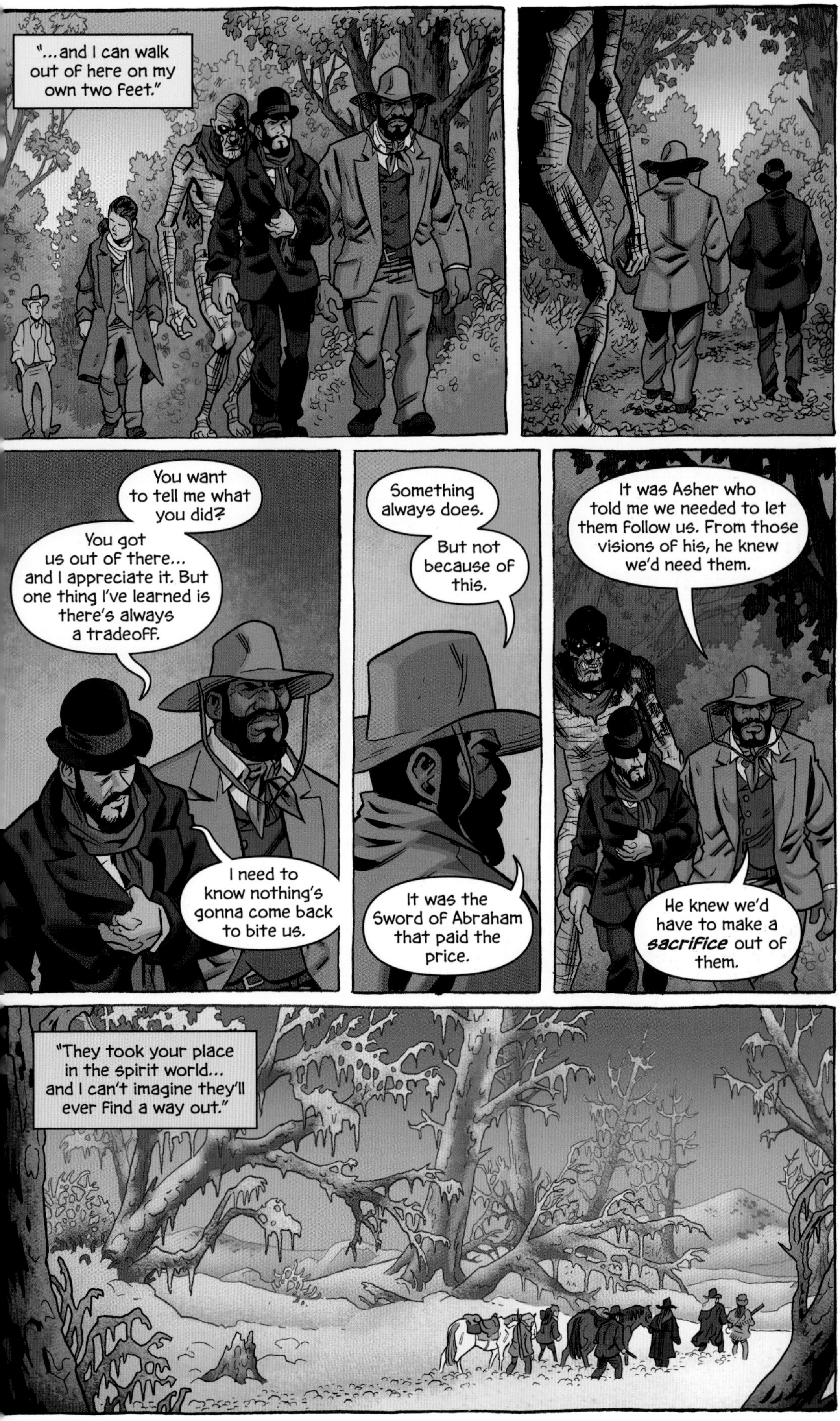
"...and I can walk out of here on my own two feet."
You want to tell me what you did?
You got us out of there... and I appreciate it. But one thing I've learned is there's always a tradeoff.
I need to know nothing's gonna come back to bite us.
Something always does.
But not because of this.
It was the Sword of Abraham that paid the price.
It was Asher who told me we needed to let them follow us. From those visions of his, he knew we'd need them.
He knew we'd have to make a *sacrifice* out of them.
"They took your place in the spirit world... and I can't imagine they'll ever find a way out."

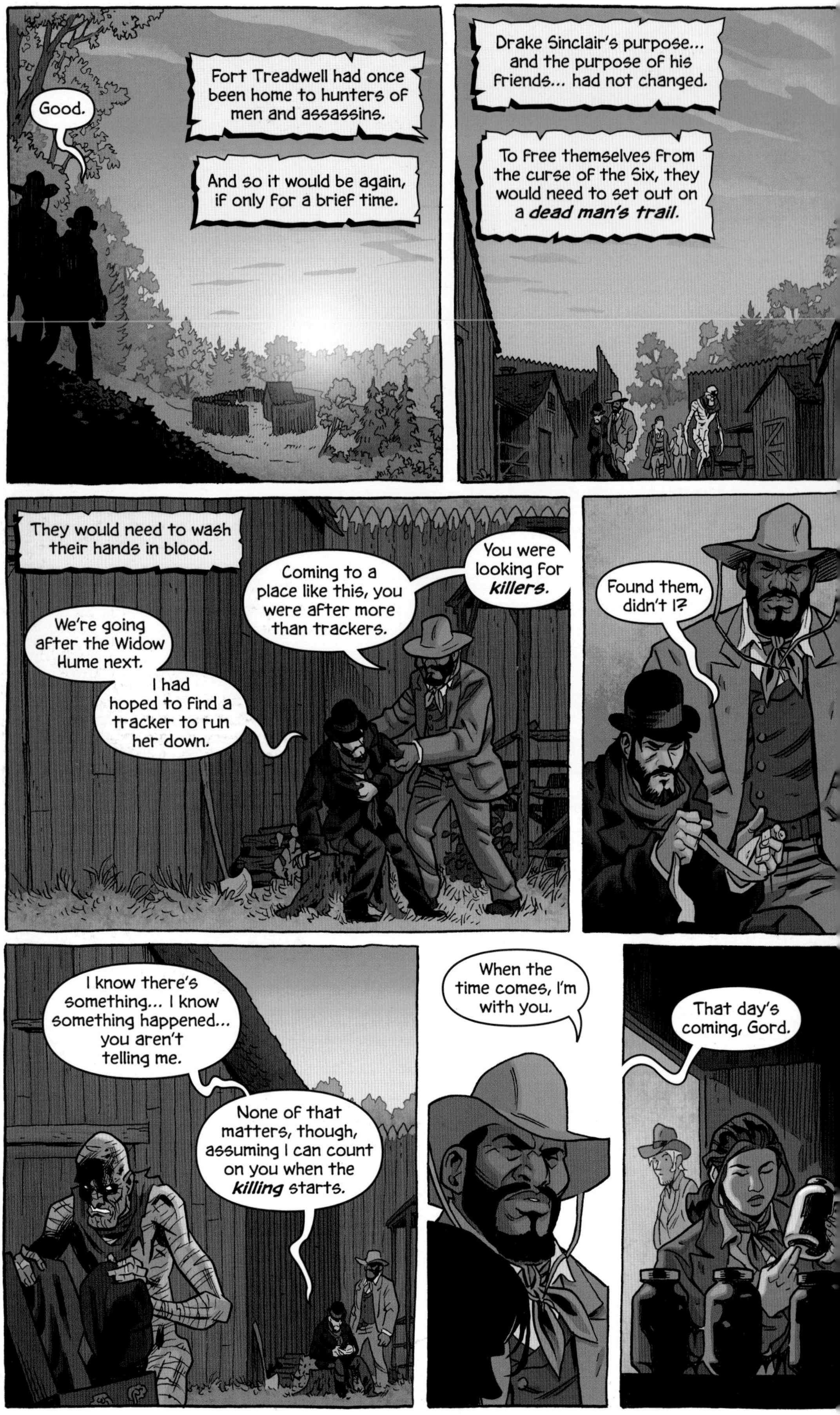
Good.
Fort Treadwell had once been home to hunters of men and assassins.
And so it would be again, if only for a brief time.
Drake Sinclair's purpose... and the purpose of his friends... had not changed.
To free themselves from the curse of the Six, they would need to set out on a *dead man's trail.*
They would need to wash their hands in blood.
We're going after the Widow Hume next.
I had hoped to find a tracker to run her down.
Coming to a place like this, you were after more than trackers.
You were looking for *killers.*
Found them, didn't I?
I know there's something... I know something happened... you aren't telling me.
None of that matters, though, assuming I can count on you when the *killing* starts.
When the time comes, I'm with you.
That day's coming, Gord.

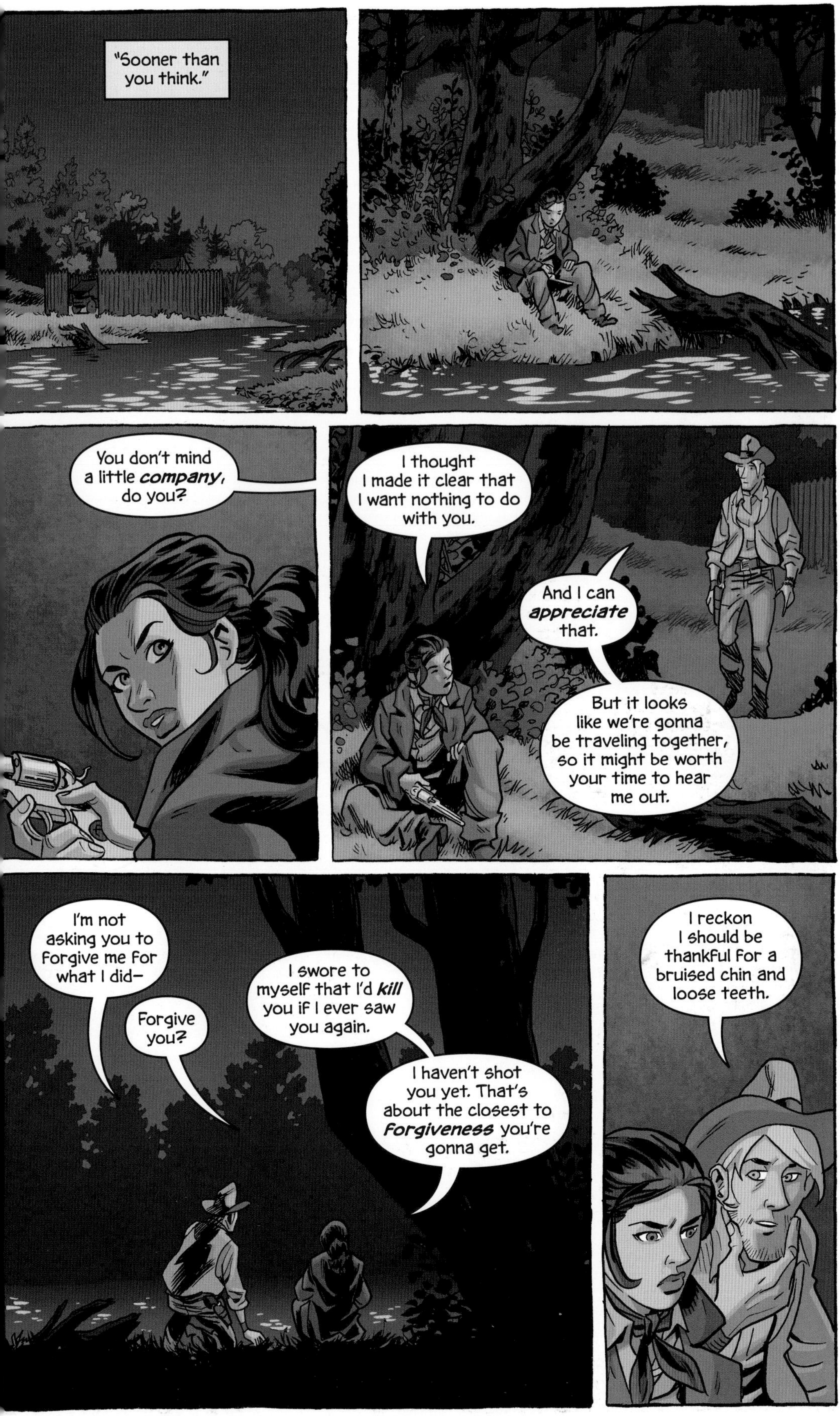
"Sooner than you think."
You don't mind a little *company*, do you?
I thought I made it clear that I want nothing to do with you.
And I can *appreciate* that.
But it looks like we're gonna be traveling together, so it might be worth your time to hear me out.
I'm not asking you to forgive me for what I did–
Forgive you?
I swore to myself that I'd *kill* you if I ever saw you again.
I haven't shot you yet. That's about the closest to *forgiveness* you're gonna get.
I reckon I should be thankful for a bruised chin and loose teeth.

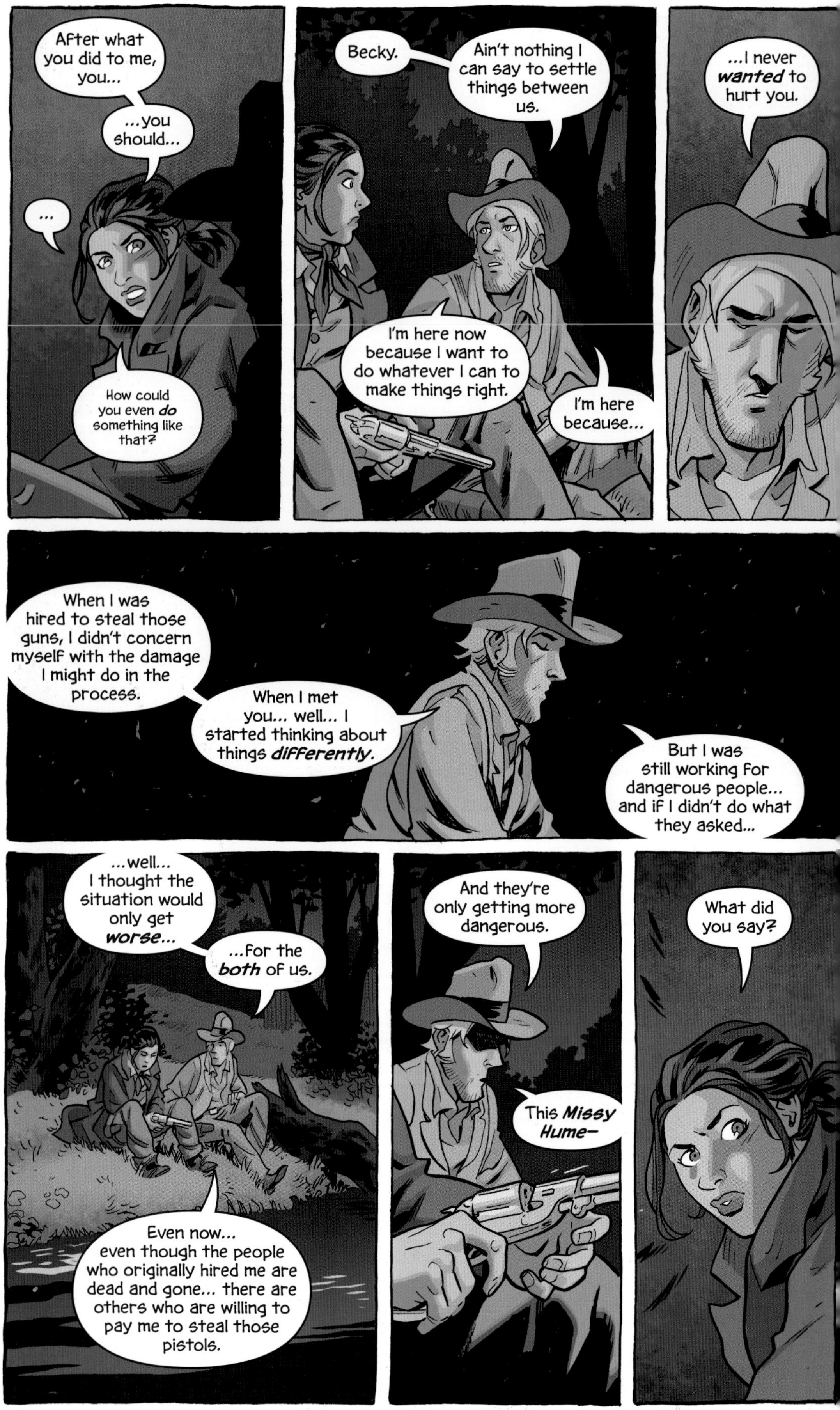

After what you did to me, you...
...you should...
...
How could you even *do* something like that?
Becky.
Ain't nothing I can say to settle things between us.
I'm here now because I want to do whatever I can to make things right.
I'm here because...
...I never *wanted* to hurt you.
When I was hired to steal those guns, I didn't concern myself with the damage I might do in the process.
When I met you... well... I started thinking about things *differently*.
But I was still working for dangerous people... and if I didn't do what they asked...
...well... I thought the situation would only get *worse*...
...for the *both* of us.
Even now... even though the people who originally hired me are dead and gone... there are others who are willing to pay me to steal those pistols.
And they're only getting more dangerous.
This *Missy Hume*—
What did you say?

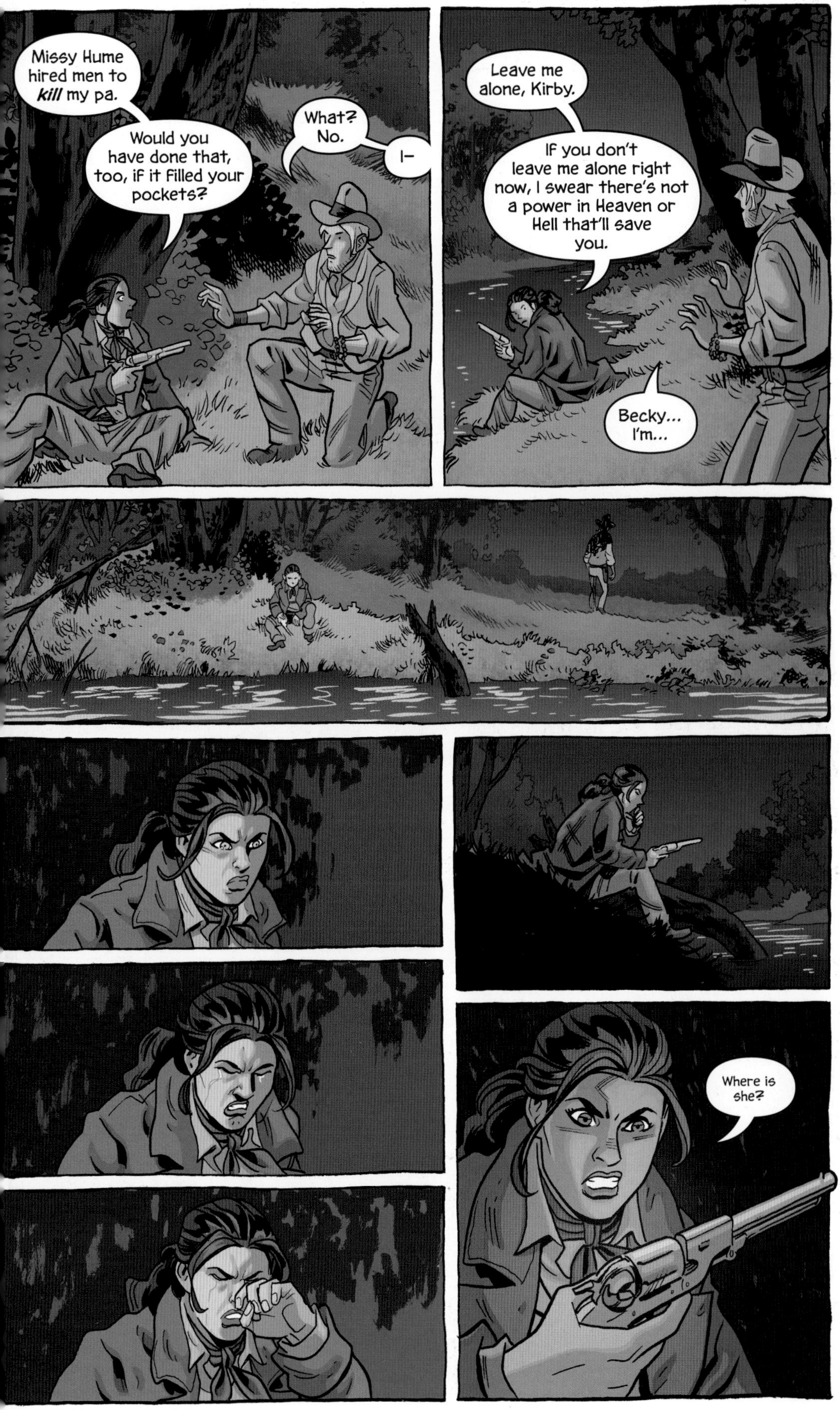
Missy Hume hired men to *kill* my pa.
Would you have done that, too, if it filled your pockets?
What? No.
I–
Leave me alone, Kirby.
If you don't leave me alone right now, I swear there's not a power in Heaven or Hell that'll save you.
Becky... I'm...
Where is she?

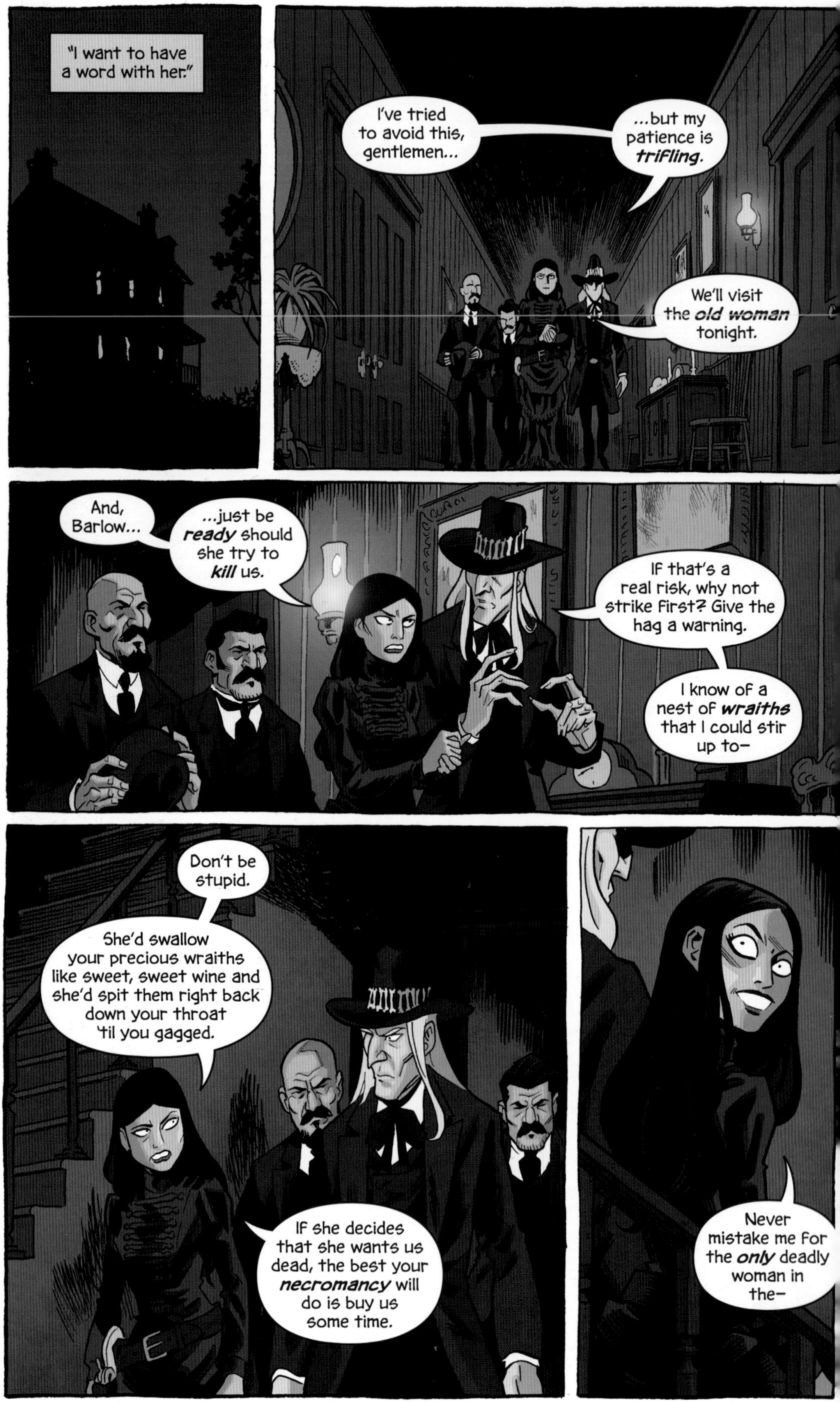
"I want to have a word with her."
I've tried to avoid this, gentlemen...
...but my patience is *trifling*.
We'll visit the *old woman* tonight.
And, Barlow...
...just be *ready* should she try to *kill* us.
If that's a real risk, why not strike first? Give the hag a warning.
I know of a nest of *wraiths* that I could stir up to–
Don't be stupid.
She'd swallow your precious wraiths like sweet, sweet wine and she'd spit them right back down your throat 'til you gagged.
If she decides that she wants us dead, the best your *necromancy* will do is buy us some time.
Never mistake me for the *only* deadly woman in the–

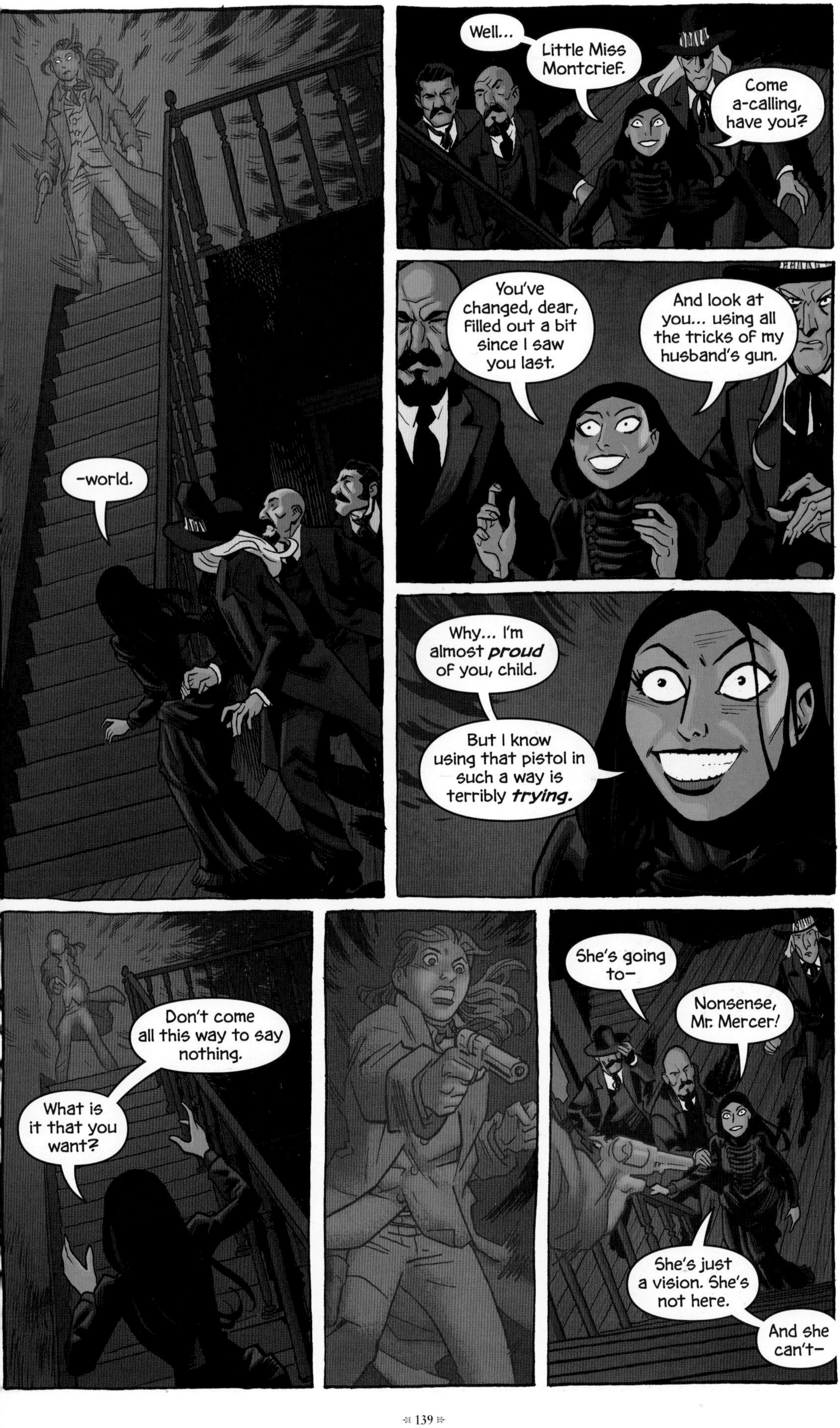

-world.
Well...
Little Miss Montcrief.
Come a-calling, have you?
You've changed, dear, filled out a bit since I saw you last.
And look at you... using all the tricks of my husband's gun.
Why... I'm almost *proud* of you, child.
But I know using that pistol in such a way is terribly *trying.*
Don't come all this way to say nothing.
What is it that you want?
She's going to—
Nonsense, Mr. Mercer!
She's just a vision. She's not here.
And she can't—

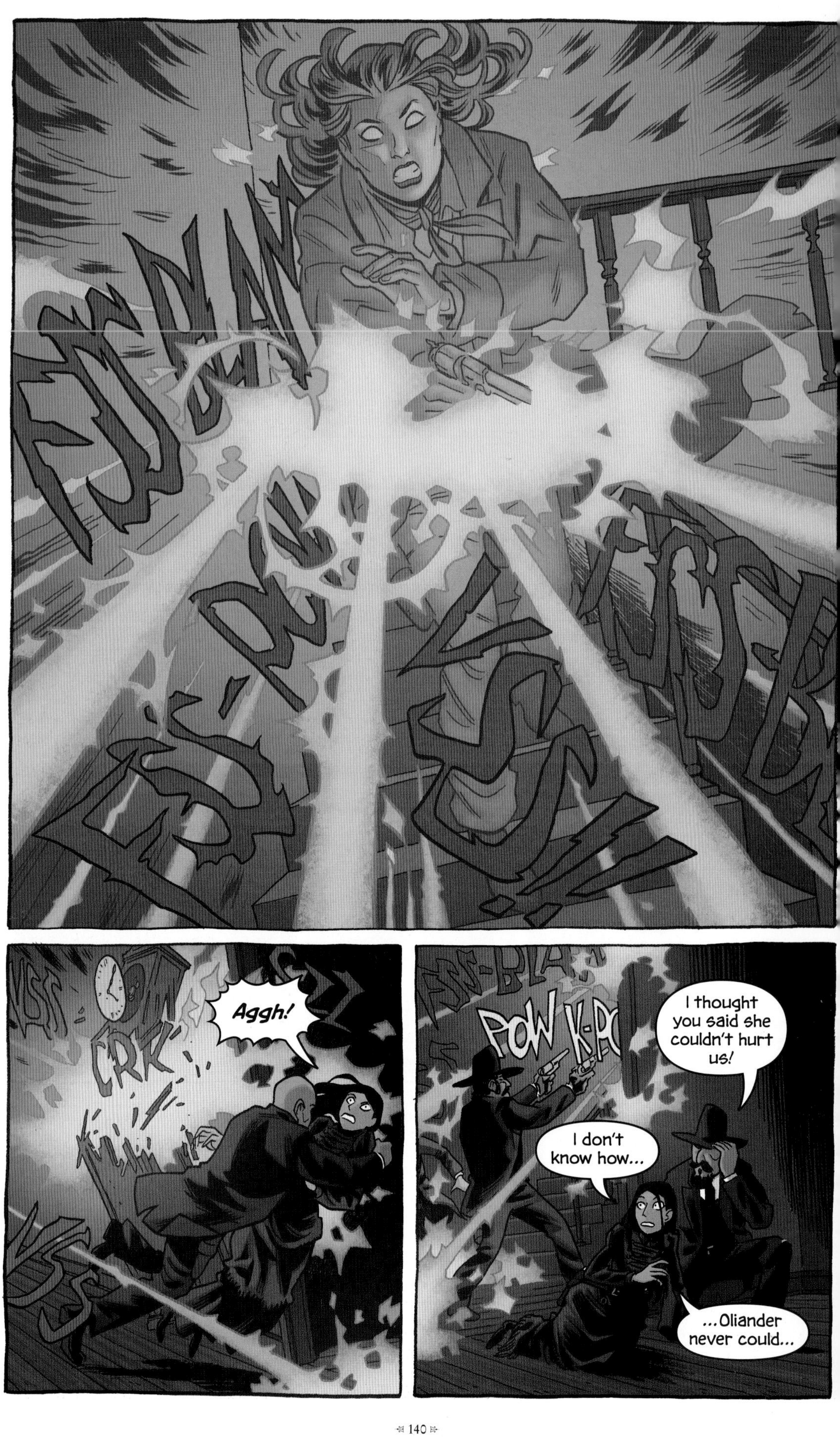
CRK
Aggh!
POW
I thought you said she couldn't hurt us!
I don't know how...
...Oliander never could...

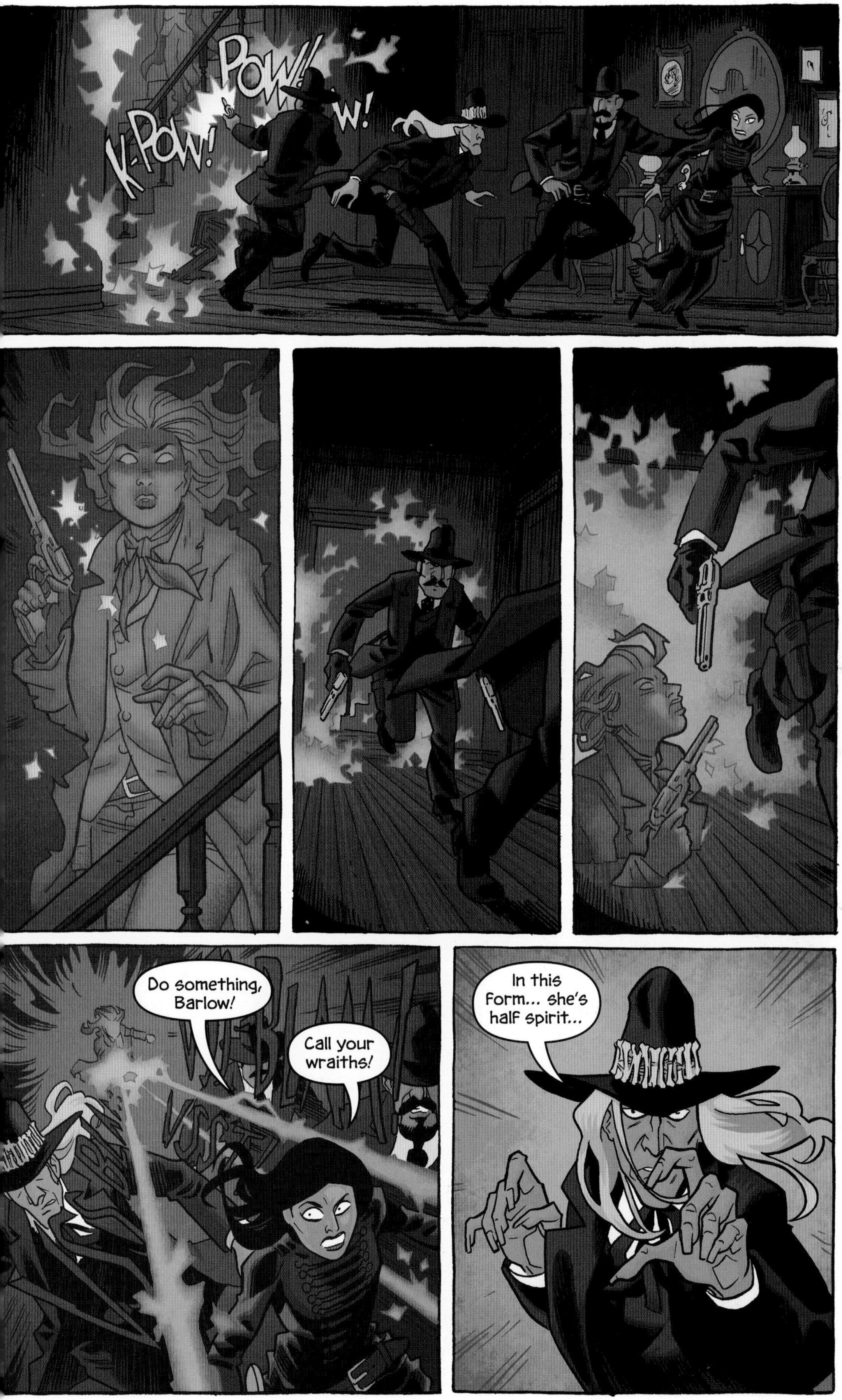
POW!
K-POW!
POW!
Do something, Barlow!
Call your wraiths!
In this form... she's half spirit...

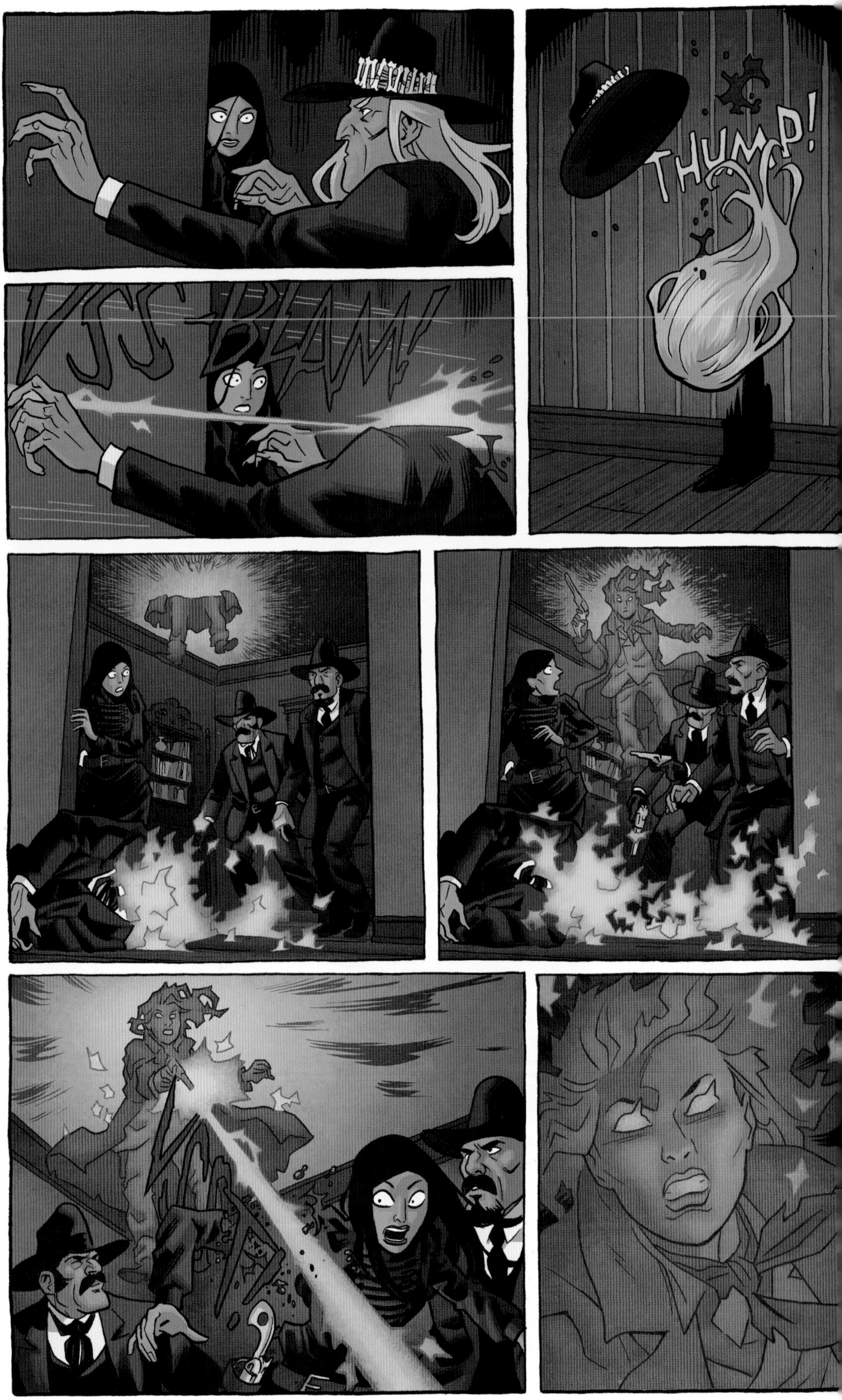
THUMP!
VSS-BLAM!

You can't kill me, witch!

You can't— *Aggh!*

I'll... ...heal.

...nnng...

I know you will.

I *want* you to.

I'm not going to kill you today... not like this.

I want to be there... really *be* there... when you get what's coming to you.

But now you know I can find you.

That gun of yours might keep you alive... but now you know... you know I can *hurt* you.

And I can see it in your eyes.

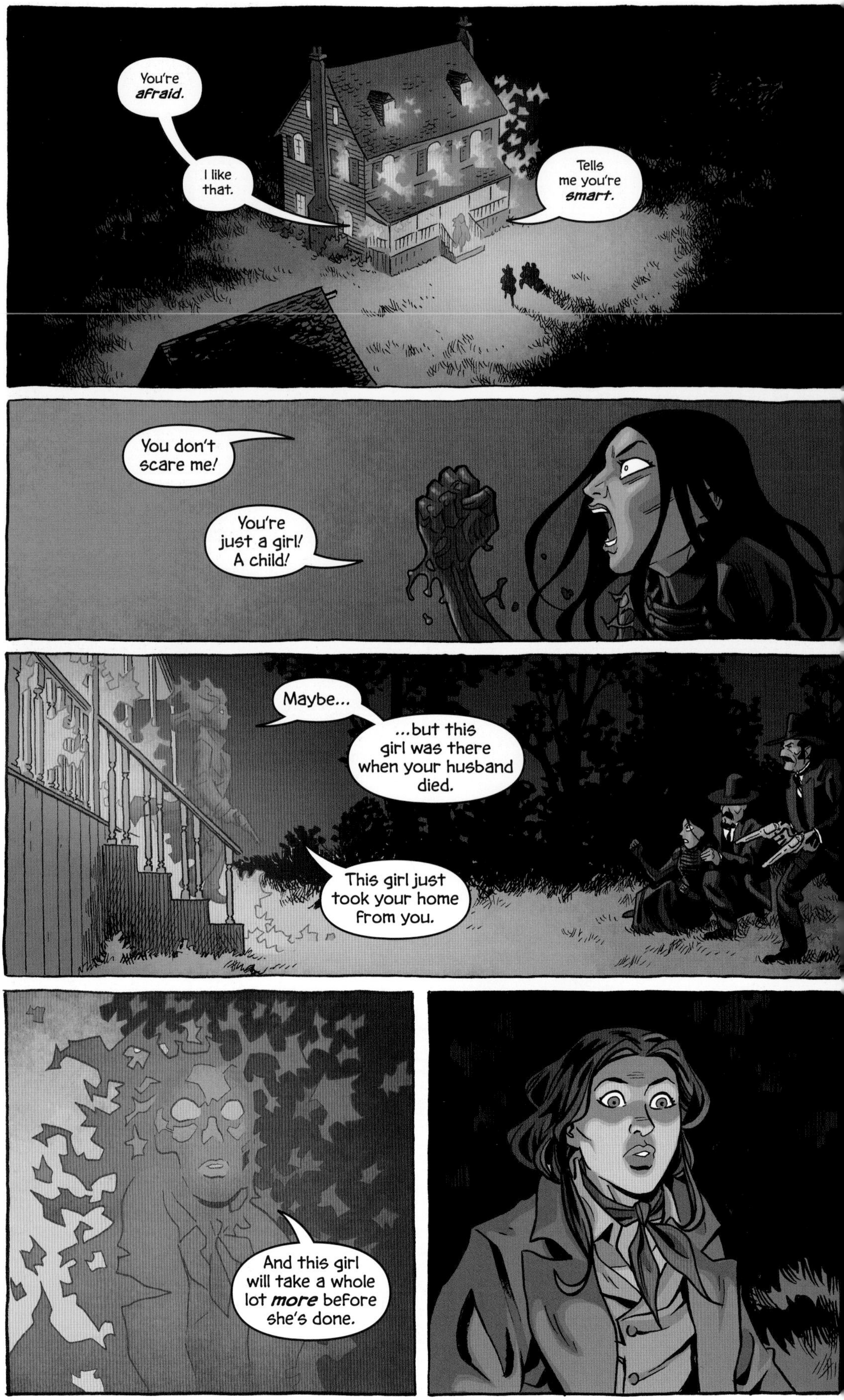
You're *afraid*.
I like that.
Tells me you're *smart*.
You don't scare me!
You're just a girl! A child!
Maybe...
...but this girl was there when your husband died.
This girl just took your home from you.
And this girl will take a whole lot *more* before she's done.

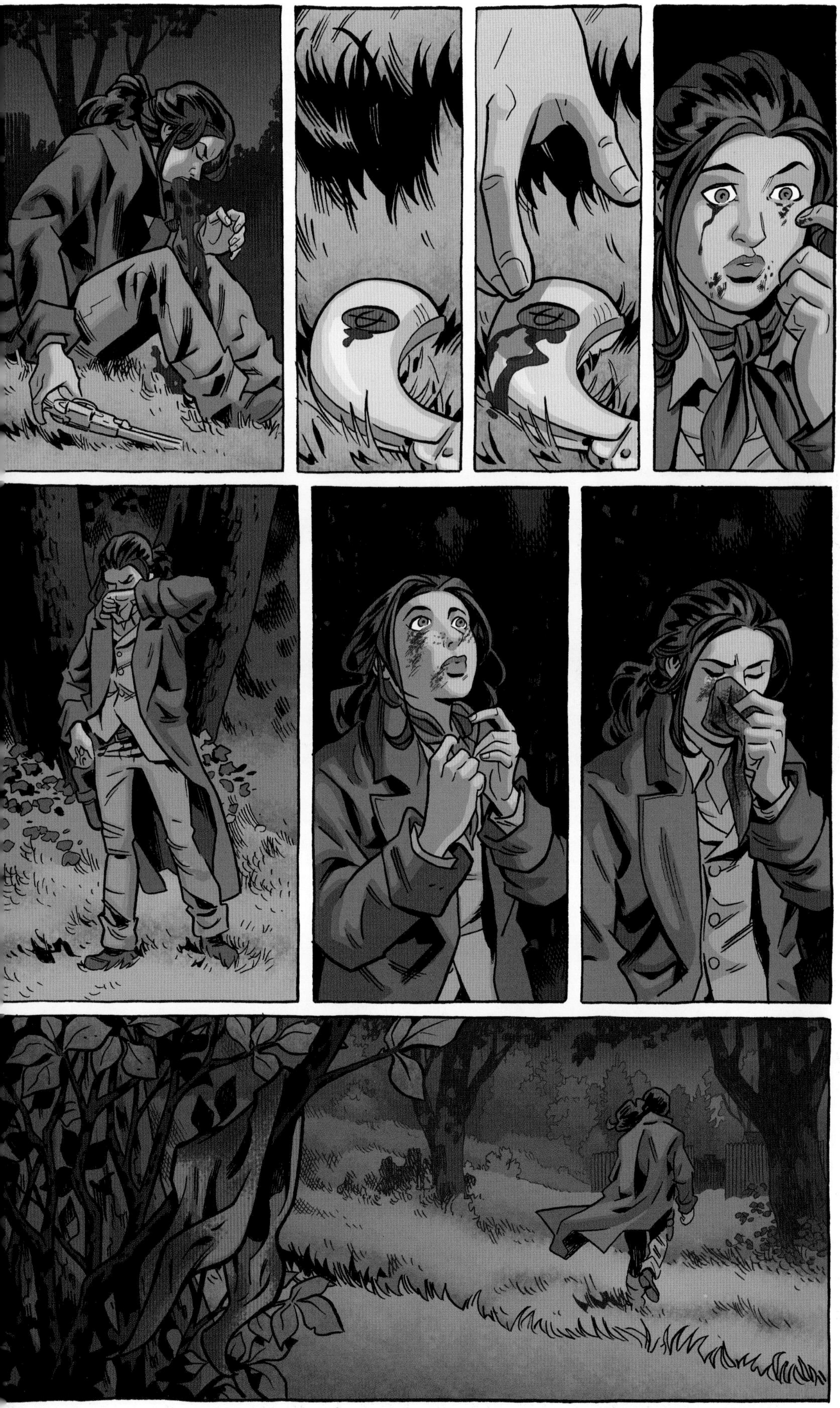

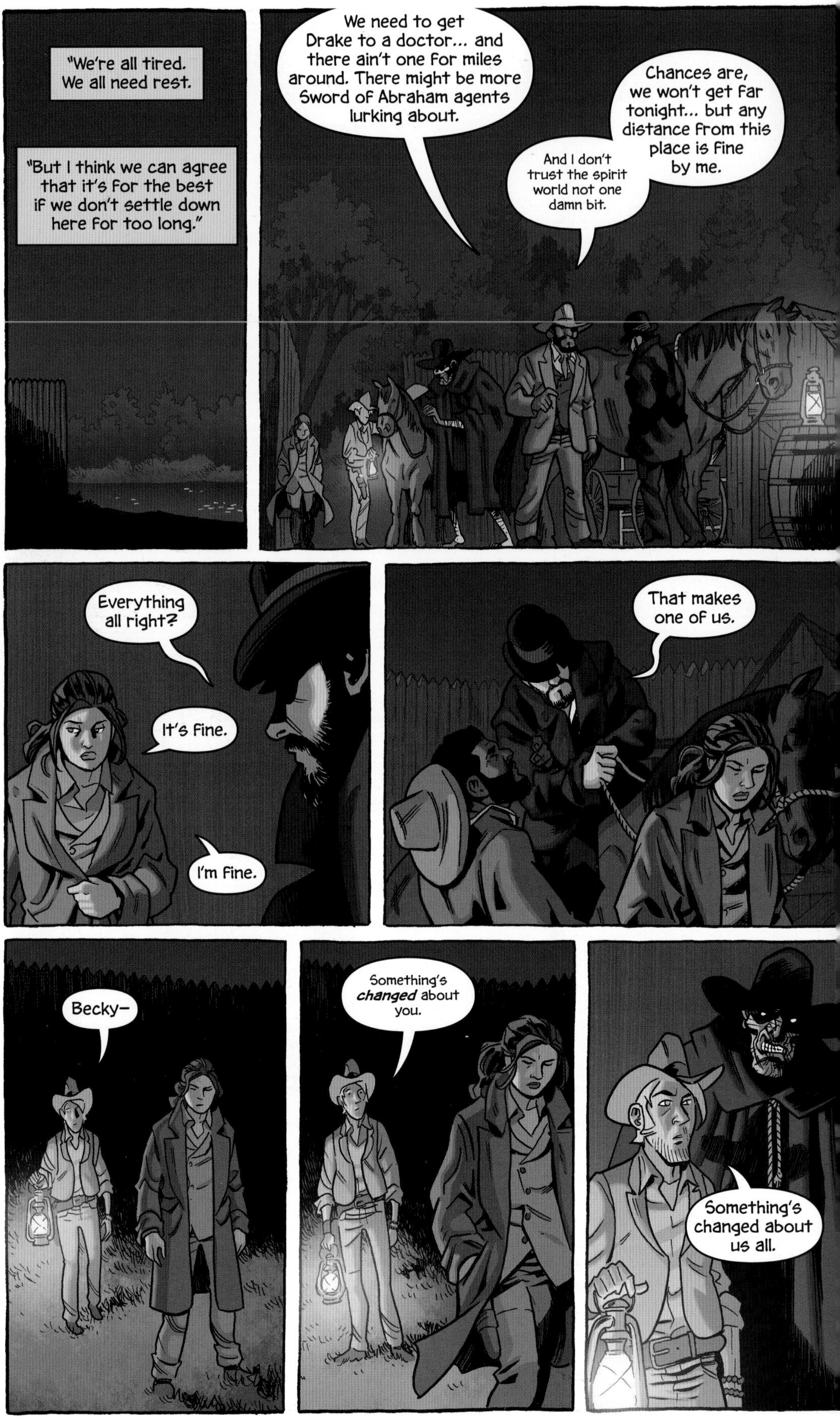
"We're all tired. We all need rest.
"But I think we can agree that it's for the best if we don't settle down here for too long."
We need to get Drake to a doctor... and there ain't one for miles around. There might be more Sword of Abraham agents lurking about.
Chances are, we won't get far tonight... but any distance from this place is fine by me.
And I don't trust the spirit world not one damn bit.
Everything all right?
It's fine.
I'm fine.
That makes one of us.
Becky–
Something's *changed* about you.
Something's changed about us all.

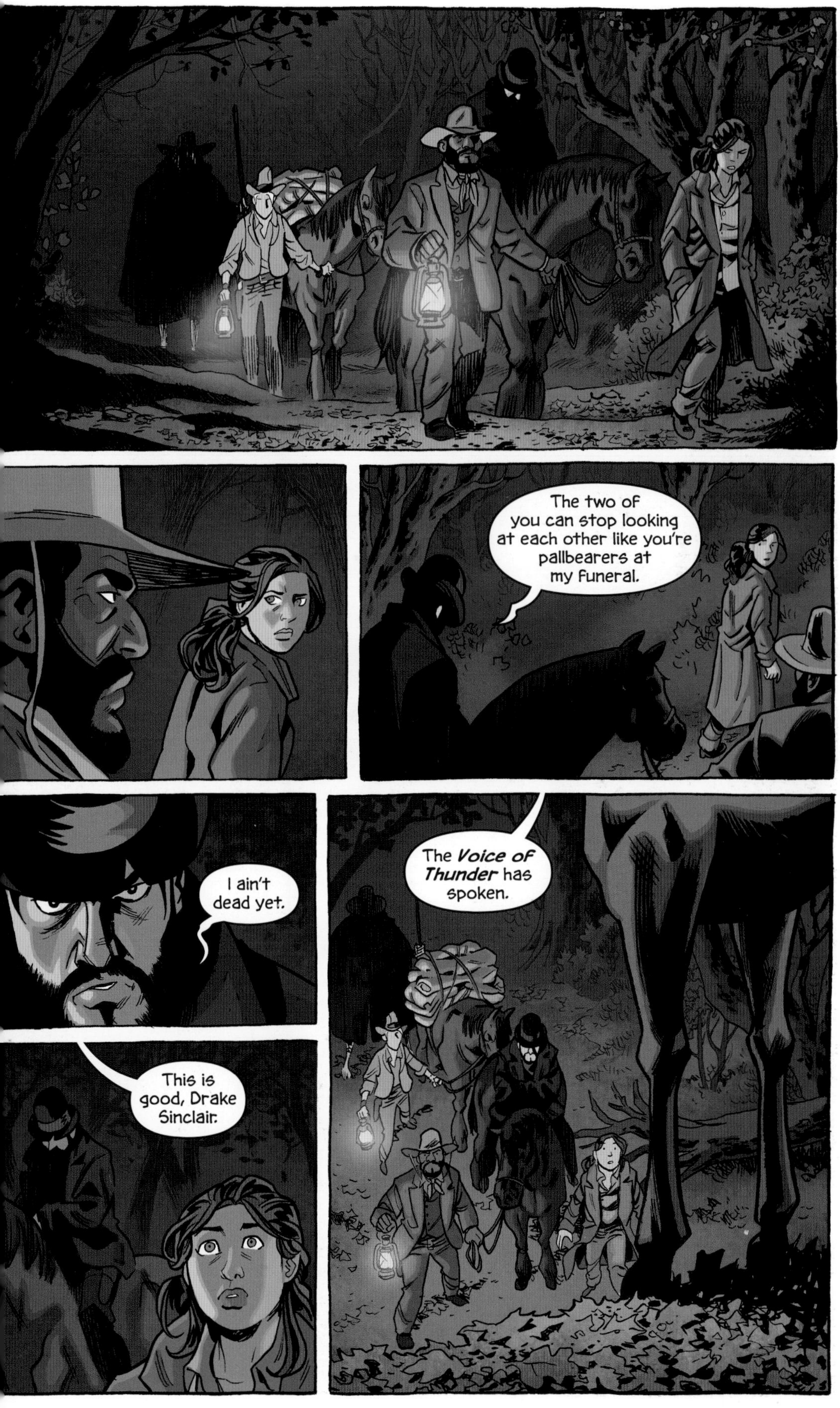
The two of you can stop looking at each other like you're pallbearers at my funeral.
I ain't dead yet.
The *Voice of Thunder* has spoken.
This is good, Drake Sinclair.

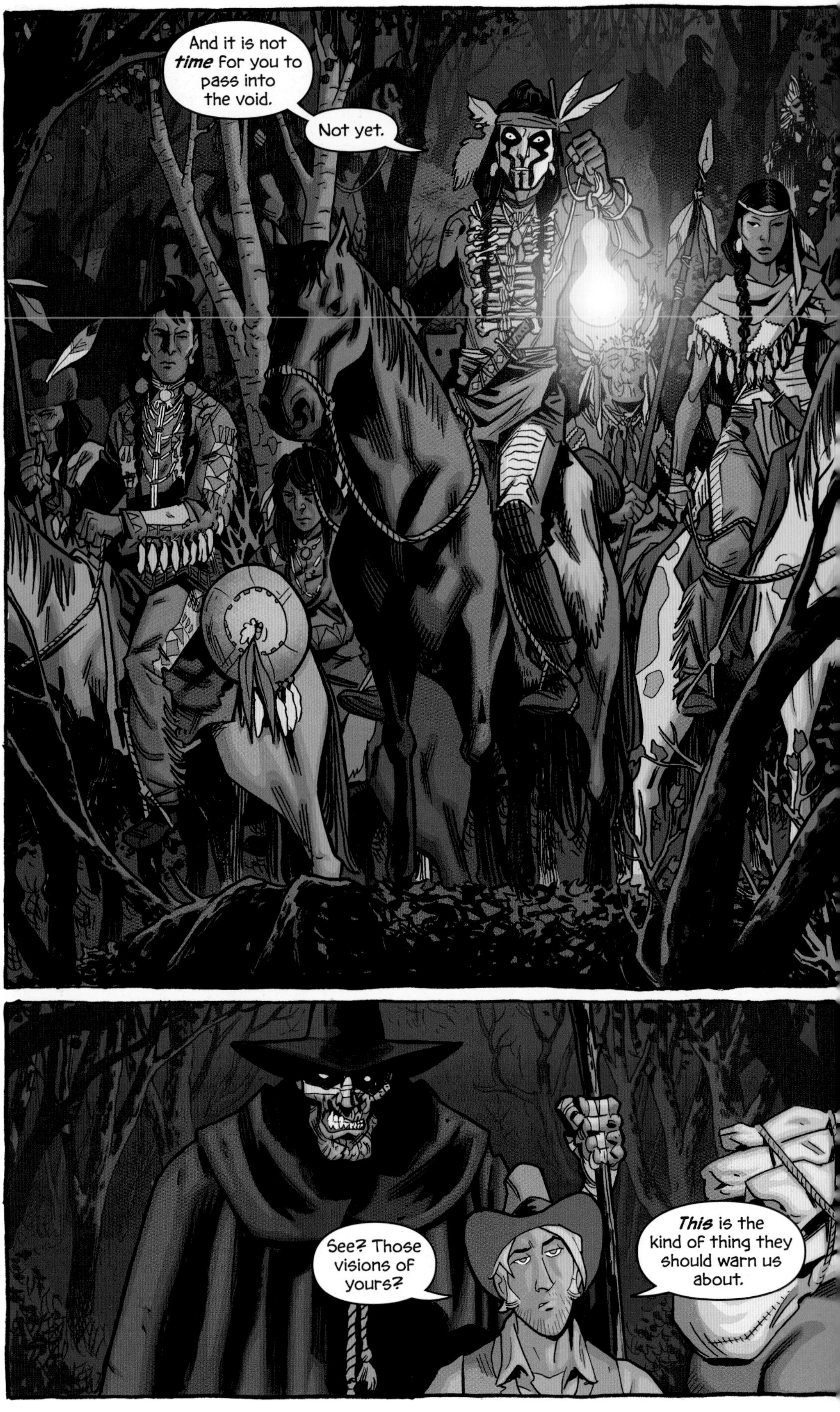

And it is not *time* for you to pass into the void.
Not yet.
See? Those visions of yours?
This is the kind of thing they should warn us about.

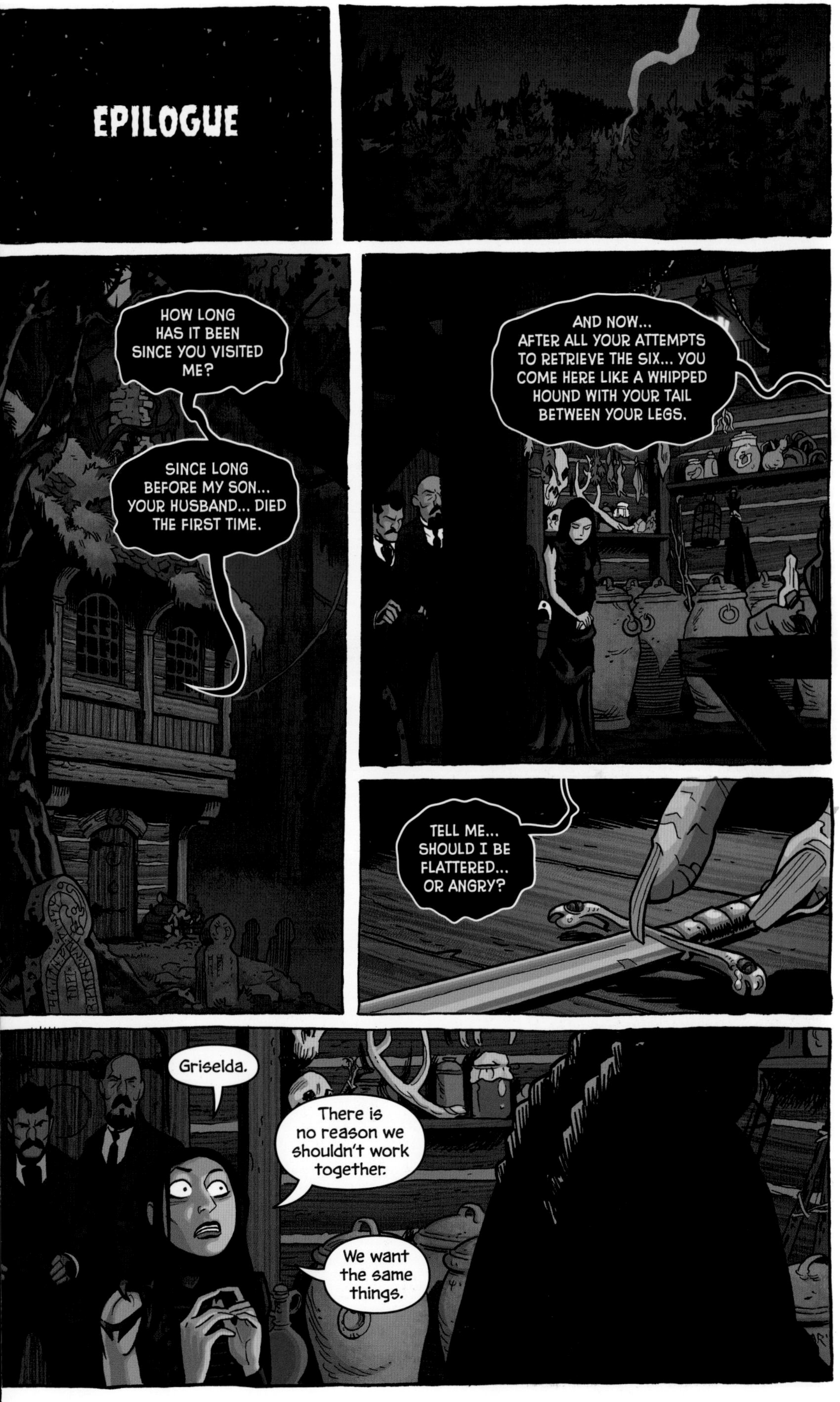
EPILOGUE
HOW LONG HAS IT BEEN SINCE YOU VISITED ME?
SINCE LONG BEFORE MY SON... YOUR HUSBAND... DIED THE FIRST TIME.
AND NOW... AFTER ALL YOUR ATTEMPTS TO RETRIEVE THE SIX... YOU COME HERE LIKE A WHIPPED HOUND WITH YOUR TAIL BETWEEN YOUR LEGS.
TELL ME... SHOULD I BE FLATTERED... OR ANGRY?
Griselda.
There is no reason we shouldn't work together.
We want the same things.

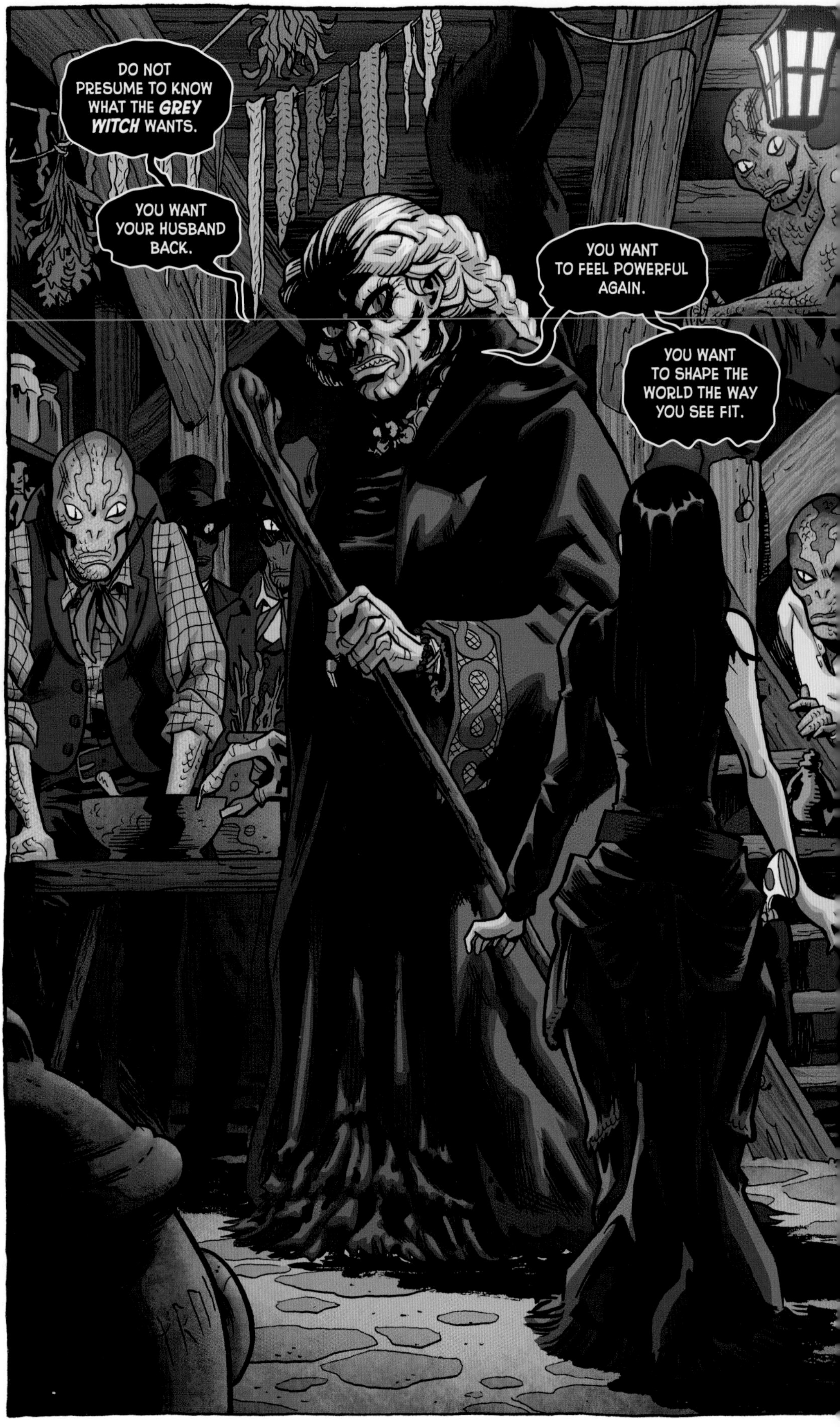
DO NOT PRESUME TO KNOW WHAT THE *GREY WITCH* WANTS.
YOU WANT YOUR HUSBAND BACK.
YOU WANT TO FEEL POWERFUL AGAIN.
YOU WANT TO SHAPE THE WORLD THE WAY YOU SEE FIT.

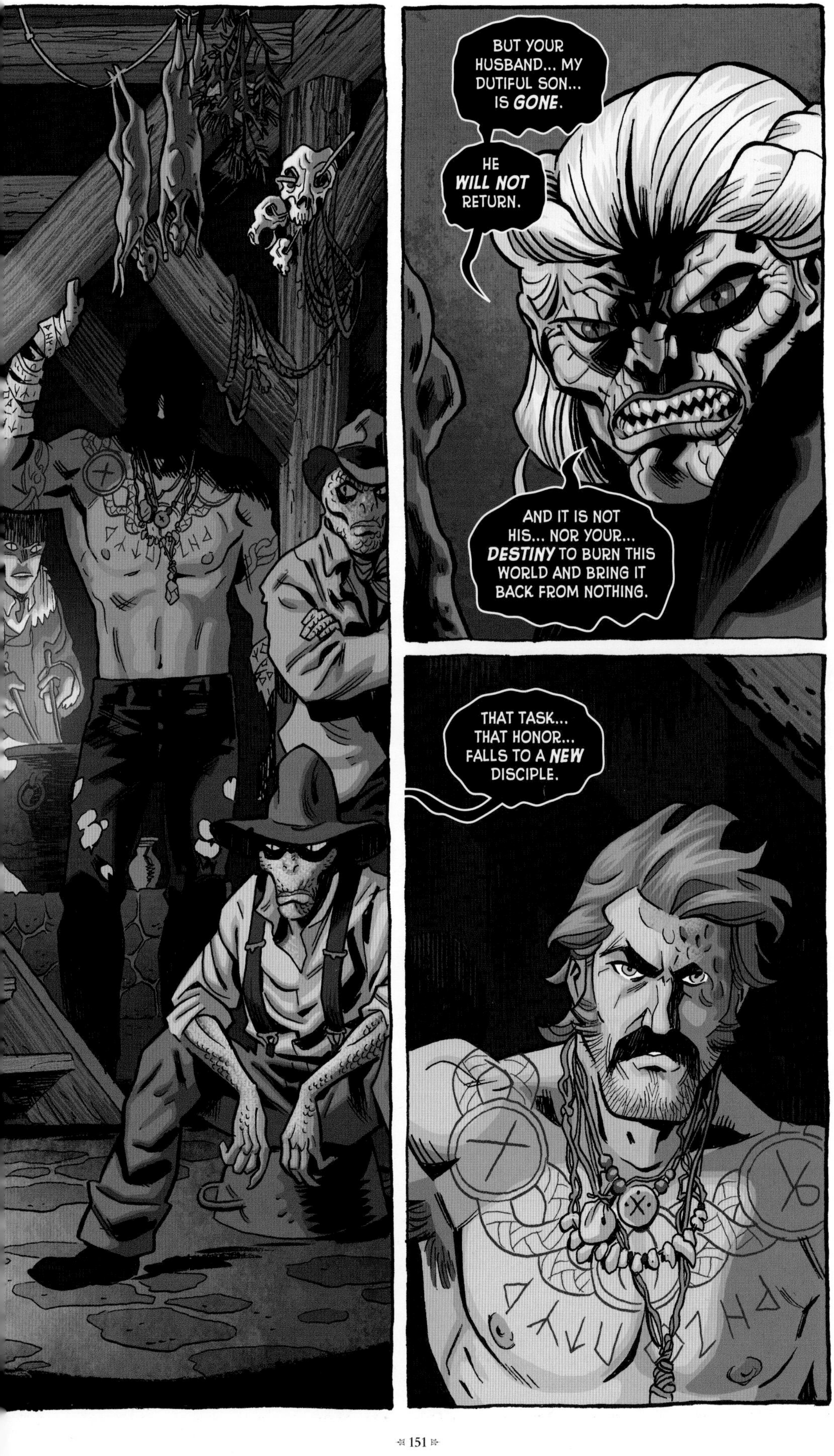
BUT YOUR HUSBAND... MY DUTIFUL SON... IS GONE.
HE WILL NOT RETURN.
AND IT IS NOT HIS... NOR YOUR... DESTINY TO BURN THIS WORLD AND BRING IT BACK FROM NOTHING.
THAT TASK... THAT HONOR... FALLS TO A NEW DISCIPLE.

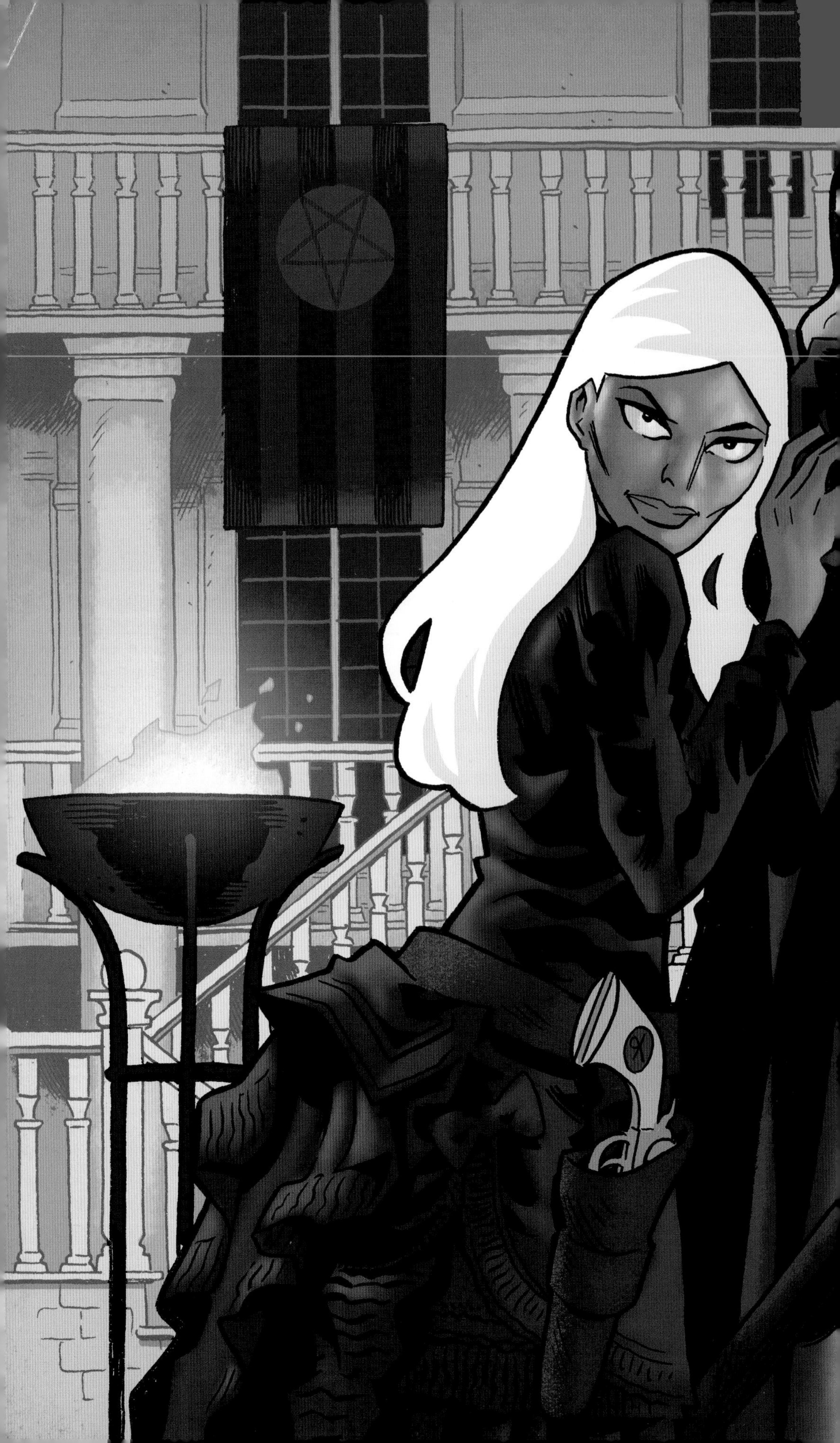

THE ADVENTURE CONTINUES EVERY MONTH!

The story of the Six is one of endings... and of beginnings. Destined to destroy the world, the weapons had passed through countless ages. And as one world dies, another is born. From one epoch to the next, the Six resurfaced... changing shapes... but endless just the same. The cycle cannot be broken, and the race to control the guns is bloody and cruel and fraught with deceit.

Becky Montcrief has used the powers of the Sixth Gun in a way only the most terrible of creatures would dare. She has one foot in the spirit world—the world she sees when the gun speaks to her. It is tearing her apart. In order to save herself, she must embark on a Ghost Dance, a journey through the past and future, through worlds that might have existed if the forces of darkness claimed the guns.

Lost and alone in the Spirit World, Becky is pursued by terrible creatures, fiendish Skinwalkers, and the most unexpected of allies. Old friends... and older enemies... choose sides in the war for all of creation.

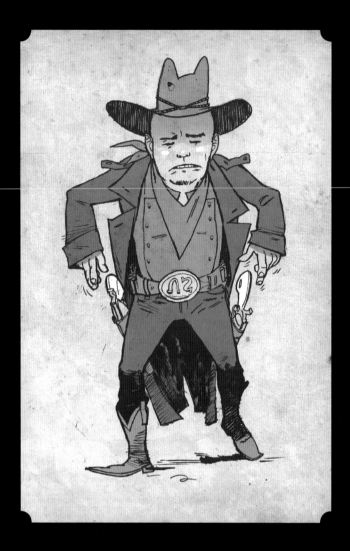

Cullen Bunn grew up in rural North Carolina, but now lives in the St. Louis area with his wife Cindy and Jackson, his son. His noir/horror comic (and first collaboration with Brian Hurtt), *The Damned*, was published in 2007 by Oni Press. The follow-up, *The Damned: Prodigal Sons*, was released in 2008. In addition to *The Sixth Gun*, his current projects include *The Tooth*, an original graphic novel from Oni Press; *Crooked Hills*, a middle reader horror prose series from Evileye Books; and various work for Marvel and DC. Somewhere along the way, Cullen founded Undaunted Press and edited the critically acclaimed small press horror magazine, *Whispers from the Shattered Forum*.

All writers must pay their dues, and Cullen has worked various odd jobs, including Alien Autopsy Specialist, Rodeo Clown, Professional Wrestler Manager, and Sasquatch Wrangler.

And, yes, he has fought for his life against mountain lions and he did perform on stage as the World's Youngest Hypnotist. Buy him a drink sometime, and he'll tell you all about it.

Visit his website at www.cullenbunn.com.

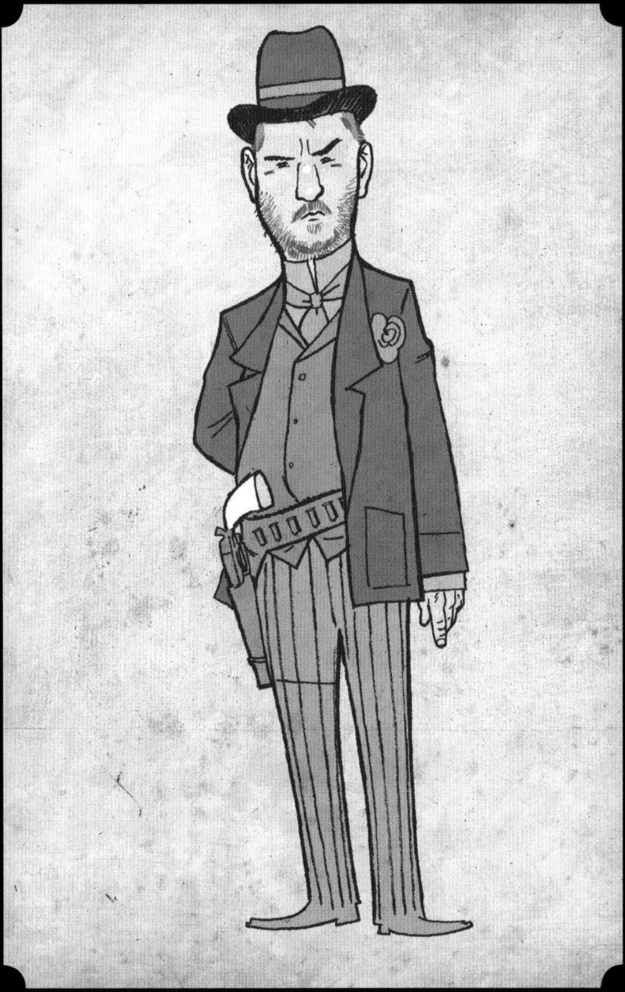

Author portrait illustrations by Jason Latour. jasonlatour.com

Brian Hurtt got his start in comics pencilling the second arc of Greg Rucka's *Queen & Country*. This was followed by art duties on several projects including *Queen & Country: Declassified*, *Three Strikes*, and Steve Gerber's critically acclaimed series *Hard Time*.

In 2006, Brian teamed with Cullen Bunn to create the Prohibition-era monster-noir sensation *The Damned*. The two found that their unique tastes and storytelling sensibilities were well-suited to one another and were eager to continue that relationship.

The Sixth Gun is their sophomore endeavor together and the next in what looks to be many years of creative collaboration.

Brian lives in St. Louis where the summers are too hot, the winters too cold, but the rent is just right.

He can be found online at thehurttlocker.blogspot.com.

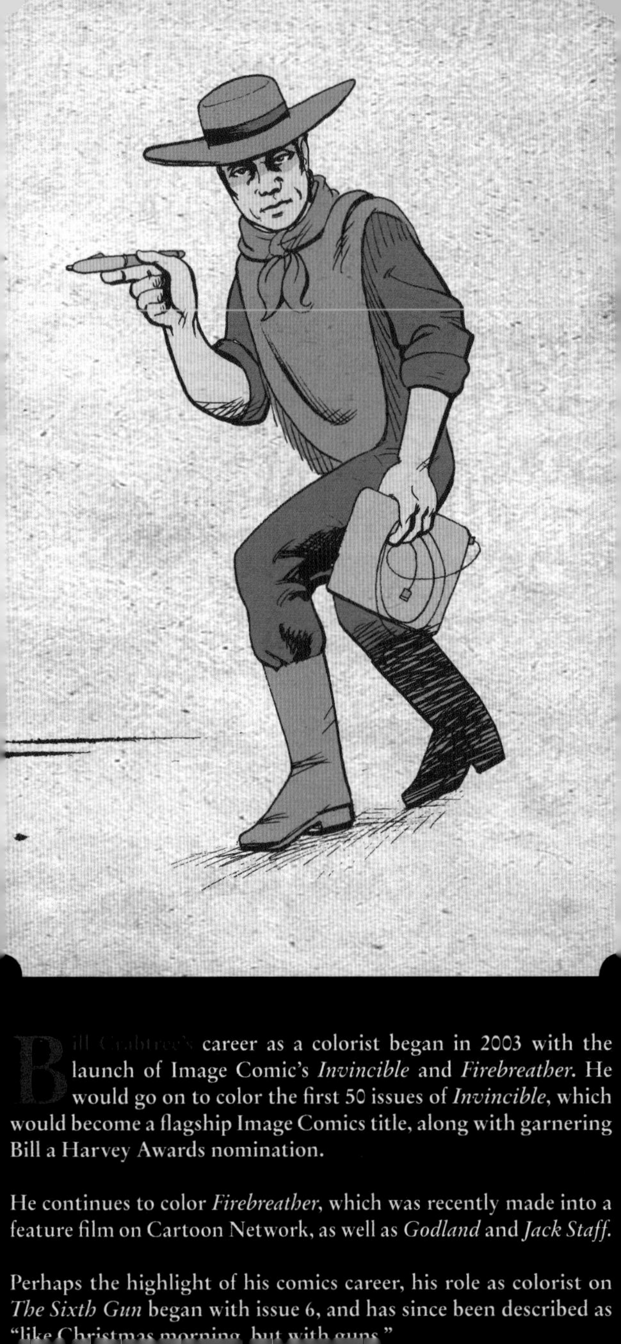

Bill Crabtree's career as a colorist began in 2003 with the launch of Image Comic's *Invincible* and *Firebreather*. He would go on to color the first 50 issues of *Invincible*, which would become a flagship Image Comics title, along with garnering Bill a Harvey Awards nomination.

He continues to color *Firebreather*, which was recently made into a feature film on Cartoon Network, as well as *Godland* and *Jack Staff*.

Perhaps the highlight of his comics career, his role as colorist on *The Sixth Gun* began with issue 6, and has since been described as "like Christmas morning, but with guns."

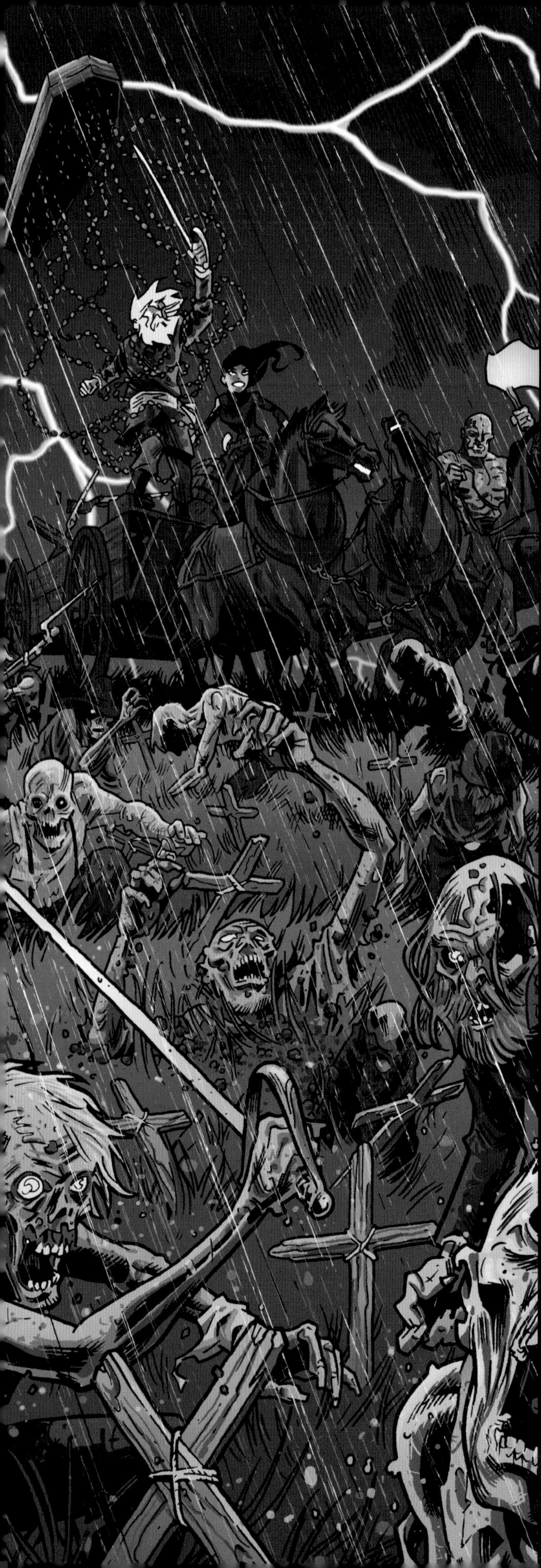

Also Available...

THE SIXTH GUN™

The Sixth Gun, Volume 1: Cold Dead Fingers
By Cullen Bunn, Brian Hurtt
& Bill Crabtree
176 pages • Trade Paperback
Color
ISBN 978-1-934964-60-6

✣

The Sixth Gun, Volume 2: Crossroads
By Cullen Bunn, Brian Hurtt
& Bill Crabtree
136 pages • Trade Paperback
Color
ISBN 978-1-934964-67-5

✣

The Sixth Gun, Volume 3: Bound
By Cullen Bunn, Brian Hurtt
Tyler Crook & Bill Crabtree
136 pages • Trade Paperback
Color
ISBN 978-1-934964-78-1

✣

The Sixth Gun, Volume 4: A Town Called Penance
By Cullen Bunn, Brian Hurtt
Tyler Crook & Bill Crabtree
168 pages • Trade Paperback
Color
ISBN 978-1-934964-95-8

ONI PRESS
REVOLUTIONIZE COMICS
www.onipress.com

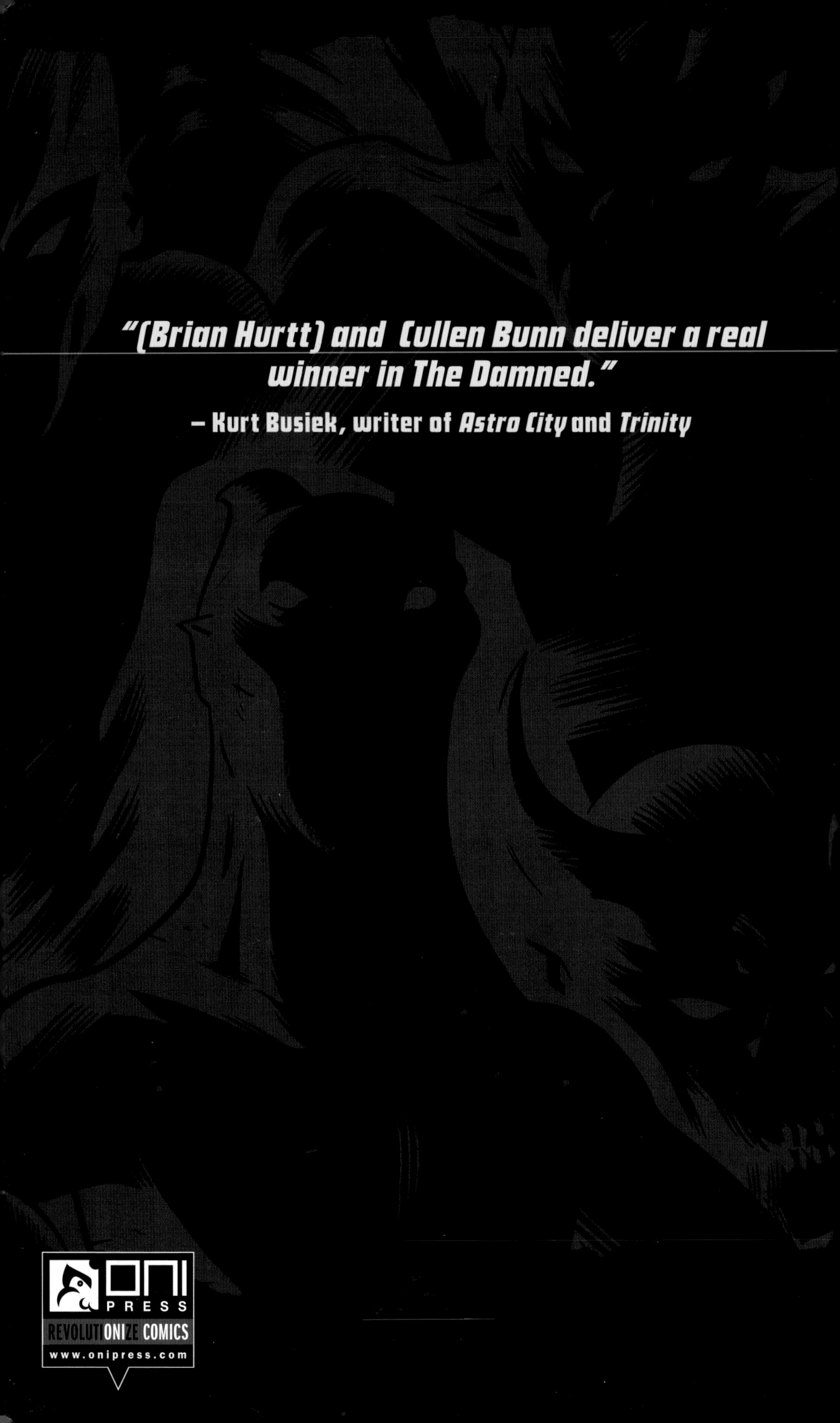

"(Brian Hurtt) and Cullen Bunn deliver a real winner in The Damned."

– Kurt Busiek, writer of *Astro City* and *Trinity*

ONI PRESS
REVOLUTIONIZE COMICS
www.onipress.com

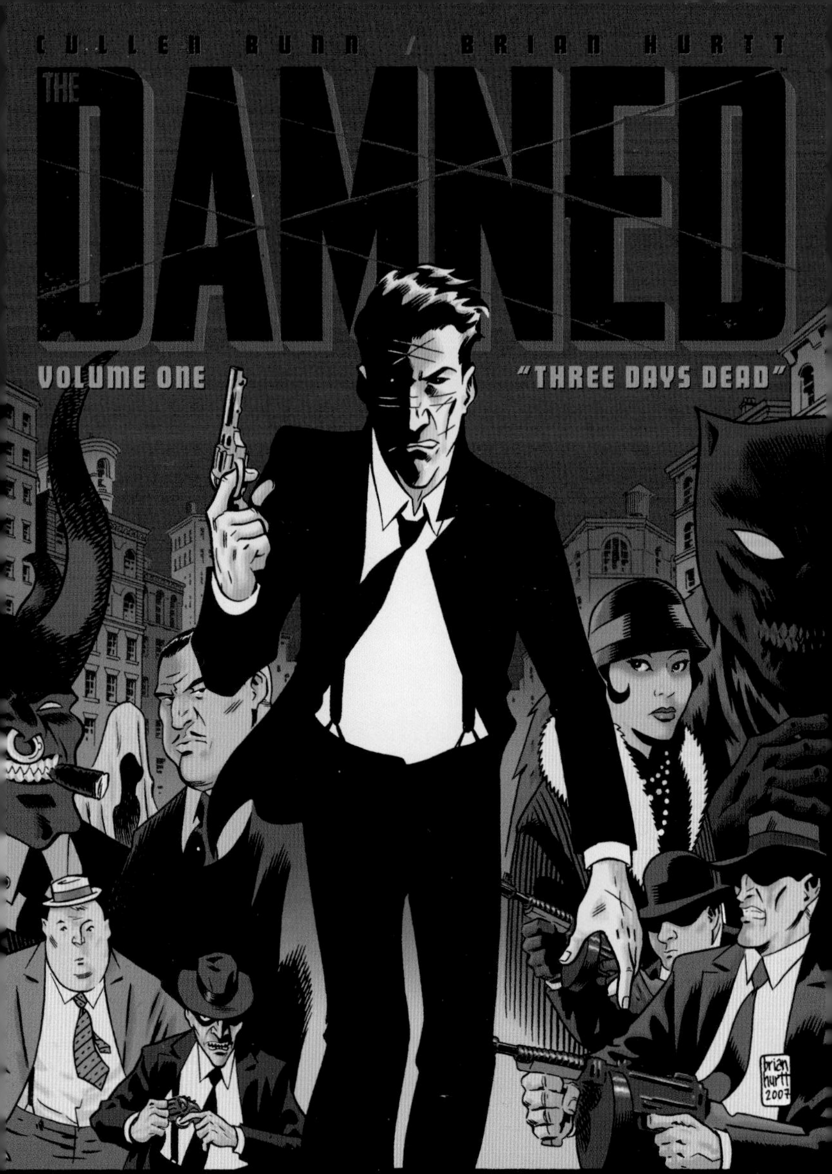
CULLEN BUNN / BRIAN HURTT
THE DAMNED
VOLUME ONE
"THREE DAYS DEAD"
brian hurtt 2007

"This is an absolutely terrific book. Tough guys, mobsters, and demons from hell. A bluesy, bitter mood and a fascinating, mysterious world. It's great to see Brian Hurtt back after the much-missed Hard Time*, and it's even better to have him doing something beautifully realized. He and Cullen Bunn deliver a real winner in* The Damned*."*

– Kurt Busiek (*Superman, Conan, Astro City*)

ISBN 978-1-934964-52-1

GHOST PROJEKT
By Joe Harris & Steve Rolston
152 pages • Hardcover
Color
ISBN 978-1-934964-42-2

GUERILLAS: VOLUME 1
By Brahm Revel
168 pages • 6"x9" Trade Paperback
B&W
ISBN 978-1-934964-43-9

PETROGRAD
By Philp Gelatt & Tyler Crook
264 pages • 6"x9" Hardcover
2-Color
ISBN 978-1-934964-44-6

QUEEN & COUNTRY DEFINITIVE EDITION: VOLUME 1
By Greg Rucka with Steve Rolston, Brian Hurtt, and Leandro Fernandez
366 pages • 6"x9" • Trade Paperback
B&W
ISBN 978-1-932664-87-4

STUMPTOWN: VOLUME 1
By Greg Rucka & Matthew Southworth
144 pages • Hardcover
Color
ISBN 978-1-934964-37-8

WASTELAND: VOLUME 1
By Antony Johnston & Christopher Mitten
160 pages • Trade Paperback
B&W
ISBN 978-1-932664-59-1

ONE SOUL
By Ray Fawkes
176 pages • Hardcover

A New Beginning! The Tooth Unleashed!

VOLUME ONE

GUERILLAS
INTRODUCTION BY JACKSON PUBLICK (CREATOR OF THE VENTURE BROS.)
VOLUME 1
BRAHM REVEL

PETROGRAD
PHILIP GELATT • TYLER CROOK

GREG RUCKA
QUEEN & COUNTRY
DEFINITIVE EDITION
VOLUME 01

"STUMPTOWN IS, FOR MY MONEY, THE PERFECT RUCKA BOOK."
STUMPTOWN
GREG RUCKA • MATTHEW SOUTHWORTH

Ray Fawkes

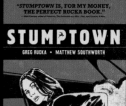